Contents

Introduction

In offering this book to those studying catering subjects we seek to emphasise the great importance we put on an extensive study of the commodities used in the kitchen.

Any Caterer who is trying to make a good meal must know all that is possible about the commodity, its storage, its variations and its purchase in order both to be able to offer the most suitable item available for the meal and to purchase and store it in the most economical manner. Any young person joining the catering industry must recognise that it is possible that he or she will have some 40 years of work before them. During this period conditions may change, and he or she may be called upon to present different types of meals from those currently planned. Supply conditions may change owing to climatic or political changes and customer demand may vary. In order to deal adequately with such changes, a full knowledge of the commodity, where it comes from and the time of year it is available is required.

Recent developments in catering have seen more and more 'Convenience Food' become available and be used. Many of these are preserved forms of normal foods, so a study as to how each food is preserved and how it can be used is included in the notes on each commodity. In order to allow the student to determine which convenience food can be used in any particular situation a short general section on these items has been included.

During our teaching of food subjects we have found that the student often finds it difficult to relate the theory of the subject to its practical use in the kitchen. In our experience this problem can be overcome to some extent, by the use of small tests which can be carried out fairly easily without using any special or expensive equipment. These tests are explained under the appropriate headings for the use of those wishing to undertake them.

In determining how far to deal with each subject we have had to be restrictive so that the reader does not have to work through pages of highly technical information to reach his or her goal. We have tried to restrict the illustrations to those which we feel are essential to the study of this work and we have aimed at the level of the normal craftsman or woman and junior management. These aims have provided us with a book which, we feel, will cover adequately the work required in the City & Guilds 705 and 706 examinations for Caterers, the Catering O.N.D. work being covered at present and the T.E.C. work which will be introduced into the Colleges in the next year or so. Much of the work covered will, we believe, be of use in various other food subject examinations.

We have based the depth and area covered on our own experiences in teaching in various Technical Colleges throughout the country over a joint period of approaching 50 years. For the reader who wishes to pursue any particular aspect to a greater depth we would recommend an approach to the local Library or College Library service for any of the specialist books on that subject.

All of the subjects covered have been dealt with by the authors in their respective teaching experiences and the remarks made are a result of many hours of teaching each item. We should also like to express our thanks to our colleagues at High Peak College, Buxton for their own comments and criticisms of our work, and, finally, but by no means least to Mrs. D. R. Harris, of the Business Studies Department of High Peak College who undertook the task of typing out and reading our work.

We have done our best to seek to eliminate errors but any that do occur are our own responsibility entirely and we should greatly appreciate corrections or comments from any reader who spots them.

M. Lingard
J. Sizer
May 1978

CHAPTER 1

Vegetables, TVP and Fungi

Vegetables are divided into various classes. The simplest way of dividing them is to state which grow above and which grow below the ground. However, it is usual to make the divisions rather closer and we propose to use the following sections:

1. **Above ground vegetables**
   Flower
   Pod
   Leaf
   Stem
   Fruit
2. **Below ground vegetables**
   Root
   Tuber
   Bulb

It is usual to cook each of the main divisions in different ways. Those growing above ground are often cooked by placing in boiling water which is maintained at a full boil; whereas those harvested from below ground are usually cooked by placing in cold water which is then brought to the boil and simmered until ready. This gives them a longer cooking period. One of the reasons for this difference is that those harvested above ground are usually more tender and need cooking quickly to retain flavour and colour while those harvested from under the soil tend to have a more fibrous content and need longer cooking to tenderise them.

It is usual to store the underground vegetables either on the farm before sales or in various types of storehouses during the journey from farm to caterer. The above ground vegetables usually perish more quickly and must be used within a few days of harvesting so any storage must be of a special type involving preservation. We shall deal with these types at the end of this section mentioning the types of preservation used for each vegetable.

Above Ground Vegetables
1. *Flowers*

(a) **Cauliflower** (Chou-fleur)
Cauliflowers vary in size according to both variety and period of harvest-

ing. They should be of good white colour, the flower should be close and firm and there should be no excessive leaf or stalk content. Before buying, a quick check on any insect or caterpillar damage or presence should be made. Any flowers showing obvious signs of damage or insect presence should be rejected. The damage will spoil the flower for service and the insect life will mean an extended examination period costing time and thus money. The flowers should be used within a day or two of taking into stock and should be firm and fresh on delivery.

Preservation methods used for cauliflowers are freezing, canning and pickling. The frozen cauliflower florets are a commonly used vegetable in many establishments using this type of supply and can give very good results.

Imported supplies come from Italy and France.

A flowering vegetable to be associated with the Cauliflower is the hardy Broccoli which supplies most of the home grown 'cauliflower' market during spring months. This is very similar to the cauliflower in appearance and taste and is available in periods when no fresh home-grown cauliflowers can be gathered. As they are used in exactly the same way our comments apply to both plants.

(b) Sprouting Broccoli (Brocoli)
These can be white, purple or green in colour and have small flowers on the end of a stalk. The purple type turns green when boiled and this, and the green sprouting broccoli, also known as Calabrese, are the ones usually served as 'Broccoli'. The individual florets of the white sprouting broccoli can be used in the same manner as cauliflower by either boiling or pickling.

Home supplies of broccoli are available in February, March and April and Calabrese, a vegetable of Italian origin, is available in August and September. This is often used in soups.

(c) Globe Artichoke (Artichaut)
This is the flower bud of a plant which looks rather like a thistle. The stalk and outer leaves are trimmed off and the artichoke now tied and poached. It may be used as a hot or cold vegetable and is also used as garnish and in hors d'oeuvres. Local crops are available June to October and imported and preserved supplies are available at other periods. The Mediterranean countries, especially Italy, produce much of our imported supply.

2. Pods (also known as the Légumes or Pulses)

The principal pods used as vegetables are the Peas and Beans. There are several important variations in varieties of which the caterer must be aware and, as with many other food plants, season of year and the time of

Pulses

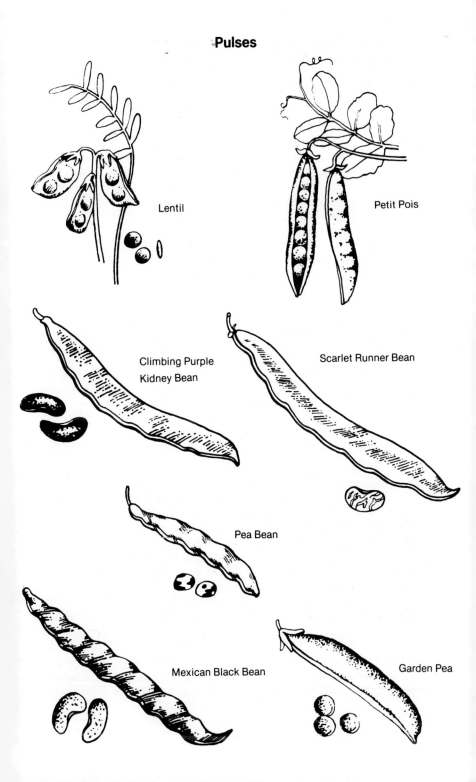

Lentil

Petit Pois

Climbing Purple
Kidney Bean

Scarlet Runner Bean

Pea Bean

Mexican Black Bean

Garden Pea

season (early or late) can have a bearing upon the quality of the vegetable offered. Preservation by drying has been practised with peas for a great many years and newer methods of drying in which the peas are quick frozen have given an entirely different product which can be used in many establishments when fresh peas are not available. Tinned peas are available for use where suitable, but it is common practice to tin beans in a tomato sauce thus providing a different dish from the normal bean. Frozen peas and beans are now available and are able to offer the caterer an excellent alternative to fresh vegetables. As the preserved types are often ready for use and require very little labour in preparation and serving they are a popular choice in conditions where labour is scarce or expensive. Any podded vegetable requires quite an amount of time before it is ready for cooking and any machinery to do this work is far too expensive for most catering establishments.

Beans

There are numerous types of beans. We propose to deal with each one independently.

(a) French or Kidney Beans (Haricot Vert)

These are the common kidney bean which is eaten in the pod. They are in a long thin pod which should have been picked when young and any of over 4″ (10cm) in length may be stringy and tough. They are widely cultivated in temperate zones and some sub-tropical zones and so are imported during many periods of the year. Local crops are available in the summer months.

(b) Haricot Beans (Haricot)

While some growing is attempted in this country the majority of these beans are grown in countries with warmer climatic conditions than Great Britain. The seeds are dried and require soaking overnight before use. A small, white coloured bean, it can be used to make the tinned 'baked beans' so well known in this country. They are used in stews and in pastry work where some chefs use the dried bean to fill pastry cases which are to be baked 'blind' for filling after baking.

(c) Scarlet Runners (Haricot d'Espagne)

Similar to the French or kidney bean but rather larger, these are named after their scarlet flowers. This is a climbing bean which is cropped in the summer and early autumn months. As with the kidney bean the larger the pods, the coarser they become, so they must be harvested small to give a tender eating bean which can be used whole in the same manner as the french or kidney bean. When large it is usual to cut them crosswise and remove the stringy section running down the side of the bean during the cleaning process. The beans are ready for harvesting when about 6″ − 8″ (15 − 20cm) long, but if left they can grow up to 24″ (60cm) in length so when purchasing choice should be restricted to the 6″ − 8″ (15 − 20cm) sized pods. The small seeds inside vary in colour with the variety of bean and can range from white through pinks to black. A white or pink seeded variety is often the choice of the discriminating caterer. They are not usually available by named variety but if there is a choice, 'Czar' is one which should give satisfaction.

(d) Climbing Kidney Beans (Rognon)

These are not commonly available but can be used to give an excellent flavour. They are purple in colour when harvested but, as with most beans, their colour changes during boiling to a green colour. Their advantage is that they are stringless and so give a more tender eating vegetable than the normal runner bean.

Other varieties of this type of bean are available from time to time and can be used to give an attractive change to the specialist menu. Among these are:

Mexican Black Bean An unusual bean with black beans in a yellow pod and a mushroom-like flavour.

Pea Bean This bean has a shorter pod than most beans of this type and its seeds are round and rather larger than normal. The seeds are white with brown patches.

Deuil Fin Précoce A French-grown bean with longer and more slender pods than is normal. They are green with violet patches.

Agricultural research has recently introduced some new varieties of French, runner and climbing kidney beans, which give tender, stringless pods of good flavour at a much larger size. The remarks on size, toughness and stringiness do not apply to these varieties.

(e) Butter Beans or Lima Beans

Grown in many tropical and sub-tropical countries, these beans are podded and dried after which they can be used in soups and stews, or served as a vegetable in their own right and used as were the haricot beans as a filler in pastry work.

(f) Broad Beans (Fève)

This type of bean has been cultivated in Great Britain for many years. It is available as a home-grown crop in June, July and August. Supplies can be imported from other European countries, but it is not commonly used out of season except in its preserved form as a frozen vegetable.

To prepare for cooking this bean is stripped from its pod, and it emerges as a flattish, almost oval-shaped bean clearly marked into two sections by a slight depression running round the edge. The size varies according to age. The larger and older bean is rather tough to eat. They are cooked by boiling. They are often served with a white sauce. Although classified as a bean it is actually a member of the Pea family in horticultural terminology.

Peas (Les Pois)

As with the beans there are a number of varieties of peas used in cookery. All can be used fresh, or preserved by drying, canning or freezing.

(a) Petit Pois
Are small peas originally of French origin but the name is often given to any variety of small pea.

(b) Marrowfats
A large, wrinkled pea which can be used fresh, but is also available in preserved forms. The older type of dried pea is known as a marrowfat. These require covering with boiling water to which some bicarbonate of soda has been added and then allowed to stand overnight before boiling. They have rather a different taste from fresh peas but are most popular in some areas. When well cooked they provide some of the 'mushy peas' becoming increasingly popular at the time of writing.

A recent introduction on to the retail market is a form of marrowfat dried pea which requires soaking for only two hours before use. When cooked this produces a type of 'mushy pea'. This type is still in its early stages of use and we expect further improvements to be made in the next few years.

(c) Blue Peas
These are a variety which have a greenish-blue colour. They are traditionally served with pork pies to provide a dish of Pie and Peas in the industrial North.

(d) White Peas
These are small white-coloured peas which are dried and used as dried split peas in stews, stocks etc.

(e) Asparagus Peas
These have no relationship to the Asparagus except by a slightly similar appearance. The pods are gathered young and are cooked without shelling.

(f) Sugar Peas or Mangetout or Edible Podded Peas
These are further varieties where, when collected young, the pods are cooked without any shelling and can provide an attractive and rather different vegetable dish.

The major use of peas is as a fresh or preserved vegetable. Fresh peas can be imported, but most used in Britain are either home-grown fresh or preserved peas. The cropping season is extended by use of different varieties with early, mid-season or late cropping characteristics. As each variety gets well into its season the peas become larger and the pods are not as crisp. Choice should be made for well-filled pods of a good green colour with no signs of browning, wilting or insect damage. Home-grown supplies are available from May until September. The early crops are the most expensive.

Others Pods and Legumes

a) Lentils (Lentille)
A small bean-like seed which is carried one or two to the pod on the parent plant and is dehusked and dried to be used in various dishes. The bean is usually split in two during the drying process. They were one of the earliest cultivated vegetables in the Near East. Lentils are mentioned in the Bible as being used in Jacob's time. They can be grown in Great Britain, but are usually imported from Egypt, Greece and other Mediterranean countries. The dried seeds are used in soups and stews and are able to offer a high protein content to dishes in which they are used. For this reason they are a popular vegetable in vegetarian cookery. The seeds can be green, brown or red, the latter being the most common.

b) Soya Beans
The Soya bean has so many uses in the food world that it is difficult to know how to classify it. It is used in its own right as a vegetable both by using the beans and by using its shoots. Sauce made from it is a traditional item in oriental service and the oils, fat and protein made from it are met with in almost every food preparing process. The seeds or beans are only used in this country in special dishes as a vegetable, but they do give us soya flour, soya bean oil and are used to make T.V.P. The young shoots of the plant are served as Bean-Sprouts in Chinese cookery.

At the moment the soya bean cannot be grown in commercial quantities in Great Britain but horticulturalists are working to develop new species which will be able to withstand our weather conditions and give us good crops. These may develop in the years to come.

3. Leaf Vegetables

These are vegetables which can have their food values greatly reduced by improper cooking. They contain an important proportion of vitamin C and, if the vegetable is cooked for too long or is stored prior to serving, a high proportion of this vitamin can be lost. In addition to their vitamin content they provide cellular matter which aids the digestive system. A number of leaf vegetables are used in salads and similar dishes. Some can be used both as salad vegetables and cooked vegetables. Where there is a choice of usage it is common to use the younger specimens of the leaf vegetable in salads. Normally a much higher proportion of the Vitamin C present is made available to the body when no cooking takes place.

Cabbages (Chou)
Various types of cabbage are available. They range from the large, almost football-like Winter, Savoy and Red cabbage to Spring cabbage,

which are plants which have not formed a heart, but are a collection of green leaves on a common stalk. The Winter, Savoy and Red cabbages have a very firm placement of large leaves on the outside with smaller, lighter coloured leaves in the centre.

a) Spring Cabbage
These are a young cabbage harvested before the heart is fully formed, — the leaves should be tender and of a dark green colour, crisp to the touch and without insect damage or wilting.

They should be used as delivered and not stored more than 24 hours before use.

b) Drumhead or Winter Cabbage
Normally a round, hard centre with a few looser outer leaves. The centre is normally much paler in colour than the outer leaves, but if the head is loose and light has been able to get into the centre leaves then a darker colour is developed. When buying, choice should be made from supplies which are clean, have no insect damage, and have a minimum of the looser outer leaves which often have to be removed. The stalk should have been cut close to the head and the whole cabbage should be fresh looking and crisp. Samples with browning and/or limp leaves should be refused. It is available, as the name implies, during the winter months.

c) Summer and Autumn Cabbage
Very similar to winter cabbage but can often have a conically shaped head. Normally available from June to October.

d) Savoy Cabbage (Chou frisé)
A similar cabbage to the round-headed winter cabbage, but having wrinkled leaves. Savoys are available from September to March and are used both as a cooked vegetable and in making up cabbage salad or coleslaw.

e) Red Cabbage (Chou rouge)
Principally used for pickling but can also be served as a cooked vegetable. The shape is again similar to winter round-headed cabbage, but this time the leaves are a deep purplish-red and their colour remains almost constant through to the centre. Home-grown supplies are principally available in the autumn months.

f) Kale (Chou frisé)
A hardy winter green leaf vegetable which produces stalks which bear early crinkled leaves somewhat similar to parsley. They are available throughout winter and the plants can produce young green shoots which can be used as spring vegetables.

g) Brussels Sprouts (Choux de Bruxelles)
A small, tight bud borne in numbers on a long thick stem. These are in season between October and March. When buying, care should be taken

to see that the vegetables are fresh and of good colour. They are often supplied in string nets holding some 20lb (10kg). It is usual to remove the outer leaves prior to cooking and use the firm heart, so again care should be taken to purchase firm specimens. Their life in normal storage is rather less than the other leaf vegetables so far mentioned so care must be taken to store correctly in a cool, dark store and to use as quickly as possible. Three days in normally the limit of storage period before the sprouts begin to go soft, brown and eventually smelly.

h) Spinach (Épinards)
Widely cultivated in temperate climates, spinach can be purchased from home-grown supplies and imported supplies. Home-grown supplies of winter spinach are available in October to March and summer spinach from May to September. Spinach is unusual amongst green leaf vegetables in having quite a high protein content. It also has an important vitamin A content. Surprisingly enough it does not have a high iron content.

The leaves are supplied loose or in clumps when bought and, as they are grown in sandy soils can have dirt adhering to them. When buying it is important to check the amount of dirt present and reject samples with an excessive quantity. Spinach does not keep long after harvesting so supplies should not be stored more than one or two days. It has an unfortunate practice of shrinking considerably during cooking and 1lb ($\frac{1}{2}$ kg) of fresh leaves will provide only two smallish-sized portions.

i) Endive or Chicory (Chicorée)
The leaves of these plants are bleached during growth and gathered as a tight clump of almost white leaves some 3 " − 4 " (7.5 − 10cm) in height and about $\frac{1}{2}$" − 2 " (1 − 5cm) across. They are used either in salads or as a cooked vegetable. To the horticulturalist these are two different members of the same family of plants, but in cookery they can be used in the same way and are therefore considered together. The chicory root is used as an additive to coffee and notes on this will be found under the appropriate heading in the section on beverages.

Chicory is available from October to May. Endive is available all the year round from home-grown sources, but is often imported as well.

When purchasing care must be taken to see that the samples are clean and fresh. They should be used within 24 hours of delivery to the store.

Storage and Preservation of Leaf Vegetables

Storage
All the green leaf vegetables should be stored in a clean, cool, dark store — an ideal temperature being in the region of 45 − 50°F (8 − 12°C) as they are all perishable and storage should be for as short a period as

possible. The firmer cabbages will keep rather longer than the less firm greens.

Preservation

Most of the vegetables listed can be canned, frozen or dried — although, at the time of writing, dried green leaf vegetables have not reached as high a quality as have some other foods. Frozen brussel sprouts have reached a very high quality and because they save loss through storage and cleaning time they have become a very important part of many caterers supplies. Red cabbage is usually the only type pickled, although some of the others are used along with other vegetables in various forms of mixed pickles.

Salad Leaf Vegetables and Salad Vegetables

The leaf vegetables used as salad vegetables are only small in number, so for the convenience of the reader we propose to deal with all the salad vegetables in this one section.

Where any one may occasionally be used as a cooked vegetable, then this alternative use will be mentioned; — where the vegetable is more usually used as a cooked vegetable but can also, on occasion, be used as a salad vegetable, then due reference will be made under the appropriate heading under general classifications.

a) Lettuce (Laitue)

The lettuce is the principal leaf vegetable used in salads and is only rarely used as a cooked vegetable.

Numerous varieties of lettuce are available both from home-grown supply and from imported supplies. In season the majority of lettuce used in catering is home-grown and as salads are usually considered a summer dish, the out-of-season supplies are not required except for special purposes. Even then hot-house supplies from the salad growing areas and from the Channel Islands are available for much of the year.

The lettuce normally used in catering is the Cabbage Lettuce with Cos Lettuce being used on some occasions. The Cabbage Lettuce, as its name implies is of a similar shape to the cabbage — a round plant with a reasonably firm heart surrounding a few looser leaves. As with the cabbage, the colour of the inner leaves is paler than the outer. As these are the younger leaves they are the more tender. When purchasing, choice should be made from samples which have a good firm heart with crisp leaves which show no signs of insect damage. The outer leaves should be clean and crisp and any stem or root present should be short and clean.

Cos Lettuce is a more oval shape and tends to be slightly looser but should still have a reasonably firm heart.

Both varieties should be purchased in a fresh condition and used within 24 hours.

b) Cress (Cresson)
Principally used in salads or as a raw green dressing on certain dishes. Cress is used as a seedling when its small cluster of leaves form at the top of a thin white stem. A different variety has crimped leaves rather like those of parsley. It is perishable and should be bought in daily and used within 24 hours.

c) Mustard (Moutarde)
The seeds of the mustard plant which are used to make the condiment are sown and allowed to grow for a few days when they produce small thin stems with two pairs of small leaves. At this period they are cut and used as a salad plant or a dressing in a similar manner to cress. In fact the two are commonly used together as mustard and cress. Again they should be ordered daily and used within 24 hours.

d) Celery (Céleri)
A blanched stem used both as a salad and as a cooked vegetable. Grows wild in Great Britain in areas near the sea and is cultivated. The cultivated variety is the type used in catering.

The plant has a blanched cluster of leaf stems surmounted by a head of leaves. When purchasing, the base should be clean and have the roots cut away. Celery can be raised under glass as well as in the field and is usually available in fresh home-grown form throughout the winter months. The best quality crops are those which have the whitest stems which are close and firm. Samples which are loose, green in colour and dirty should be rejected.

Celery seed is used as a spice (see Herbs and Spices section).

e) Florence Fennel (Fenouil)
A salad variety of the fennel which can be used by slicing into salads or hors d'oeuvres. It has a bulb-like appearance, the leaves being cut off. Originally of Italian origin it is now grown in Great Britain.

f) Radish (Radis)
The radish is a root salad vegetable. Various varieties are grown in Britain — the more common being the small round red variety known as Scarlet Globe. The longer cylindrical type which is half red and half white is usually the French Breakfast variety. The round red and white variety known as Sparkler is rather larger than the Scarlet Globe. A white radish with various names is also available and a larger black radish known as the Round Black Spanish variety is sometimes available. This is a winter variety which can be stored in cool stores or in clamps. Radishes will keep rather longer in the caterer's store than most other salad vegetables. When purchased they should be clean, sound and have had the leaves removed. If the leaves have been cut too close to the root this may

have caused damage and will reduce the keeping quality so such radishes should be rejected. The younger radish is more tender to eat and variety is important. We have listed the principally-grown varieties but others in the same classification are available and can be stronger or weaker in flavour. Care should be taken in purchasing so that the type chosen will be suitable for the work intended.

g) Spring Onions (Ciboule)
These are a special variety of small onion which are gathered early and eaten with part of the leaf. They are usually purchased as gathered, i.e with the full leaf and the roots still attached. Care should be taken to select samples of a medium size which have not too much soil still present. They should be freshly gathered so that they have a crisp firm leaf and bulb. The lower portion of the leaf and the bulb should be white in colour and any showing green or yellowing at this section should be rejected.

h) Chives (Ciboulette)
An onion-like plant also used as a herb. The fresh chives can be gathered and used as spring onions or the leaves can be chopped and added to dishes such as salad and hors d'oeuvres to give an onion-like flavour to the dish. The bulb is rather stronger in flavour than a spring onion so it is usual to use only the leaves in salads but the bulb can be used in certain cooked dishes.

i) Welsh Onion
It is not a commonly available member of this group. The Welsh onion is not one which comes from the Principality but from Eastern Asia originally. It grows in clumps rather like chives but is rather larger and has a brown outer skin. When this skin is removed it can be used in the same way as spring onions.

j) Cucumber (Concombre)
Used for salads, garnishing and pickling. Home-grown cucumbers are commercially grown in heated greenhouses and available during the whole of the year with winter and spring supplies being more expensive than those in summer and autumn.

There are differences depending on the variety but these do not concern the caterer who normally buys in bulk. As with all vegetables the cucumbers should be as fresh as possible when purchased. A size of 12" − 15" (30 − 40cm) in length is one which will allow for economical usage without the toughness of ageing in the plant.

Outdoor varieties of cucumber are available but as these are normally smaller in size, they are rarely used for commercial sales.

Kept in a cool store, cucumbers will maintain good condition for up to a week or ten days. Therefore it can be an advantage to buy sufficient to extend over that period.

Tomato (Tomate)

The tomato is a fruit vegetable used in many different ways in the kitchen. As a salad vegetable it adds colour to any salad dish. As a cooked vegetable, often served with stuffing, it again adds colour and a rather distinctive flavour and texture to a dish. As an ingredient it is also very important. Raw it provides vitamins A, C and some B groupings as well as some protein and minerals. As it has a low carbohydrate content it has wide uses in dietetic work.

All this makes the tomato extremely difficult to classify, but we shall deal with it firstly as a salad vegetable and secondly as a fruit vegetable.

The type of tomato normally used in salads is the red tomato, which can vary in size from quite small (about $1\frac{1}{2}''$ (4cm) diameter) up to large samples of 3" (7.5cm) and over in diameter. The smaller ones usually have the better flavour. A good evenly-rounded tomato should be looked for and the short stalk should still be in position. There are many varieties producing some excellent fruits, which can be used to give interesting variations to dishes without additional cost or labour. These include the Yellow or Golden tomato, the Pear-shaped tomato and the small Cherry tomato.

Tomatoes are mainly produced for commercial sale in heated greenhouses and are available all the year round. Crops from the Channel Islands and the Mediterranean area, particularly Italy, are also available. In order to maintain the best flavour it is important to use the tomato intended for salad dishes as quickly as possible after picking. So, although tomatoes for cooking purposes can be kept in good condition for a week or more in a good cool store, it is considered better to order only sufficient for a day or two's usage and then re-order. In the summer months when locally grown supplies are available the caterer can maintain a high standard of freshness and thus flavour by using these supplies. When purchasing, the fruit should be firm and of good colour. The red tomatoes should not show green or yellow patches.

Stem Vegetables

Two of the important stem vegetables, Celery and Fennel, have already been dealt with under the heading of Salad Vegetables. Others in this grouping include the following:

a) **Celeriac** (Céleri Rave)
A close relative of the celery plant, sometimes called turnip-rooted celery, this has a turnip-like root which is served as a cooked vegetable with melted butter as a sauce or is used in broths and similar dishes. It is grown commercially in Great Britain and is available during the winter months as a fresh vegetable. When purchasing the root should have had the leaves trimmed off about $1'' - 2''$ (2 – 5cm) above the root and there should be a minimum of dirt etc. on the root. The sample should be firm and free from damaged portions.

b) Kohlrabi (Chou de raves)
This plant is closely related to the cabbage family and is sometimes known as turnip-rooted cabbage. There are three varieties: — white, green and purple. It is available at most periods of the year. When selecting samples they should be about the size of a small orange; larger specimens tend to become woody when cooked. The root actually appears below the swelled stem and is cut off when preparing for cooking. The stem and root should be sound, firm and free from excessive soil and should not show harvest damage.

c) Leeks (Poireau)
A blanched elongated bulb with long green leaves which should be trimmed off before purchase just above the blanched section. Leeks vary in size according to variety, growth area and time of year. It is locally grown in Britain and imported from various Western European countries. The traditional plant of Wales, it is used as a vegetable in its own right and as an important part of a number of traditional dishes. A good sample should be about $1\frac{1}{2}'' - 2''$ (4 – 5cm) across and some 6" (15cm) in length. The bulb should be an even white throughout and the short leaf left on should still be crisp and firm. A careful inspection should be made to ensure that there is neither excessive dirt or damage due to insects or careless harvesting.

Fruit Vegetables

Tomatoes and cucumber have already been mentioned as salad vegetables. The cucumber may be stuffed and boiled as a cooked vegetable.

Tomatoes, are, as already mentioned, used in a great many ways in the kitchen. When used as a cooked vegetable or in soups and similar dishes it is often accepted that the tomato need not be quite as firm as when required for salad purposes. The stalk should be intact and no serious deterioration showing.

Green tomatoes are used in making certain pickles and the size of the fruit can be allowed to vary subject to a good quality being maintained. In cooking it is important to have a tomato with a tender skin. Some varieties have a firmer, almost rubbery skin and these produce difficulties in use.

a) Aubergine or Egg Plant (Aubergine)
Although some supplies are available when grown under glasshouse conditions in this country, the majority of aubergines used by the caterer are imported from Asia and other tropical and sub-tropical regions. In season during the late summer and early autumn the fruit is purple in colour and should have a rich deep colour to show full ripeness. It has poor keeping qualities and should be used within 3 days of purchase. They can be truncheon-shaped or round and are used as a cooked vegetable by sautéing or by stuffing.

14

b) **Marrow** (Courge) **and Courgette** (Courgette)

The courgette is the small vegetable marrow so we deal with both under the same heading. The fully grown fruit is used as a vegetable in its own right or can be stuffed and roasted after removing the seeds from the centre. The courgette is a small marrow of some $6'' - 7''$ ($15 - 18$cm) length and about $1\frac{1}{2}''$ (4cm) diameter which are often skinned and then boiled whole or in strips. Various sauces are used to finish off the dish. Marrows are grown in this country and available in early autumn and are imported.

The marrow can be of any size from $8'' - 10''$ ($20 - 25$cm) and $3'' - 4''$ ($7.5 - 10$cm) across, — the smaller, and therefore younger, fruit is the more tender. The skin may be white, green with white stripes or deep green in colour. Imported supplies come from near continental countries.

Marrows of both types should be used fresh; when selecting samples they should still have a short portion of the stalk attached and should have no bruises on the skin.

c) **Pumpkin** (Potiron)

These are grown in Britain under sheltered or glasshouse conditions. Home supplies are available in the autumn and imported supplies can be obtained throughout the winter. It is a large round fruit of up to $12'' - 18''$ ($30 - 45$cm) in diameter. It is used with other ingredients in pumpkin pie, or boiled as a vegetable or made into soups. On its own it is rather watery and tasteless. The young shoots of the plant can be boiled and used in the same way as spinach.

When buying, the fruit should be sound and firm to the touch and should be used within 2 to 3 days.

d) **Gherkin** (Cornichon)

A small cucumber-type fruit used in pickling and in hors d'oeuvres and some other dishes. Imported supplies can be obtained from the USA and Poland; the Polish supplies are often preserved in salt.

Selection and storage points are as for Cucumbers.

e) **Sweet Peppers or Pimentoes**

The fruit is imported from Southern Europe and the USA. It may be red, yellow or brown in colour when ripe and can also be picked unripe in a green condition. It is used in salads and as a decorative addition to many dishes and can be served as a vegetable after boiling or can be stuffed. The fully ripened sweet peppers are also used as a spice and known as pimento or allspice. It has a high vitamin C content and is in season from mid-summer to November.

Below Ground Vegetables
Roots

a) Carrots (Carotte)

Home-grown carrots are available in all seasons of the year. The main crop can be stored either on the farm or in suitable premises until required for use and thus last throughout the winter months. New carrots are young, small and tender and are available in the spring months.

Different varieties give stump-rooted and long-rooted types and although the main colour is a reddish-orange, white and yellow-coloured supplies are available as specialist crops.

Carrots should be bought with the minimum dirt and with no harvest damage. An even shape and similar size means less work in preparation. They can be used as a boiled vegetable, in mixed vegetable dishes and in soups, stews, etc.

A very important feature of the carrot is its high content of carotene, which can be converted in the body to vitamin A.

b) Parsnip (Panais)

The parsnip is widely grown in Great Britain and is also a popular crop in most other European countries. The British crop is available from November to March and can be stored in the ground or in clamps if harvested early in the season. The root is rather larger than the carrot, but similar in shape to the long carrot. Whiteish-yellow in colour, good samples should be clean with the leaves trimmed off close to the top of the root without damaging the root itself.

c) Swede (Rutabaga)

This is a recently developed vegetable, probably starting in the 17th century, grown for both human and livestock feeding. They are round with a purple or yellow top half and vary in size from 4″ − 9″ (10 − 22cm) in diameter. The lower half is usually white or yellow on the outside. The leaves should have been trimmed off, but the root is often still present. The larger types are usually the stronger in flavour. When young they provide a tender eating vegetable, but when older they tend to go 'woody', that is to say the flesh takes on a stringy appearance and becomes harder to chew. They are used as separate vegetables or in mixed vegetables or in various stews. They may be purple, white or yellow in colour. The flesh may be white, or more usually, a deep orangey-yellow. They are in season from early autumn throughout the winter and can be lifted and stored until required.

d) Turnip (Navet)

The turnip has been known as a vegetable for thousands of years. The swollen root has a white flesh and its green tops can be used in early spring as spring greens. Actually it is a member of the wallflower family. The swollen root can be of various shapes, is usually round and normally white but some samples take on a yellowish colour. Size varies with variety ranging from the small turnips weighing 3 or 4oz (200 – 250g) to large ones weighing up to 1 lb ($\frac{1}{2}$kg) or more. Flattened varieties have found favour with some growers and users and others have taken almost a cylindrical shape. Their season extends from summer through the winter.

Both swede and turnip have the same purchasing and storage requirements. As root crops they may be damaged in harvesting or, if harvested in wet conditions, may be dirty.

Smaller vegetables are usually sweeter eating and larger ones tend to become 'woody' if old but particularly in the turnip this must depend to some extent upon the variety sown.

e) Turnip-rooted Parsley
Not commonly grown in Great Britain but quite well-known in Germany. This has a root rather like a small parsnip but with a similar flavour to celeriac.

f) Turnip-rooted Chervil
This a plant with grey coloured skin and a sweet yellowish-coloured flesh. It is found in southern Europe. They may be served as a boiled vegetable or used in soups and stews. The plants are harvested in the summer and can be stored for use over the winter months.

Tubers

a) Potatoes (Pomme de Terre)
As the potato can be served at breakfast, lunch, dinner and high tea and is often consumed as an evening meal in the form of chips, its importance in the catering industry cannot be over emphasised.

Potatoes are divided by season of cropping, by colour of skin and by variety and each division must be considered as having some importance in the selection for use in the kitchen.

We propose to deal with each division in turn as listed.

Season of cropping
Potatoes are available from British farms as new or early potatoes and are for sale in the months of May, June and July. Second early are available in July, August and early September. Main crop is available as a fresh crop from August to November and then available from store throughout the rest of the year until well into the new potato season.

Some early potatoes are imported from Egypt and other Mediterranean areas, then from the Channel Islands before the start of the mainland harvest is ready. The first mainland crop comes from the South Coast areas followed by those from Pembrokeshire, Cheshire, Lincolnshire and Ayrshire.

Main crop potatoes come mainly from Wales, the Northern Midlands and Scotland but local grown crops are available throughout the country.

Skin colour

The principal skin colours used in this country are red and white, but it must be remembered that yellow and blue skinned potatoes are grown as speciality crops here and in other areas of Europe.

The red potatoes can be a deep red, a pink or a basically white skin with red or pink patches.

Reds are usually considered as 'soft' potatoes and are used to make fondante and purée. If they are to be used as boiled potatoes, after an initial quick boiling period of some three or four minutes, they must be cooked more slowly to prevent them breaking up in the pan.

The whites, actually having a light brown coloured skin, are considered as 'hard' potatoes and are used for boiling, chipping and sautéing.

Some of both types are good commercial potatoes which can be used for most potato dishes.

Varieties

There are, in all, probably some 70 – 80 varieties grown in Great Britain — the most popular are possibly Arran Pilot as earlies, Craig's Royal as second early and King Edward and Majestic as main crops. We list below a number of the more popular varieties together with brief comments upon their uses.

Variety	Comment	Use
Early		
Ulster Premier	Red, medium to large size, shallow eyes.	All round
Arran Pilot	White, medium to large — good for chipping in late season, shallow eyes	Boiled in early season, frying and chipping when larger.
Home Guard	White oval potato, good shape	Poor storage
Epicure	White, texture waxy, deep eyes	General purpose
Second early		
Craigs Royal	White splashed with pink nutty flavour, shallow eyes	Good all-round use
Red Craigs Royal	All pink skin — otherwise as above	
Ulster Dale	White shallow eyes. Yellowish flesh	All-round use

Variety	Comment	Use
Maincrop		
King Edward	Medium sized, white splashed, pink, shallow eyes	Very good — all-round potato
Redskin	Pink skin, shallow eyes. Very popular in Scotland	Best used as jacket potatoes or in soups
Kerr's Pink	Pink skin, deep eyes.	Good for boiling and mashing.
Majestic	Medium to large. Kidney-shaped. Shallow eyes. Good keeper	Good for frying.
Dr McIntosh	Oval shape. Shallow eyes	General purpose, very good for frying.
Golden Wonder	Small sized. Kidney-shaped.Shallow eyes. Nutty flavour	Very popular as an all-round potato in Scotland. Good for frying.

Other varieties will be available in different localities. We have stressed the depth of the eyes in every case. This is important because if the potatoes are to be peeled in a machine, a deep-eyed potato will require considerable hand labour in cleaning out the eyes unless a deep skin is taken off in the machine, obviously a waste in either case.

Other factors to look for in selecting potatoes are the following:
1. There should be a minimum of dirt and stones in the delivery.
2. There should be no unsound potatoes in the delivery.
3. There should be no harvesting damage seen.
4. There should be no green potatoes in the delivery.

Green potatoes contain poisonous alkaldois known as Solanines which can, in extreme cases cause poisoning to the human body. In addition to this they can taste bitter so green potatoes should not be accepted by the careful caterer. In actual fact the poison can be cooked out during boiling but as so many potatoes are prepared by other means a risk remains which should not be accepted.

Potatoes can be stored in the kitchen or general store for a reasonable period if given the following conditions:
1. Absence of any faulty stock.

2. Dry storage.
3. Cool store with fresh air supply (approximately 40°F (5°C))
4. Darkness
5. No strong-smelling goods in the same store.

b) Jerusalem Artichoke (Topinambour)
Home crop available November to March. It is also imported from the Americas. A whiteish or yellowish-coloured tuber which is sometimes tipped with pink. It has a flavour similar to the true artichoke; is club-shaped with short branches and up to 4″ (10cm) long and 2″ − 3″ (5 − 8cm) across. They are used as a boiled vegetable, in soups, stews and baked. Will keep well in a good cool store.

c) Sweet Potatoes
No close relation to the true potato — this has a large red-skinned root which may be round or tubular shaped. Usually imported from warmer climatic countries, the sweet potato must be used within a day or two of delivery as it is a poor keeper. Usual use is boiling and mashing.

d) Yam
A vegetable popular in certain tropical countries, but not often used in catering work in this country. It has a tuber which may be round or tubular, has a brown skin and a white or yellow flesh. Growing areas are Asia, Africa and the West Indies.

e) Oca
Another unusual vegetable to the British taste, the Oca is mainly used in South America. They can be dried in the sun after harvesting and then eaten in the same manner as dried figs. They have a rather similar flavour to the fig.

f) Ulluco
Grown mainly in South America, this plant produces a small pink or yellow tuber which can be boiled and eaten as a vegetable.

g) Ysano
Again a South American vegetable, this time a rather unusual method of cooking is adopted. The tuber, yellow in colour with purplish specks is boiled and then frozen before eating. If eaten immediately after boiling the flavour is unacceptable to many palates. An alternative method is to dry them before eating.

Bulbs

a) Onions (Oignon)
Onions are grown in many countries in Western Europe. Britain grows some of her own and imports from Spain as well as some other European countries.

The English onion has traditionally a stronger flavour than the Spanish onion although this does vary with variety. Ailsa Craig, Bedfordshire Champion and Giant Zittau are all well-known varieties of onions but the caterer has not usually the opportunity to specify variety. Onions should be clean, dry, free from excessive root or leaf and have no signs of new growth starting from the top of the bulb.

They will store quite well if kept in a dry, dark, cool store. Spanish crops can be bought in a string or in netting bags.

b) Chives (Ciboulette)
A bulb used in cooking and surveyed under Herbs

c) Spring Onion (Ciboule)
Young onions usually served as a salad vegetable

d) Shallot (Échalote)
A variety of onion grown mainly for pickling

In this section we have dealt with a great many vegetables. In every case they offer a pleasant additional component of the main meal and in a great many cases their correct use is a great help in balancing the diet and in offering an attractive meal with various colours, flavours and textures to attract the appetite.

It is essential that cooking is done correctly in order to present the dish in the best manner and to retain the maximum food value in the meal. Possibly the most important point is not to overcook or to store in a heated condition for a long period as this often causes a reduction in the food value available. This is particularly so in those vegetables which contain vitamin C.

In order to help the reader we list below the food values of the more common vegetables used in the catering industry in Great Britain.

Vegetables — Food Value

It must be remembered that variations will occur according to the age of the vegetable, the storage conditions under which it has been kept and the growing conditions under which it has been produced. The values quoted are intended as a guide and, should the reader wish to obtain exact food values for use in dietetic cookery, then a more exact list should be obtained from a book such as *The Composition of Foods* by McCance & Widdowson.

21

	P	F	CHO	Calcium	Iron	A	D	C	Thiamine	Riboflavin	Nicotine Acid
Beans — runner	*	0	*	+	*	+	0	+	*	*	*
Beetroot boiled	*	0	*	+	*	0	0	+	*	*	*
Brussels Sprouts boiled	*	0	*	+	*	++	0	++	*	*	*
Cabbage boiled	*	0	*	+	*	++	0	+	*	*	*
Carrots	*	0	*	+	*	++	0	*	*	*	*
Lettuce (raw)	*	0	*	+	*	*	0		*	*	*
Peas (fresh) boiled	**	0	*	*	*	*	0	*	*	*	*
Potatoes (old) boiled	*	0	***	*	*	tr	0	*	*	*	*
Spinach boiled	*	0	*	+	*	*	0	*	*	*	*
Tomatoes (fresh) raw	*	0	*	*	*	*	0	+	*	*	*

Carbohydrate, Protein and Fat are noted as follows:
0   None present or only a trace
*   Under 10% present
**   10 to 25% present
***   25 to 50% present
+   50 to 75% present
++   75 to 99% present
+++ 100% present
Minerals and Vitamins
0   None present
tr   Trace
*   Small amount present
+   Plentiful amount present

Vegetable Experiments
Potatoes

Take samples of a number of varieties of potatoes.
Weigh 4lb (2kg) of each variety. Attempt to obtain a fair sample of the potatoes in the container.
Wash each sample and dry. Re-weigh noting any loss.
Pass each sample through a potato peeler, making certain to stop the machine as soon as possible.

Remove all eyes, green sections, damaged or bruised sections and any other unusable parts and then re-weigh.

Calculate the percentage loss of (a) dirt (b) peelings, etc.

Divide each sample into 5 sections by weight.

Make sample

(a) into chips and pass through a deep fryer at a set temperature.
(b) place in the steamer, cook until tender.
(c) place in a roasting tray with a measured amount of fat. Cook at a set temperature until tender
(d) place in an earthenware dish, cook in the microwave oven until tender.
(e) place in an earthenware dish with sufficient water to cover. Cook in the microwave oven until tender.

Note the time taken for each operation.

Weigh each section after cooking and calculate the percentage of cooked potato produced by each from prepared potato.

Compare the finished potato dishes noting the following points:

Quality, Quantity, Flavour, Colour, 'Eatability', Texture, Suitability for purpose required.

Allow the dishes to stand in a *bain-marie* for 15 minutes and note if there is any variation in any of the above factors.

From your comparisons determine which varieties of potato are most suitable for which purpose. Is any potato variety suitable for general purpose use?

Green Vegetables

Obtain a 4lb (2kg) sample of as many green vegetables as possible (all in the fresh state).

Check that the weight is exactly 4lb (2kg). If it be necessary to cut any sample to obtain an exact weight take care to cut an even sample with dirt, outer leaves etc. in the same proportion as in the main supply.

Wash, clean and prepare for cooking and then re-weigh.

Note the percentage loss of each vegetable in preparation.

Divide the sample into equally weighed portions and put sample A into a pan to boil, sample B into a steamer to steam and fry sample C in shallow fat.

It is essential that if salt is added, the exact quantity is added to each sample and that the water in which the boiled samples are cooked is at the same temperature and the same measured quantity for each sample.

All pans must be of the same type and size and, ideally, all should be cooked at the same time over an identically heated area.

Time each cooking operation and when the vegetables are fully cooked empty from the pan and taste each. Make particular note of any variations in tenderising and flavour and appearance.

Weigh the finished products before tasting and calculate the weight lost in cooking and the amount of raw vegetable required for a $3\frac{1}{2}$oz (100g) portion of each vegetable.

Root Vegetables

Repeat the above experiment using samples of root vegetables.

In both experiments the experiment could be carried further by boiling all samples vigorously in the first experiment and then in a second experiment bring to the boil and simmer until cooked.

Does the cooking method give any variations in the cooked flavour of the finished dish?

Texturised Vegetable Protein

Texturised Vegetable Protein, usually abbreviated to TVP, is a recently introduced commodity in this country. It was developed in the 1950s mainly in the USA and was introduced to the market here in late 1959. Since that time a number of firms have produced their own types of the product and each firm has offered it in various flavours and sizes. Recent introductions include canned foods for the domestic market which use only vegetable proteins mixed with various other flavoured foods as a complete meal or as the protein portion of a meal.

The reason for the development of TVP as a food is mostly claimed to be the far greater amount of protein for the human diet which can be produced in vegetable form than the quantity which can be produced in meat form from the same area of land. As the majority of the world's underfed areas are short of protein and as it is anticipated that by the year 2 000 most of the world will be suffering from malnutrition due to protein deficiency, then it is obvious that some thought must be given to the production of additional protein.

Various methods of providing additional protein, in the form of animal or fish proteins, have been attempted — deer farming in Great Britain's highlands — kangaroo farming in the Australian outback — fish farming in the oceans and in certain large inland lakes; and even the use of waste products from the oil refineries to feed yeasts on and so produce a powdered protein product have all had various degrees of success. It is not our purpose to develop these points here. We point them out to those readers who wish to look into the matter further.

The development of vegetable proteins in various forms was practised for a number of years before TVP came onto the market. These included the protein content of the groundnut and other nuts from which oil had been extracted and which had previously been used as animal food. One project took groundnuts, removed the oil, the starch and the protein. The oil was used in the manufacture of margarines etc. The starch was used to make various non-food products and the protein was provided as a powder form to add to soups, stews and other dishes in the nutritionally deprived areas of Africa to improve the native diet.

All of these schemes have, as we say, had various successes but none have provided a viable substitute for red meat in the eyes of the housewife of the western world. TVP is an attempt to do this.

Figures to show the reasoning behind the use of vegetable proteins may be useful at this stage. We quote information supplied to us from various sources.

If one were to feed ten normal men, the following list shows the number of days during which ten acres of land could provide sufficient protein for their needs from one year's cropping.

Soya Bean Protein	2,200 days
Peas	1,600 days
Wheat	900 days
Rice	650 days
Milk	235 days
Pork	130 days
Beef	77 days

From this it will be seen that soya beans can provide the maximum feeding period of the foods listed.

One point which must be considered, however, is the type of protein supplied by these foods. Proteins are a combination of amino acids. There are in all some 20 amino acids. Of these 8 are essential for adults and these, together with another one, are essential for children. The ones essential for adults are

Isoleucine	Phenylaline
Leucine	Threonine
Lysins	Tryptophan
Methionine	Valine.

In addition to these, Histidine is essential for the growing child. Those protein foods which supply all of the essential amino acids are known as first class proteins or, by a newer term, proteins of high biological value. Those which do not supply all of the essential amino acids are known as second-class proteins or proteins of low biological value.

The vegetable proteins used to make texturised vegetable proteins are selected for their high biological values and therefore TVP products are able to offer first class protein to the diet.

In the manufacturing process the protein content of the vegetable is extracted from the fat and carbohydrate content. The fat content is often used for making up our commercial oils and fats and is referred to in the appropriate chapter. The carbohydrate content is used in various ways, some for food and others for various industrial processes.

The treatment next given to the protein is most important. There are two different methods used. The one which gives the most meat-like result is the 'extrusion process'. In this the protein is mixed with water, colour and any flavouring and then cooked before being extruded into pieces of the required size and dried. When rehydrated this product takes up water, swells and assumes a gel-like structure with a very similar eating quality to cooked meat.

In the second process the vegetable protein is spun through a machine to produce fibrous matter in a similar manner to the way of producing artificial textile fibres. This does not produce as satisfactory an eating quality when used as a meat extender in dishes such as pies, stews etc.

The method of using vegetable protein varies in different situations. The two major uses are either as an extender for meats or in its own right as a protein food.

Both methods have been used for a number of years and many developments have taken place over those years.

If the TVP is to be used as a meat extender it must be remembered that, by law, certain dishes must contain a minimum meat content. This is meat and not protein, so the TVP used must be extra to this figure. The regulation concerned is a complex one indeed. There are a number of such regulations mostly under the Food and Drugs Act. They include:

The Sausage and other Meat products regulations.

The Meat Pie and Sausage Roll regulations.

The Labelling of Food regulations and their amendments.

Any caterer intending to use TVP should provide himself with copies of these regulations or seek advice upon them.

Particular items of reference include the following dishes with a specified required meat content.

Beefburgers	80%
Beef Curry	35%
Boeuf Bourguignon	40%
Cottage Pie	25%
Goulash	35%
Irish Stew	25%
Lancashire Hot Pot	25%
Meat Stews	35%
Savoury Mince	35%
Shepherds Pie	25%
Steak & Kidney Pie or Pudding	25%

These are just some of the dishes specified, not a complete list.

Any TVP used in these products must therefore be in addition to the meat required to fulfil the laid-down conditions.

If it is intended that less than these amounts of meat must be used and the balance made up with TVP then the name of the dish must be changed and the name used must not be one to indicate a major component of meat.

The alternative, and one which may become necessary at some time in the future when more TVP is required to be used in our products is to make up dishes entirely from TVP as the protein content.

A typical example of this is one we have developed ourselves. We quote recipe and method to illustrate our point.

'Peakburger'

10lbs rehydrated beef-flavoured TVP mince
8 oz finely chopped onion.
1lb finely chopped part-cooked carrot
3lb dry breadcrumbs
Salt, pepper and mustard to taste
Eggs to bind
Soak the TVP in boiling water for 30 mins. and then cook for 10 mins. Strain any surplus liquor and allow to cool. Sweat the onions in dripping. Boil the minced carrot in water for some 10 mins. or use carrot which has already been cooked.

Mix all together, bind with egg — adding any liquor from the TVP if required, to moisten the breadcrumbs.

Divide into suitable sized portions. Mould, round and flatten to an appropriate thickness. Cook as required in a frying pan or on a hot-plate.

The exact method of preparation required by TVP will vary both according to the product used and to the dish or manner it is to be used in. The wise caterer will always take due regard to any suggestions made by his supplier at the same time still being prepared to try a sample made in another fashion.

From our own work, and from the advice of many friends, we would offer the following methods as ones which have proved to be useful.

(a) Soak the chunk type in cold water for $\frac{1}{2}$ hour before use. The exact amount of water varies slightly but is usually double the weight of the TVP giving of course 3lb ($1\frac{1}{2}$ kg) usable TVP from 1lb($\frac{1}{2}$ kg) dry weight.

(b) When using mince or powdered TVP this can be added to the appropriate amount of boiling water, mixed together and used immediately.

(c) When using chunks or smaller sizes it is often possible to add the dry TVP to any stew-like mixture and cook in the normal manner. It is important in this case to make certain there is sufficient moisture present in the dish to allow for the absorption by the TVP of approximately twice its own weight of moisture.

One suggestion to give a different flavour is to use a braising technique. In this chunks of TVP are fried in hot oil or fat until they take on a light golden-brown colour. They are then dealt with by adding to the dish in the case of stew-type mixtures or by so boiling water for some 15 – 20 minutes.

In general TVP requires less cooking than raw meat so it is often possible to reduce cooking time for many dishes. The mince type of TVP product is fully cooked in 5 minutes and the chunky types in 15 – 20 minutes. If the TVP is required to take up flavours from the other ingredients in the dish then this cooking time may require to be extended. We have found that TVP chunks retain their shape and eating quality after 2 hours of cooking so there is little danger of over cooking if reasonable care is exercised.

A research programme is, at the moment, under way in Great Britain trying to find a suitable vegetable to produce a sufficient quantity of protein to enable its commercial use in making TVP. Recent reports show that lupins are being tried for this purpose. The seeds have a high protein content and if cropping results can be improved upon this may well provide us with locally grown TVP.

Texturised Vegetable Protein Experiment

Examine as many samples of Texturised Vegetable Protein as possible both by eye and under the microscope.

Take $2 \times \frac{1}{2}$ oz(10g) samples of each and place each in a small dish.

Pour boiling water on one sample of each so that it is adequately covered.

Pour cold water on one sample of each to cover.

After 5 minutes re-examine all samples.

Make up the following dishes, using a standard recipe in each case.

(1) Beefburgers — for beef flavoured and neutral flavoured types.

(2) Stew — with the appropriate meat for Beef, Chicken, Lamb types

(3) Pork Pie and/or sausages with Pork flavoured types.

Now replace the meat in each recipe by 25 per cent, 50 per cent and 75 per cent TVP

Compare the results obtained.

Make up a dish to the given recipe using TVP as the only protein content. Compare the finished dishes for flavour, eating quality etc. noting at what stage, if any, the use of TVP became apparent.

The experiment can be extended by increasing the weight of samples treated and obtaining the opinions of various people who do not know TVP is added to the finished dish.

Edible Fungi

Fungi grow in a wild state in all parts of the world and in Britain we have a large number of varieties. It is of supreme importance to remember that some are edible, some mildly harmful and some are dangerous when

Edible Fungi

Morel

Blewit

Field Mushroom

Cep

eaten. The caterer should always restrict his purchase of fungi to sources which can assure him that all he receives are good quality edible fungi. There are many firms specialising in cultivated fungi and most wholesale suppliers obtain all their stocks from such sources. An alternative, where possible, is for the larger user to buy direct from such organisations.

Mushroom (Champignon)
Like most of the fungi the mushroom has only a small food value and its principal use in meal preparation is to add decoration and eating quality to the dish. When served as a separate item the method of cooking and the sauce served with them are of prime importance.

Both field and cultivated mushrooms are available (the points made above should be carefully noted). Grades available are Button, the small unopened mushroom, Small Caps, a mushroom which is rather larger and starting to open and Large Caps the large, fully opened mushroom. Buttons and Small Caps are preferred for many catering uses, particularly where the mushroom is to be presented in a whole or half form. The large caps are better used where they are to be cut up into small pieces or puréed.

Mushrooms are usually used in fresh condition the day they are received, but preserved supplies are available in either frozen or canned form when fresh supplies are not available. For many jobs these will provide a very satisfactory substitute for fresh supplies, although in the case of the more delicately flavoured dishes many chefs prefer to use fresh supplies.

Oyster Mushroom
Rather similar to the field mushroom, but growing on trees or fence posts. It has a cap which starts a bluish-grey in colour changing to a pale brown with age. They are usually fried.

Beef Steak Mushroom
Similar to oyster mushroom. Best eaten young. Has a beefy flavour. Grows on dead wood.

Ceps (Cèpe)
A mushroom cultivated in France. It can become quite large with age. It has a nutty flavour and is used in all ways listed for field or cultivated mushrooms.

Truffle (Truffe)
Found in Perigord and Piedmont districts of France, and also grown in Britain, the truffle is considered a delicacy. The French truffle is considered to have a superior flavour to the British product. It grows underground in woods, often near beech trees, in an irregular globe shape from 1″ to 4″ (2.5 − 10cm) across. It has dark brown skin with white flesh which soon turns buff coloured with white veins showing. It may be used

fresh or in tins — the tinned variety being imported from various parts of the world. Truffles are used as a decorative medium in many dishes on the cold buffet table and in classical dishes such as Sole Cubat and Poulet Sauté Archiduc.

Chanterelle
A funnel-shaped cap — egg yellow in colour with a base which extends down the stalk and an odour faintly resembling apricots. It is found in British woods in summer and autumn. The chanterelle can be rather tough and so needs lengthy cooking to tenderise.

Morel
Spring growing in clearings in woodlands — an acorn-shaped or oval cap with a criss-cross of brown ridges with darker brown hollows. The stalk is pale pink becoming redder when old. These can be fried for service with breakfast dishes in a similar manner to the mushroom.

Blewits
Mushroom-shaped with a grey or pale brown cap with a purplish tinge to the stem. Grown in open grass in the autumn and used as mushrooms.

Shaggy Parasol
This type is available in a number of varieties. Care must be taken in using them because some are poisonous. The two types mainly used are:
1. Shaggy cap — This is rather similar to a large mushroom and has a shaggy cap up to 8″ (20cm) across. The cap is an even brown colour all over.
2. The Parasol — This has a paler coloured cap, with a smooth brown centre with paler scales on the edges. The stem is tough and has shaggy scales on the surface.

Puff ball
This is a white ball fungus found growing in woodland and pastures. It can grow up to 4′ − 5′ (122 − 152cm) across if left unpicked. Young puff balls are the ones selected for eating and when sliced and fried provide a pleasant additive to the breakfast or high tea grill menu.

CHAPTER 2

Fruits and Nuts

The fruits have various important parts to play in the workings of the body. They provide important vitamin content to the diet, their cellulose matter is of importance to the digestive system and they have important mineral contents which are also required.

Most fruits have only a small carbohydrate fat and protein content and so are of prime importance in dietetic work.

To the caterer, fruits may be either fresh or preserved. Preservation may take any one of a number of forms and some preserved fruits alter completely after certain types of preservation. The most important of these are the dried fruits of the vine which give us our currants, sultanas and raisins and the candied peels provided by preservation of citrus fruit skins. Other methods of preservation are canning, freezing and bottling — all of which have an important part in catering supplies and, finally, the preservation of some fresh fruits by storage in special ways — such as in carbon dioxide gas to delay the final ripening process.

We will refer to the methods of preservation when dealing with each fruit and then summarise these methods at the close of this section.

Fresh fruits are divided into five main categories:

Soft fruits such as the berries and the red, black and white currants
Stone fruits such as plums, apricots, cherries
Hard fruits such as apples and pears
Citrus fruits such as oranges, lemons and grapefruit
Tropical fruits and others which cannot easily be classified under other headings and include bananas, dates, figs, melons, and rhubarb.

Soft fruits

These are grown in Great Britain and are available during the late summer season. At other times they are imported from other countries. The imported crops are considerably dearer than the home-produced, but as supplies of the latter are not so widely available imported produce has to be used by the caterer who has need of fresh fruit for a particular occasion.

The currants

The principal uses of the currants are in pies and puddings. Typical dishes are the fools, ice cream dishes and fruit pies and flans. They are also used in flavouring various jellies.

Red Currants (Groseille rouge)
They are similar in size to the blackcurrant but with a rather acid taste. The red currant is used in many different catering dishes.

Blackcurrants (Cassis)
They are traditionally a very good supplier of vitamin C and are also used as a basis of speciality blackcurrant juice drinks.

White Currants (Groseille blanche)
These are not easily available, but when they can be bought, may be used to form the basis of very pleasant speciality dishes.

The berries

Bilberry (Airelle Myrtille)
Also known as Blaeberry or Whortleberry. The bilberry is native to Great Britain and other European countries. This blue-black berry is round and about $\frac{1}{4}''$ (0.05cm) across. Preserved fruits in cans or bottles are imported from various European countries including Poland. They are used, like many soft fruits, in pie fillings and puddings.

Blackberry (Mûre de Ronce)
This is a berry of some $\frac{1}{2}''$ (1cm) in length by $\frac{1}{3}''$ (0.82cm) across. The blackberry is a cluster of seed-holding bags joined firmly together on a single stalk. The cultivated berry is far superior both in size and quality to the wild one which is seen growing in a great many parts of Great Britain and is available in August to October. Its uses are again the dessert course dishes, such as fruit flans and pies, puddings and fools and the ice-cream desserts.

Cranberries (Canneberge)
They are grown in Europe, North Asia, America and Russia. The cranberry is mainly used to make cranberry sauce and jelly for serving with turkey and venison. It is a rounded berry, bright red in colour and about $\frac{1}{3}''$ (0.82cm) across. British crops become available in late summer and at other times of the year. Either fresh imported supplies or canned or bottled fruits are usually used. Frozen supplies are also becoming increasingly available.

Dewberry
Rather similar to the blackberry but is rather smaller. The dewberry ripens earlier than the blackberry so, when available, can be used to provide the same type of dish at an earlier period in the summer.

Gooseberries (Groseille à Maquereau)
They are grown in many parts of Europe and good local crops are also

available in Great Britain. The berry is oval-shaped with a firm flesh covered by a hairy skin. Gooseberries are available in two types — a rather larger, often red-coloured dessert gooseberry and a harder, smaller green-coloured cooking gooseberry. The dessert gooseberry can be used uncooked in fresh fruit salads or served as a dish in its own right. The cooking gooseberry, being hard and rather tart, requires cooking with sugar and is then used in a similar manner as that already described for blackberries. Some dual-use fruits are also available. Local crops are available from July to late September.

Loganberries (Ronce-framboise)
A hybrid berry, rather larger than the raspberry, but of similar shape, rather darker in colour and with softer flesh — often seedless. The loganberry is cultivated in Britain and used in a similar manner as the other soft fruits. Crops available June to September.

Raspberries (Framboise)
Grown in most Northern European countries, the raspberry is a soft fruit of some $\frac{1}{2}''$ (1cm) long by a $\frac{1}{3}''$ (0.82cm) across. Like the blackberry it is a collection of small seed-holding segments attached to a single stalk. The fruit needs careful handling if it is not to be damaged. The British crop is available from June to September. The first crops come from the south country with the later crops coming from Scotland. Both white and red raspberries are available, the red type being the more common. They are used in dessert dishes such as pies, flans, and puddings as well as being a dish on their own with cream.

Strawberries (Fraise)
The strawberry is unusual among the soft fruits as it is the only common fruit which carries the seed on the outside of the skin. The common strawberry is bright red, varying slightly with different varieties, and is a rounded heart shape. The first British crops are available in June and go on through until September. Sizes of berries vary according to the variety. The caterer prefers the medium-sized fruits. Again their main use is in pies, flans and puddings. Strawberries are frequently used on their own and served with cream. Occasionally they form, with cream, the filling of a sandwich cake.

Storage and Purchasing

All soft fruits are extremely perishable so they should be bought daily for use when fresh. Storage for the period until use should be in a cool dry and dark place and a refrigerator at 40°F (4.5°C) is ideal.

When purchasing, care should be taken to examine the fruits. They should be fully ripened, but not over ripe. Dry, clean fruit of a suitable size should be selected; any showing green patches on red, white or black fruit indicate that they are not yet fully ripe. Colour is a good indication of ripeness.

In selecting the fruits, some regard can be paid to variety where this is known. Many of the fruits have different characteristics in each variety, so we list below some of the more common varieties available on the British market. It may be that the packs available in the wholesale fruit market do not name the variety offered and then the only way to select is on the points made above.

Fruit	Variety	Cropping	Comment
Blackcurrants	Laxton's Giant	July	Large berries — good flavour
	Boskoop Giant	July	Large berry
	Wellington XXX	Sept	Thin skin — good for eating raw.
	Daniel's September	Sept	Medium size
Red Currants	Redlake Earliest of	July early	Good flavour
	Fourland Laxton's	July late	First crops
	Perfection Mammouth	July early Sept	Large berry Large berry
White Currants	White Versailles	early July	First cropper
	Transparent	July	Clear skinned
	White Grape	July	One of the best flavoured
Blackberries	Himalayan Giant	late July	Large berry — good flavour
	Bedfore Giant	Sept	Large berry — later cropping
Gooseberries	*Cooking types*		
	Careless	June	Old type — good flavour
	Lancashire Lad	June	Green if picked early. Turns red and is used for desserts if left to grow
	Dessert		
	Crown Bob	June	Red
	Whinhams Industry	June	Large soft-skinned berry
	Leveller (yellow type)	June/ July	Yellow skin, dessert or cooking
	Whitesmith (white-skinned type)	July	White skin (pale green) For cooking, jam-making or bottling.
Loganberries	Thornless	July/Aug	Sweet eating — juicy
Raspberries	Laxton's Bountiful	June	Good eating
	Lloyd George	July	An old variety — still very well thought of

Fruit	Variety	Cropping	Comment
	Malling Exploit	July	Large, well-flavoured
	Norfolk Giant	Aug	Large fruit
	Malling Jewel	Aug	Large fruit — good flavour
	Hailsham	Oct	Good eater
Yellow	Golden Everest	July and	Good eater — colour
Raspberries		Aug	offers a good contrast
Strawberries	Red Gauntlet	June	Good colour — pleasant eating.
	Talisman	June	Fine flavour
	Royal Sovereign	late June	Old variety still very well thought of
	Stirling Castle	July	Medium size
	Auchincruive	July	Crops late in month
	Climax Huxley	July	A large berry which has a poor flavour
	Baron Stolmeir	Sept	A small berry which is not popular with commercial growers, but will crop until the frost comes

It must be remembered that the lists given above cannot cover more than a small number of the varieties grown at the time of writing. Horticultural research is continuing to go ahead with improving cropping of fruits, so new varieties, some of which may be better than any listed, are constantly being introduced. One difficulty is that improvements in cropping, quality or quantity can, at times, leave a fruit which has lost some other important factor — such as flavour. It is up to the caterer to select the fruit which will give the desired results.

Preservation

All soft fruits are preserved in a similar manner, by freezing, canning or bottling, canning usually in a syrup and bottling usually in water. Both involve heating the fruits to a temperature at which any putrefactive bacteria are killed off and this has the tendency to make the fruits rather soft and unsuitable for eating unless cooked further. Domestically the canned fruits are used by the housewife for serving as they are — but it is anticipated that the caterer would wish to offer a better article when this is possible. Uses of canned fruits are in flans, pies, trifles, jellies etc. Bottled fruits often do not have sugar added and are used for items in which the required amount of sugar will be added in a cooking process such as in making fillings for flans and used in pies, puddings, etc.

Frozen soft fruits are improving with research and the flow method using nitrogen gives a good quality fruit which can be used in its raw state for many dishes, for which fresh fruit is usually used.

Stone fruits

Plums and cherries are the major stone fruits grown in this country. Peaches, apricots and nectarines are imported for commercial use, although small quantities are grown in southern England.

Apricots (Abricot)
Apricots vary in colour from pale yellow to deep orange with a red flush. They also vary in size, flavour and tenderness. The skin is smooth and the flesh is pale to deep yellow surrounding a central stone. Apricots are imported from China, Japan, North Africa and California. They are packed in an unripe form so that they can ripen during shipment and storage. They are available during May to September as fresh fruit.

Peaches (Pêche)
Peaches vary considerably in their season of ripening, size and colour. Their velvety skin can vary from a pale green to golden yellow with a pink flush. The colour of the flesh may vary from a greenish colour through yellow to white with the yellow flesh being considered to give the best results in canning and the white flesh said to give the best flavour when used as a dessert fruit. Imported supplies come from the Mediterranean areas, the United States, Africa, China, Japan, Australia and New Zealand. Crops are available in the summer and autumn months.

Nectarines (Brugnon)
These are really a type of peach with a smooth skin of brighter colour and smaller in size. They are imported from similar areas to the peach, and are available during a similar period.

Cherries (Cerise)
They are members of the plum family, but smaller in size. The cherry is attached to a long thin stalk which should still be in position when the fruit is bought. Cherries may be imported or grown in Britain. There are two types — the sour cherry and the sweet cherry. The sour cherry is used to flavour liqueurs. Sweet cherries can be black or red in colour with a few white ones becoming available at times.

As with the peaches, the cropping period varies with the area of growth but the following are some suggested varieties which are well recommended:

Early White	Frogmore Early
Early Black	Early Rivers
	Bigarreau Schrecken
	Merton Favourite
Mid-season White	Kent Bigarreau
Mid-season Black	Waterloo
	Merton Bounty
	Merton Premier

Mid-season Red	Bigarreau de Mezel
Late season White	Florence
Late season Black	Hedelfinger
Late season Red	Napoleon

Plums (Prune)

Plums are grown in the northern hemisphere. There are good home produced crops in season and in both early and late season, imported supplies arrive to supply the market.

There are a number of different types of plums used in catering. The main ones are: the blackthorn or sloe, used in making wine and gin; the damson, a small plum used mainly in cooking and jam-making; the gages, the common type of which, the greengage, can be used in the same manner as the normal plum; the cherry plum, as its name implies, a small plum which is not often used in cooking and the European plum of which there are a number of variations.

We propose only to deal with the damsons, gages and plums in detail.

Damsons (Prune de Damas)

Available on the British market in September and October. A small plum used either for dessert or cooking according to variety. Examples of well recommended varieties are:

Cooking	Farleigh — available mid-September
	Merryweather — available late September and October
Dessert or	Bradley's King — available September
Cooking	Frogmore — available late September

Gages

As we have already said the Greengage (Prune de Reine-Claude) is the most commonly used variety but the yellow gages are also available.

First crops come through in mid-August and continue until October with British supplies.

Noted varieties are:

Cambridge Green Gage	Mid-August
Comte d'Althan's Gage	Mid-September
Early Transparent Gage	Early August
Golden Transparent Gage	Early October
Green Gage	Early September

Plums (Dessert varieties)

The normal dessert plum varies in colour from a blue-black through yellow to a full deep red.

British crops come onto the market in early August and then quantities increase until late September when they fall off. Sometimes late supplies continue until October.

Typical varieties are:

Victoria	Possibly the best thought of plum, gives excellent results both as a dessert plum and as a cooker. Crops in early September.
Coe's Golden Drop	A yellow plum with red patches. Crops in late September and is mostly used for dessert.
Laxton's Delicious	A yellowish-green colour used for dessert or cooking. Ready in mid-September.

Hard fruits

Apples (Pomme)

Apples are available in many varieties and, as they can be imported from all over the world without too much difficulty, they are readily available in all seasons of the year.

There are three major types. Those which one uses only as dessert apples and are normally called eating apples; those which may be used for either dessert or cooking — eat or bake; and those which are used only for cooking and are known as baking apples or cooking apples. The English crop is grown in many areas of the country and is available throughout most of the year by being given the correct storage. Some apples are ready for use immediately they are gathered from the tree. These come onto the market in August. Others crop later and become available in September, October and early November. Some varieties require storage for a period to complete their ripening and these become available from October and go on until the early summer months of the following year. There are various methods of storage. The caterer can purchase apples in boxes and store these in a cool, dry, dark place for a number of months, or the farmer or wholesaler can store in the same manner. An alternative is to delay ripening by storage in carbon dioxide gas. In this type of storage the apples are packed onto trays or shelving in a gas-tight store shed which is then filled with carbon dioxide gas thus delaying ripening by some months. In this way early ripening types can be made available almost throughout the year. Other methods of storage include bottling, tinning and freezing. Bottled fruits are well-known for their good quality and the A6 tins of canned apples, usually imported from other countries, have long been used in situations where the quantity can be used within two days.

The choice of which variety to use is important. The two most popular apples are probably Cox's orange pippin for eating and Bramley seedling for cooking. Both give excellent results, but there are others available at various times of the year and, in the choice of the dessert apple, it is important to appreciate that some people prefer apples of different coloured skins so a selection of red, red and yellow, yellow and green dessert apples both look attractive and at the same time offer choice to the customer.

We list below some of the more popular varieties with a brief description of each and the season they are mostly available.

Name	Type	Description	Home or Imported	Home Crop Available
Cox's Orange Pippin	D	A reddish-orange colour. Good flavour	H	Nov-March
Egremont Russet	D	A greenish-brown apple with slightly roughened skin	H	Sept-Oct
Golden Delicious	D	A yellow-skinned apple becoming more popular in recent years on the British market	H & I	Sept-Dec
Gravenstein	D & C	A larger type of apple with a sweet yet acid flavour and a strong aroma	I	Aug-Sept
James Grieve	D	Another acid dessert apple, but a very popular one. Has a skin with patches of red and yellow colouring	H & I	Sept-Oct
Ellison's Orange	D	A rich red-coloured fruit which was developed from Cox's orange pippin and so has many of the same characteristics	H	Aug-Oct
Laxton's Parmain	D & C	A small apple with a greenish-yellow skin flushed with red	H	Mar-Apr
Bramley's Seedling	C	The best cooking apple. It has a good shelf life and when used in cooking keeps its body well so gives a good filling to pies etc.	H & I	Dec-Jan
Laxton's Fortune	D	Another apple which has Cox's orange pippin as a parent and has very similar characteristics	H	Sept

Name	Type	Description	Home or Imported	Home Crop Available
Blenheim	D	A large apple with yellow skin flushed with red	H	Nov-Jan
Bismarck	C	A vivid crimson cooking apple	H & I	Nov-Feb
Laxton's Superb	D	Another apple with many of the characteristics of Cox's. It is very popular on the British market as the second choice to the Cox's pippin	H	Oct-Jan
Sturmer Pippin	D	A late apple which is better in imported crops due to weather	I	Sept-Oct
Granny Smith	D	Another late apple This time green-coloured with a golden tinge	H	Feb-Apr
Beauty of Bath	D	A green apple which has only a short storage life under normal conditions	H	Aug.
Stirling Castle	C	Has a pale green skin with a golden flush	H	Aug-Oct

Pear (Poire)

Pears, like apples are available in both dessert and cooking varieties with some varieties usable for both purposes. The usual choice for a dessert pear to be eaten raw is one which has a very juicy flesh which keeps soft without collapsing and for most people the William (correct name Williams' Bon Chrétien) is the one chosen. This is also used for canning when it is known as the Bartlett Pear. Preservation methods are similar to those already listed for Apples so we can proceed immediately with a list of the varieties available.

Pears are available from both home and overseas. The major countries from which we import pears are France, Germany and Belgium in Europe, and South Africa and Australia.

There is usually a period in late spring when supplies of dessert pears are very short so prices are high.

As with the apples, the pears vary in their keeping qualities. Some mature quickly and will only keep for a few days after gathering. Others require storing for weeks or even months before they are fully ripened and ready for eating.

Name	Type	Description	Home or Imported	Home Crop Available
Williams' Bon Chrétien or Bartlett	D or C	A yellowish-orange skin with red flushes. The flesh is a soft, very juicy quality with a fine flavour	H & I	Sept
Conference	D or C	Possibly the second most popular pear, widely grown in England. Will store for 2 to 3 months	H	Oct-Nov
Hazel	D or C	An older type not easily available. The pears are small but when ripe have plenty of juice	H	Sept-Oct
Beurre Hardy	D	An early cropping pear with good flavour	H	Sept
Doyenne du Comice	D	Another popular pear with a good eating, juicy flesh	H	Nov
Catillac	C	A hard pear which requires cooking. Stores well	H	Dec-Apr
Uvedale St Germain	C	Very similar to Catillac	H	Oct-Mar

Citrus Fruits

The citrus fruits used in catering are all imported. The fruit requires tropical or sub-tropical conditions for its growth and so no commercial growth is carried on in the United Kingdom. The major fruits in the group are the orange, lemon, grapefruit, lime and tangerine. All can be used as fresh fruit or they may be preserved in various ways. The main methods of preservation of interest to the caterer are canning (principally orange and grapefruit), bottling after preservation (lemon slices) and the preservation of the juice of the orange, lemon and grapefruit by canning, bottling or freezing. The skin of the fruit is crystallised into candied peel. All citrus fruits are important suppliers of vitamin C in the diet.

Orange (Orange)
The orange is available in two forms, the sweet orange and the bitter orange. The bitter orange is used to add flavour to marmalades and occasionally for the same purpose in a few dishes. Its major area of production is Spain. An alternative name is the Seville orange. The sweet orange is

available in various sizes and is imported from Spain, Israel, Florida, California and South Africa with smaller supplies coming on occasions from Australia, Brazil and some North African Countries.

Various types are available, Seedless oranges are popular for use in fresh fruit salads. Blood oranges have a red flesh and a reddish tint to the skin. One of the best-known names is the Jaffa orange, a large seedless variety with a high juice content.

With such a wide area of growth, supplies are available in fresh form in all seasons of the year. Other than names such as Jaffa and Seville, oranges are not often chosen by named variety but rather by the general descriptions quoted so we propose not to describe in detail the various varieties.

Lemon (Citron)
Widely grown in the Mediterranean and sub-tropical regions, the lemons used in Great Britain are mainly imported from Italy, Israel, Spain and California. Again several varieties are available but the caterer does not often purchase by name. With a wide area of growth fresh supplies are available in all seasons. The juice is composed of a large proportion of citric acid and has a bitter taste so is only rarely eaten as a fresh fruit. Its principal use is as a flavouring ingredient especially as a flavouring/ decorative ingredient on fish dishes.

Grapefruit (Pamplemousse)
The important producing areas of this fruit are in Florida, California, the West Indies, South Africa and Central America and again fresh fruits are available at all seasons of the year. Their principal use in catering is as a breakfast dish or starter course to a main meal when it may be served either as a half fruit, or in segments, or mixed with oranges as Florida cocktail or as fruit juice. Seedless types are available and these are the ones usually used when the half fruit is served.

Lime (Limon)
Not usually used as a fresh fruit but only as a flavouring or in the making of dishes and drinks. Its main growing area is in the tropics. The main centre for exporting to this country is Dominica in the West Indies.

Tangerine or Mandarin (Mandarine)
An orange-like fruit also known as Satsuma. The tangerine is a smaller fruit than the dessert orange, somewhat softer and principally used as a dessert fruit or for canning for use in fruit dishes.

The main areas of production are South Africa, USA, China, Japan and Spain and the main crop becomes available in this country during the Christmas period.

Citron
Not used as a fresh fruit in catering but the preserved peel provides an attractive decorative medium. The peel is much thicker than that of any

other citrus fruit and when preserved by candying has an attractive green colour. A traditional use which is not often followed today was to place a thin slice of the peel on the top of madeira cakes before baking. It is also used in mixed cut peels and in various other mixtures of preserved fruits.

Tropical and other fruits

Banana (Banane)
Grown in Central America, the West Indies and West Africa with some cropping in South Africa, Australia and the Fijian Islands. There are numerous types of the banana grown. Two main varieties are dessert and cooking bananas but the cooking variety are mainly consumed in the growing areas and are little used in Europe. Dried bananas are available but again are of little use in the catering industry. The major use then is as a dessert fruit when they may be served in a mixture of fruit or as an individual dish. Other uses are as fritters and as a garnish to poultry such as Chicken Maryland.

Pineapple (Ananas)
Native to South America and now grown widely in the tropics — the pineapple is available in all seasons, but at its best during our summer months. Fresh pineapples are used as a dessert in many sweet dishes and as a garnish to some meat dishes and as a fritter.

Grapes (Raisin)
The grape is used both as a fruit in fresh or preserved form and as a dried fruit it is the fruit used to produce currants, sultanas and raisins (see notes on preserved fruits). Another very important use in connection with the catering industry is in winemaking. It is in this respect that types, growth areas and climatic conditions are of supreme importance. Much could be said on this point but as it is so complex we would recommend any reader wishing to pursue the matter further to consult a book on wines and winemaking. Both black and green grapes are available and, although those sold in the United Kingdom are mostly imported there are home grown supplies of certain types available. The normal area of growth outdoors for the hardier grapes is south of a line drawn approximately from the Wash to Liverpool; north of this point glasshouse cultivation is required. The most popular type grown in this country is possibly Black Hamburgh, a fine black grape of good flavour. The green grape considered the finest is muscat of Alexandria, which, even in the southern areas is best grown where some protection and some heat can be given to it. These are the two types mainly used as dessert fruits — but for winemaking a great many other varieties, often giving their name to the wine made from them, are grown. With the wide area of growth and the use of

protection and heat, grapes are available in all seasons of the year — but local crops only in the autumn when imported crops are considered to be at their best and at their lowest price.

Melon (Melon)

Melons are closely related to cucumbers, but we deal with them under fruits as they are principally used in catering as a fruit or starter course. Three main types are used: honeydew, charentais and cantaloupe. Each comes from a different area and has different characteristics, so care must be taken in obtaining the correct types for the dish to be made. Melons can be grown in the United Kingdom, but this is only done in small quantities and very little of this production is available on the home market.

Honeydew or Winter Melon These are long, oval-shaped and with a dark green skin and a white flesh which is scented. They can be stored for a while and so are a good melon for transport. Main imports into this country are from Spain in late summer, autumn and winter.

Charentais Small, round, with a green/yellow skin and orange-coloured flesh — they are imported from France and Spain in late summer.

Canteloupe Large, round melons with a skin which has regular grooves and an orange-coloured flesh turning to pink. They are imported from France and Holland in late summer.

When buying melons a careful check must be made on them. If for immediate use, they must be fully ripened and a slight pressure with the thumb at the top or base of the fruit should show a slight degree of softness. The stalk should be sound and fully attached as when it is broken or removed, the melon begins to soften and go bad.

Water Melons This is a different plant from the other melons, but can be used in a similar manner, although possibly more popular as a dessert fruit. The seeds, which are a provider of oil, are eaten with the flesh. Commercial stocks are imported from sub-tropical and tropical regions in many parts of the world. The melon has a green skin with a thin yellow lining and a soft watery and red-coloured flesh inside. They often reach 9" − 12" (20 − 30cm) across and must be fully ripened before eating. This is the traditional melon seen in the American South films etc. where the pieces of melon are eaten from the skin and stretch from ear to ear.

Rhubarb (Rhubarbe)

Probably the largest area of commercial rhubarb growth in Great Britain is in Yorkshire, where both outdoor and forced rhubarb is grown. The forced variety is available soon after Christmas and the field grown from April to June, with the later crops tending to become rather coarse and acid tasting. Varieties have different flavours and appearance, ranging from Champagne — a variety which is used in winemaking and is a delicate pink colour with a mild flavour, to Early Albert — which has a tendency to be yellow-pink and to Victoria, a well-used main crop variety which tends to be reddish green in colour and has a more acid taste. It is important when using rhubarb that no portion of the leaves are used as these contain poisonous oxalic acid which has, on occasion, caused the death of people eating rhubarb leaves. Its principal use is in fruit pies, fools and as stewed rhubarb. It may also be used as an additive to other fruits.

Figs (Figue)
These may be used fresh or dried. The fresh figs are served as a starter course or a dessert course. Dried figs are used by the pastry-cook in pastry work and in puddings and tarts. Although figs were grown in Britain in the Roman times, there is no commercial production listed in modern times. Imported supplies come from the Eastern Mediterranean countries, — Italy, Algeria and Portugal with some supplies from California. Fresh supplies must, of course, be brought in by air, and therefore are expensive. Dried figs are in supply throughout the year. Fresh supplies are mostly available in the summer months. Canned fresh figs are also available.

Dates (Datte)
Dates are a principal crop in many of the countries on the Southern Mediterranean coastal strip and are also grown in California and Arizona in the USA. There are three types of dates eaten. The first are the soft dates, usually eaten as gathered in the countries of production. The second are semi-dried dates which are the ones usually used in this country and are available in boxes often with the fruits still attached to the stalk. The third are dried dates. These can be stored for long periods and form a valuable reserve food store in the producing areas. Whole dates can be served as a dessert in their fresh state. Stoned semi-dried fruits are used in pastry work in short pastry filling, in date puddings and, when coated with boiled sugar they are served as glazed fruits.

Both dates and figs have a high energy value because of their high sugar content, so they form a valuable dietetic source of energy.

Preservation

As already mentioned, fruits are preserved in many ways. We propose to deal briefly with the main methods of preservation and leave it to the reader to refer to the type of fruit preserved under the appropriate heading.

Bottling
Sound fruit is selected and after any appropriate cleaning, skinning and dividing up into smaller pieces is packed into sterile bottles. Sufficient water is added to cover the fruit and then a lid is applied and held down with a spring clip. The bottles are then heated in a hot chamber to semi-cook the fruit and to destroy any bacteria. Steam generated during this

heating process is able to pass out of the jar by forcing up the lid against the spring clip. After the appropriate time has passed, the jars are allowed to cool and in this cooling a vacuum is created under the lid thus sealing it on. The fruit may then be stored in a normal cool, dry store without strong light from many months. Cases have been known of such fruit being in good condition for over 5 years after bottling. The fruit is in good condition for most catering uses.

Canning

The canning process is basically similar to the bottling one with the exception that, while most bottled fruits are bottled in water, most canned fruits are canned in a sugar syrup. The density of the syrup is varied for each fruit. After a careful selection of the fruits — cleaning, peeling and dividing as required — the cans are filled with fruits and syrup added. The lids are then applied and the fruits heated in reduced pressure and a vacuum applied. The lids are then sealed and the fruits passed through a further heating process to cook them. After cooking, the cans are quickly cooled, labelled and packed ready for despatch. Canned fruits can be stored in a dry, cool store for a number of years, but good stock rotation is still desirable, so that the oldest is used first.

Freezing

Again the fruits are prepared in a similar manner to that already described. The best method of freezing is when the fruits can be frozen individually, so the new method of flow freezing is ideal. Most fruits are frozen unsweetened but some are often sweetened, so a careful check should be made to see which method has been used. Once frozen the fruits are packed in various sized cartons and must be stored no higher than $14°F$ (approximately $-10°C$) until required for use. Most fruits will give very good results after freezing, but one or two of the soft fruits are not of too high a quality after defrosting, so are not normally used as dessert fruits.

Drying

Various fruits are dried. The hard and the stone fruits can both be dried and made available for use in seasons of shortage. They are then soaked in water for a period to reproduce the fruits which may be used in many cooking processes. One dried stone fruit which is of importance is the dried plum. These do not reconstitute to the original form and are used in their own right as Prunes — a popular dish served for breakfast with or without cereal; as an additive to rice pudding and with custard or cream as a dessert dish.

Another fruit which is of supreme importance when dried is the grape, for dried grapes give us Currants, Raisins and Sultanas. Basically all dried fruits follow the same process. The fruit is gathered, cleaned, and then laid out on racks to dry — either in the heat of the sun or in artificial heat. After drying they are collected, packed and are ready for despatch. Almost all of our dried fruits are imported. Dried grape fruits are supplied by the Eastern Mediterranean countries — currants being an important export of Greece and sultanas coming from Turkey. Raisins are available from California and the Australian fruit grower has developed his crop and its quality greatly in post-war years and he is able to send us very high quality dried fruits.

The choice of variety is important in the dried fruits and particularly so in the vine fruits. Greek currants are graded by name — Vostizzas being the highest quality followed by Gulf, Amelias, Patras and Pyrgos. Australian currants are graded by crowns with 5 crowns being the best and one crown being the lowest quality.

Raisins are again graded in a similar manner with the best Mediterranean crop being Alicante and the Australian raisins being graded by crowns. South Africa exports us some good quality fruits in this range.

The best Sultanas should be light-coloured by natural means. Low quality fruits may have been bleached, so an examination should be given to any suspect goods and any with a smell of sulphur rejected. Smyrna sultanas are of the highest quality, as are Californian seedless. Again the Australian crop is of high quality and graded by crowns.

Candied Peels

We have already mentioned that the peels of the citrus fruits are preserved by candying. A thick-skinned fruit is chosen, cut in half and the pulp extracted and used for other purposes. The caps are placed in a brine solution for a few days and then, after washing, placed in successively stronger sugar solutions until they are thoroughly saturated. They are then dried off on wire trays, after which they are ready for supplying as drained caps or processing into mixed cut peel or a named type of cut peel.

Glacé Cherries

These are prepared by boiling in a thick syrup after the stones have been removed. A colouring is often added during this process to give them a brighter appearance. They should be stored with some of the syrup until required for use but care must be taken, in many uses, to wash the fruits to remove the syrup or this may spoil the appearance of the finished product.

Fruits — Experiments

In considering what experiments to undertake on fruits we would suggest that the basic factors of the fruits are those which should be researched.

(a) Colour and cooking ability.
(b) Flavour — raw and after cooking.

(c) What wastage is there:
     (i) in cooking
     (ii) when left standing

These may be carried out on different varieties of the same fruit or to consider how the different fruits compare for a similar use.

For the second question, the best way, we would suggest, would be to take equal weighted samples of different fruits and use them in a basic recipe.

Example:

Prepare four flan cases. Take an equal weight of raw apples, apricots, strawberries and banana. Prepare the fruit for use and cut into suitable sizes. Weigh the amount of fruit available for use. Fill the flans using pastry cream or jelly as a base and finish off for use in the restaurant.

Sample the flans — noting flavour, eating quality, portion size etc. Compare the results and determine a future usage policy.

Note

One variety of each of the four main groups has been suggested. This may be further developed by using four soft fruits, stone fruits, etc. or by giving variations in cooking time — nil, 10 mins, 20 mins, 30 mins etc.

Another point to be considered is whether there is any point in purchasing fruits by named varieties. This could be determined by the following experiment:

Take four different apples, one of which should be a cooking apple, one a cook or eat and one a dessert apple. The fourth could be any available apple or a canned brand of apple.

Firstly compare them for size, shape and for the amount of damaged sections in the apples.

Take an equal weight of each apple — possibly 7oz (200 g).

Note If the apples can easily make up this weight or if one has to be cut to make up a specific weight — would this cause further wastage?

Peel, core and cut the apples into sections (possibly 8) *Note the weight*

Note the colour and a description of each apple.

Taste each apple and note flavour and eating quality raw.

Cook each apple with the addition of a weighed quantity of sugar and water.

Note if there is any collapse or if the sections remain whole.

Weigh and taste after cooking and note results.

Now take a whole apple, core and place a lump of sugar in the hole created.

Bake for a set period. Note if each apple is cooked and if it can be served as a baked apple. Again test flavour.

Peel, core and section a sample apple of each variety and divide into four sections. Stand one in sufficient plain water to cover the apple.

Stand the second in sufficient water to cover but add 2 oz (56.7g) sugar to each pint of water used. Stand the third in sufficient water to cover the apple but add 1 oz (28.35g) salt to each pint of water and allow the third apple section to stand without water added. Note how quickly the apple section deteriorates. How they deteriorated etc. after a period of at least one hour. Cook the apples in water and note the results.

From these experiments the following points should be made:

1. Does the amount of wastage vary according to variety, size, quality, etc.?
2. Do cooking apples give a different result after cooking than the other types?
3. Does a similar variation occur when baking apples?
4. Is there a method whereby apples may be prepared prior to use and will remain in good, usable condition for a period?

A further development of the final point could be to extend the standing period overnight to see if it would be a reasonable proposition to prepare apples in a slack period during the previous day.

Nuts

Nuts are used in catering both as a dessert item and as an ingredient, or a decorative medium in the kitchen. They are an important item in the vegetarian diet because of their high protein content and are used in many vegetarian dishes. When served as a dessert the nuts are usually served with their shells on. When used in the kitchen, the shell is usually removed and the nuts must then be stored in clean, airtight containers. Because of their high fat content they will quickly go rancid if badly stored, so it is important they be kept in a cool, dry store until required for use and that large stocks are not kept for a long period.

Most nuts are imported, but some are home produced and notes will be given as to the appropriate source with each nut.

Almond (Amande)
Mainly imported from Mediterranean areas and Mexico.
Two types available — sweet and bitter. The bitter almond is used as a flavouring in some products, but is not commonly seen in the kitchen. The sweet almond is used as a dessert nut and in various forms in cookery.
Whole Almonds The whole almond with its brown outer skin after the outside shell has been removed.
Blanched Almonds The whole almond after dipping in boiling water and removing the brown outer skin.
Split Almonds Blanched almonds split in half.
Flaked Almonds Blanched almonds cut into flakes.
Strip and Nibbed Almonds Blanched almonds cut into strips or nibs.

Nuts

Hazel

Brazil

Filbert

Almond

Walnut

Chestnut

Ground Almonds Blanched almonds ground into a fine granular powder.

When purchasing, it is important to check that the product supplied is whole almonds, — some of the cheaper mixtures may contain groundnuts or hazel nuts or peach-kernel. These will not give the flavour required.

Whole or split almonds may be salted for use in cocktail bars, etc.

Whole almonds are used in cookery as a decoration, either before or after cooking.

Split almonds — as whole.

Strip and nibbed almonds — used mainly in decorative work, but can also be used in dishes where suitable.

Ground almonds — the main types used in dishes. Typical uses — rich fruit cakes; rich fruit puddings; filling for pastry goods, such as almond tarts; to make marzipan and almond paste; to make praline for various uses and as a coating for various items.

Brazil Nut (Noix du Brésil)
Used as a dessert nut

Coconut (Noix de Coco) This is principally used as a decorative medium and in some speciality dishes. It is also offered for service with curry dishes. The coconut is provided in dessicated form and is available in various grades — usually coarse, medium and fine. The type used can be varied with the dish being made, but the fine or medium is the more popular. When used as a decorative medium, it can be roasted by placing the required quantity on a clean tray in a warm oven and turning frequently until it all reaches the colour required or it may be coloured by adding a small quantity of liquid colouring to it and mixing well through. The chief supplies are from the South Sea Islands and the Indian subcontinent. All imported coconut must now be treated to remove any bacterial contamination before it is allowed into the country.

Chestnut (Marron) One of the few locally grown nuts. Supplies are also imported. There are two types — the sweet chestnut and the horse chestnut. Only the sweet chestnut is used for food. Crops are principally available in the autumn period up to Christmas and catering uses are in ice creams, as a stuffing for Turkey, and as a puree.

Hazel Nut (Noisette) As already mentioned, these are used by some people as a replacement for the more expensive almonds. They are available ground, nibbed or whole. Their principal use in catering in addition to this is in praline and as a dessert or as a decorative medium. A good quantity of local supplies are available from Kent in the late autumn and additional quantities are imported — mainly from Turkey.

Filbert (Aveline) This is a very similar nut to the hazel. It is also grown in Kent and is imported from South East Europe.

Pistachio Nut (Pistache) These are small green nuts which are cultivated in the Mediterranean countries. They are mainly used as a decoration on various gateaux, cakes and ice creams. The outside is brown, but this skin is removed by blanching as with the almond — the inner green flesh being used either whole or chopped.

Pea Nut or Ground Nut (Cacahuète) Pea nuts or monkey nuts as most of us have known them are really known as ground nuts, as they grow into the ground before harvesting. They are used, often salted, as a cocktail bar dainty and can be ground and used as a ground almond substitute. Their principal interest is their high oil content which is used as a cooking oil and in margarine.

Walnut (Noix) Available both locally and from many countries in Europe, Asia and China. The walnut is used as a dessert nut, as a decoration and as an ingredient. Pickled walnuts are also available. The principal uses are in dessert dishes, in salads and as a decoration for various cakes and sweet dishes.

CHAPTER 3

Dairy Produce and Eggs

Under this heading we propose to deal with milk, cream, butter, cheese and eggs, to show the variations between various types of each of these main commodities and to list preservation methods applied to those which are available in a preserved form.

Milk (*Lait*)

Milk is secreted by the lacteal glands of the female mammal for the complete sustenance of the young during the early period of its life.

Milk is therefore a complete food in itself and contains essential carbohydrate, protein, fats, mineral salts and vitamins for the growth of the young mammal. The milk of the beef cow is the type usually used in catering in this country but it must be recognised that all milks have the same basic background and the milk of some other animals is used in some countries. These animals include the goat, the ass, the yak and the camel. Goat's milk is sometimes prescribed in certain illnesses as is asses milk so the caterer in a hospital diet kitchen may be required to make up dishes using these milks.

The use of milk as an ingredient in dishes improves the flavour and the sugar content can cause cooked dishes to brown more easily.

Fresh cow's milk can vary in quality according to certain conditions. Amongst these are:
The breed of the cow
The food of the cow
The season of year
The time of day the cow was milked
The length of time since the cow had a calf

The breed of cow
Cows are classified into three main types:
1. Those which are bred for **beef production** — these will be dealt with in more detail under Meats. They have a low milk yield and are not usually kept on dairy farms.
2. Those which are **dual purpose** animals and will give a good milk yield over a fair period and still give a good carcase for use as Beef.
3. Those which are kept for their **milk producing** capabilities.
Typical of these classes are:

Dual Purpose Breeds

Dairy Shorthorn   Lincoln Red
Red Poll   Welsh Black
North Devon

Milk Producing Breeds

Jersey — the Jersey cattle produce milk of a very high quality which has a cream content higher than normal. It is usually sold at a higher retail price because of this factor.

Guernsey and South Devon — these breeds are similar in performance to the Jersey and produce milk of a similar quality.

Others kept for their high milk yields are — *Kerry Ayrshire* and *British Friesian*. This latter is also a good beef cow.

The cow's food

In most parts of Great Britain cows are put out to pasture in the summer months and the fresh grass they then eat probably contributes considerably to the increased quality and yield of the milk produced during the summer months. In the bad weather and winter months most cows are kept indoors and fed on cattle cake and other manufactured foods.

Season

As we have mentioned above, the quality of the milk increases during the summer months. At this period the cows have long periods of daylight during which they consume the grass which is turned into their milk. This together with the increased sunlight has its effect upon the quality of the milk.

Time of Milking

It has been recorded that milk from the morning milking is of superior quality to that from the afternoon milking.

Length of time since calving

The cow will give milk for a long period after giving birth to a calf. Towards the end of this period both quantity and quality begin to decrease and the cow is taken out of the milking herd and prepared for having another calf.

Fresh milk sours easily owing to the lactic acid bacteria present in the milk. These bacteria feed on the lactose (milk sugar) and convert it to lactic acid. This reacts with the milk protein causing it to coagulate and produce curds. The milk also has an acid taste and is known as sour milk.

As with many bacteria the lactic acid bacteria have a temperature range in which they work. At a temperature below 50°F (10°C) the bacteria only act slowly. At 70° to 80°F (20° − 25°C) they are fully activated and work quickly. At 150°F (65.5°C) they are killed. This factor is made use of in the pasteurisation process, the normal method used in this country for improving the keeping qualities of fresh milk.

In the original process milk was heated to 150°F (65.5°C) and kept at this temperature for 30 minutes, cooled rapidly to 40°F (4.5°C) and stored at 40°F (4.5°C) when it will keep for a number of days. A newer process is now usually used. The milk is heated to 161°F (71.6°C) kept at this temperature for 15 seconds and then cooled rapidly to under 50°F (10°C). This process is know as the High Temperature Short Time process (abbreviated to HTST). There is a danger of coagulation of the milk proteins which coagulate at 158°F (70°C) but the time at the high temperature is so short that it is possible to avoid this risk. The milk is then ready for bottling and despatch.

Composition of Milk

Fresh, full cream milk is required by regulation to reach a certain standard. These vary in different parts of Great Britain but in England and Wales milk must have a butterfat content of 3 per cent and a milk solids not fat content of 8.5 per cent

A pint of milk has an average content as follows:

Protein 18g	Vitamin A	258 μg
Fat 27g	Thiamin	0.2 mg
Carbohydrate 27.6g	Riboflavin	0.85 mg
Calcium 680 mg	Nicotinic Acid	5.2 mg
Iron 0.4 mg	Vitamin B12	1.8 μg
Phosphorus 540 mg	Pantothenic Acid	2.0 mg
	Biotin	11.4 μg
	Vitamin C	5.9 mg
	Vitamin D	0.29 μg

This is for summer milk; the quantity of some items falls in winter.

Milk Processing

Milk is processed in various ways to offer a longer storage life. Pasteurisation has already been dealt with. Other methods applied to liquid milks include sterilisation and the newer process of Ultra Heat Treatment (UHT).

Sterilisation

The milk is homogenised, that is mixed together so that the cream will not separate out, then heated to 212° to 240°F (100° to 115°C) in sealed bottles and held at this temperature for a long enough period to kill off all bacteria in the milk. It is then cooled and may be stored at normal temperatures of some 70°F (20°C) for some time without any souring taking place. One difficulty in this process is that the milk takes on a particular taste. This is liked by some people and not by others so if this milk is used as a beverage the flavour is changed. It is however, a flavour which will prove to be acceptable to many people in dishes such as milk puddings.

Ultra Heat Treatment

In this the milk is heated to a temperature of 275 − 300°F (135 − 149°C) for a few seconds and then rapidly cooled. This milk can then be bottled or packed in cartons when it can be kept under normal storage conditions for a long period (usually up to six months).

UHT milk does not have the flavour of sterilised milk and can be used in most catering items without any problem.

Other processes used to provide a milk with a longer storage period include Drying, Evaporation and Condensing.

Dried milks

The milk may be full cream or skimmed milk. Skimmed milk is the name given to milk from which the cream has been removed.

Two processes can be used, by driving off the water content by passing the milk over heated rollers (roller drying process) or by passing a spray of milk into a heated chamber (spray dried milk).

The roller process involves the danger of burning the milk sugar content and so has now largely been superceded by the spray dried process.

A form of dried milk not used in the industry to any great extent is special full cream milk. This is used for certain dietetic conditions and for feeding babies in certain conditions. Additional cream is added to the milk before drying. All dried milks are reconstituted by adding 2oz (56.7g) dried milk to 1 pint ($\frac{1}{2}$ litre) of cold or luke-warm water (1lb ($\frac{1}{2}$ kg) to each gallon) and whisking together. There is a danger of lumps if the milk powder has been stored in a damp atmosphere so sieving the milk powder before reconstitution is recommended. Once reconstituted the milk must be stored in a cool place and used quickly as its keeping qualities are only the same as those of fresh milk. In view of the hygiene problems it is recommended that a fresh supply of milk be made up for each usage and not a full batch made up for the day's work. In many items it is possible to mix the milk powder into the other ingredients in its dry form and allow reconstitution to take place when water is added in the mixing process.

Evaporated milk

The milk, usually full cream milk, sometimes skimmed milk and sometimes milk which has been treated to increase the vitamin D content, is prepared, and placed in a sealed chamber. The pressure is reduced until the milk can be heated to a temperature at which the water content will turn into steam without the temperature being too high so as to coagulate the proteins. As water boils (turns into steam) at a lower temperature when the pressure is reduced this is possible. The steam created is taken out by an extractor fan and the process continues until some 60 per cent of the water content is removed. The milk is then run off into cans, sealed, labelled and is ready for despatch. The cans are of various sizes,

57

small ones for domestic use and larger cans holding the equivalent of a number of gallons of milk for various industrial uses.

Condensed milk
This is produced in a similar manner to the evaporated milk but taken a little further. Sugar is added before canning. When using this type of milk in catering due allowance must be made for the sugar content.

Both types of milk are packed in cans with full instructions printed on the label as to the normal method of reconstituting the milk back to standard milk. These should be read before use.

Cream (*Crème*)

Fresh cream is available in various types. It is usually pasteurised. The thickest cream normally used by caterers is double cream which has a butterfat content of at least 48 per cent. Whipping cream has a butterfat content of at least 35 per cent and single cream that of 18 per cent. Other types are available but are not generally used in catering.

In some situations a stabiliser is added to cream to improve its whipping properties. These are strictly controlled by the Food and Drugs Acts. The ones permitted at the time of writing are:
a)   sodium alginate
b)   a mixture of sodium bicarbonate, tetrasodium pyrophosate and alg̈inic acid
c)   sodium carboxymethyl cellulose
d)   carageen
e)   gelatines in quantities which in total do not exceed 0.3 per cent of the weight of the cream.

Butter (*Beurre*)

Butter is made from the cream of milk. Again the cream can come from various animals although in this country butter from the cow's milk is the most common with Goats' milk butter being used occasionally for special dishes and for diets.

In the butter-making process the selected cream is washed by steam, rested for a period and then churned for some 30 to 40 minutes. During this churning the fat gathers together leaving the major liquid portion of the cream. This liquid is known as buttermilk and is used in some catering and bakery work for speciality dishes.

After the churning process the buttermilk is run off and the fat cooled and washed by adding chilled water. After this stage, salt and colour may be added. The exact amount of each added will vary according to both the type of milk used in the first instance and the type of butter required as the end product. After a final mixing in the churn the butter is then removed and taken to a packing plant for packing into domestic or commercial packs as required. Typical packs are the individual portions used with rolls etc., half pound or one pound blocks and 28 or 56lb ($12\frac{1}{2}$ – 25kg) cases. Butter was at one time also packed in barrels but these are only rarely seen these days.

The butter sold in this country must conform to certain legal limits. The most important of these is that it must not contain more than 16 per cent water. The fat content will be over 80 per cent and the salt, colouring matter and small quantities of milk protein in the form of curds will make up the remainder. An average analysis of various popular butters are as follows:

	English	Danish	Australian	New Zealand	Siberian
Fats	82	83.5	84.5	85.8	86
Water	14	13.5	13	11	11
Curd	1.5	1.25	1.25	1.2	1.25
Salt	2	1.75	1.5	2.25	1.5

(These do not necessarily add to 100 per cent because they are an average of a number of analytical surveys).
Butter is imported from countries other than those listed including many Western European countries. Special brands may vary from the national average figures quoted above.

Siberian butter is included because of its special qualities. The monoglycerides in the various butters will vary according to the milk used to make them, from a larger proportion of the softer monoglycerides to a larger proportion of the harder ones. Siberian butter contains a relatively high proportion of the harder glycerides and is thus an ideal butter for puff pastry and danish pastry work and for modelling work.

Cheese (*Fromage*)

Cheese is again made from milk. The milk is delivered to the cheese-making factory in large tankers. (A little cheese is still made on farms, but this is only a small quantity and is mostly sold through farm gate sales or in specialised retail outlets.) After testing, the milk is placed in large containers. The milk is warmed by pipes which pass round the container and then a souring organism is added. This is a type of rennet, often specially cultivated in the cheese factory so as to produce a cheese of a particular quality. The milk is soured and turns into curds and whey. The whey is separated out and is used for other purposes and the curds cut up to release any whey imprisoned inside the curds. The curd is now gathered together into blocks which are allowed to stand to drain being continually turned during this standing so as to expel any remaining whey. This is known as cheddaring. The exact manner in which it is done varies with each type of cheese. The curd is now cut up by machine into small pieces and salt mixed into it. Colour if required, is also added at this stage. The curds are now packed into moulds, pressed for 24 hours and then stored for a period until they are ready for use. Most cheeses are graded for quality before being sent out of the factory for sale.

Variations in the cheeses are made by altering the above processes and also by allowing other developments. Most of these will be referred to in the descriptions of the major cheeses which follow, but special reference must be made to the blue cheeses. These have blue veins running through them. This veining can be caused by mould being allowed to develop in the cheese, by either packing a mouldy item when the cheese is being packed into the moulds before pressing (Roquefort has mouldy bread crumbs packed into it) or by injecting moulds into the cheese, as is done with Stilton cheese.

One point should be remembered — many of the cheeses are available in more than one form, e.g. blue and white Stilton, white, red and blue Cheshire. When ordering a cheese the order must clearly state the type required and when labelling them on a cheese board the same care must be taken.

Buying and Storage

With the large number of cheeses and the wide variation between them it should be obvious that only a general guide can be given in this section.

There should be no over-strong smell for the type of cheese under survey, an indication of an ammonia-like smell indicates a bad cheese.

The skin or rind should not show any damp patches or moulds. When the cheese is cut it should not be dry in a semi-hard or blue-vein variety and should not be runny in a soft cheese.

The outer crust should not be dirty.

Unless very good storage conditions are available cheeses should not be stored for a long period. Where storage is possible this should be in a cool, dark store at a temperature of about 50°F (10°C) the cheeses must be turned every week and used in correct delivery order. Once cut the cheese should be used as soon as possible. It is possible to extend the storage life of a cut cheese by covering the cut surface with a muslin cloth which has been dampened with a salt water solution.

Cheese will give off smells and take them in so any cheeses in store should be kept out of the way of all other foods.

Refrigerated storage at a temperature of 40°F (4.5°C) is good for a few days but should not be used for long-term storage. Deep freeze storage may be suitable for some cheeses but is not generally recommended for all cheeses.

Cheese is used as a dish in its own right, as an ingredient in many dishes and as a dressing and a sauce. The cheese usually used as a dressing is grated Parmesan cheese.

A modern development in cheese production has been the availability of crustless cheeses in block or round form and of processed cheeses. These are good cheeses for many uses but to a great many people they are not widely welcomed on the cheese board.

Cheeses are classified either by their country or area of origin or by their type, the types being:
1. Hard cheese.
2. Semi-hard cheese.
3. Soft or cream cheese.
4. Blue veined cheese.

British Cheeses

1. Blue Vinney (Blue Dorset)
Made in Dorset from skimmed cow's milk. White in colour, blue vein, hard texture, rather strong flavour.

2. Caerphilly
Originally Welsh, now also made in Somerset, Wiltshire, Devon and Dorset. A whole milk cheese, pressed only lightly, which can be eaten when only 10 days old. Soft and white, creamy, mild flavour, and best used uncooked.

3. Cheddar
Originally made in Somerset. Now produced all over the world by the 'cheddaring' process. A hard, yellow, slightly salty cheese; varies in flavour from mild to strong. Equally good cooked or uncooked.

4. Cheshire
Said to be oldest English cheese. Hard but crumbly with a mild and mellow flavour. Three varieties: the red, which is artificially coloured, the white and the blue. The red is normally milder than the white. Some cheeses are allowed to turn blue and develop a very fine rich texture and flavour. Equally good cooked or uncooked.

5. Derby
A hard close-textured, white cheese, mild in flavour when young, but developing a full flavour as it matures.

6. Sage Derby
Derby cheese, layered with sage leaves to give green bands through the cheese. Very pleasant cheese, not widely available.

7. Dunlop
A Scottish cheese, originally produced in Dunlop, Ayrshire, but now fairly general throughout Scotland. Not unlike Cheddar, but moist and of a closer texture.

8. Double Gloucester
An orange-yellow cheese with a close, crumbly texture and a good rich flavour rather similar to that of a mature cheddar.

9. Lancashire
A fairly hard cheese, crumbly in texture when cut. When new it has a mild tangy flavour, which develops considerably as it matures. Can be eaten uncooked and is an excellent cooking cheese.

10. Leicester
Hard cheese, orange-red in colour, and a mild, slightly sweet flavour.

11. Blue Stilton
Stilton is in Huntingdonshire but genuine Stilton is also made in Leicestershire and Derbyshire. Probably the greatest of all cheeses. A white, double cream cheese (produced from the richest milk and the cream of other milk may also be added). Made only from May to September — needs 6 – 9 months to ripen — at its best when fully ripe. The cheese is semi-hard with blue veining, caused by innoculation. The veins should be evenly distributed. The rind must be of a dull, drab colour — well crinkled, regular and free from cracks.

12. White Stilton
Stilton cheese is also available as a white cheese; again it has a very fine flavour.

13. Blue Wensleydale
Made in the valley of Wensleydale in the Yorkshire Dales. Originally it was a double cream cheese, cylindrical in shape, matured until it became blue. It was considered second only to Stilton.

14. White Wensleydale
A mild, creamy cheese with a flaky texture. It has become more common in recent years.

Continental Cheeses

Italy
1. Bel Paese Rich, creamy cheese of mild flavour. Made in various parts of Italy, usually from October to June. The cheeses weigh about 5 lb ($2\frac{1}{2}$ kg).

2. Gorgonzola Semi-hard, blue veined, sharp flavoured — made around Milan.

3. Parmesan Hardest of all cheeses; specially processed, the curd is broken up, heated, packed into a large mould the shape of a large millstone and matured for at least two and usually three years. When ripe the crust is almost black, but the cheese itself should be a pale straw colour and full of pinprick holes. A strong distinctive flavour and is used as an accompaniment for minestrone, pasta and rice dishes.

Switzerland

1. Gruyère A hard, large cheese, weighing anything up to 100lb (45.5kg). Originally from Switzerland, it is now made in France, Italy and other parts or Europe. Pale yellow in colour, honeycombed with 'eyes' or holes, caused by the rapid fermentation of the curd. It has a distinctive and fairly sweet taste. It is served uncooked, but it is also used in such classic dishes as Fondue.

2. Emmenthal Similar to Gruyère but larger and slightly softer in texture with larger 'eyes'.

France

1. Brie A soft-textured cheese, produced in the north of France. Made from whole milk; is mould innoculated. Flat and round, usually 14" (35.5cm) across — $1 - 1\frac{1}{2}$" (2.5 − 3.5cm) thick and about 6Ib (3kg) in weight. A brownish, slightly mouldy crust instead of the more usual hard rind. Should be eaten fresh; does not keep well.

2. Camembert A soft-textured cheese, made from cow's milk, the curd being innoculated with a white mould. The cheese was made originally in Camembert, but is now made in other parts of Normandy. The best is made from the richest milk during the summer months. Camembert is at its best when it begins to get soft. If it is allowed to over-ripen it becomes too soft and gases are generated, giving it a smell which many people find unpleasant.

3. Demi-sel A soft cream cheese, usually sold in small square foil wrapped packets. Made mainly in Normandy.

4. Fontainebleau A soft, fresh cream cheese. Made around Fontainbleau. Produced mainly in the summer.

5. Petit Suisse An unsalted cream cheese, cylindrical in shape, mild in flavour. Often sold in small foil-wrapped packets.

6. Pommel A double cream cheese, unsalted, and not unlike Petit Suisse. Made all the year round.

7. Pont L'Évêque A semi-hard, yellow cheese, about 4" (10cm) square $1\frac{1}{2}$" (3.5cm) thick. Made practically all the year round in the Pont L'Évêque area of Normandy. Salted repeatedly while maturing.

8. Port Salut A semi-hard cheese, round in shape, made originally by the monks of Port Salut. Now made elsewhere in France and Belgium.

Creamy-yellow in colour and has a mild creamy flavour. Should be eaten slightly soft.

9. **Roquefort** Made from ewes' milk. Made during lambing season in village of Roquefort in the mountains of Cevennes. Only made in this area, partly because the sheep grazing is suitable but also because of the limestone caverns of Roquefort itself, where the cheese is matured. Mouldy breadcrumbs (containing the same mould as that used in the making of Stilton) are introduced into the curd as a maturing agent.

Denmark

1. **Danish Blue** A white crumbly cheese with a blue mould veining and a sharp salty taste.

Holland

1. **Edam** A ball-shaped cheese, bright red skin, deep yellow inside, about 5Ib ($2\frac{1}{2}$ kg) in weight. Firm in texture and a mild flavour. Imitations are made in Germany, Belgium and Yugoslavia.

2. **Gouda** Similar to Edam in taste and texture, but flatter in shape with a yellow skin and very much larger. There are also small Gouda about 1Ib ($\frac{1}{2}$ kg) weight known as 'Little Dutch'.

Belgium

1. **Limburger** A semi-hard, whole milk cheese made from December to May. Full flavoured, strong smelling.

Norway

1. **Mysost** (Gjetost) A whey cheese, principally made from goat's milk. Hard and dark brown, with a sweetish flavour.

Milk Experiment

To introduce the student to the various types of milks and to show how the processing they have received alters their flavour.

Milks suggested for sampling

A.   1 pt ($\frac{1}{2}$ litre) Pasteurised Milk

B.   1 pt ($\frac{1}{2}$ litre) Sterilised Milk.

C.   1 pt ($\frac{1}{2}$ litre) Homogenised Milk.

D.   1 pt ($\frac{1}{2}$ litre) Long Life (UHT) Milk.

E.   2 oz (56.7g) Dried Full Cream Milk.

F.   2 oz (56.7g) Dried Separated Milk.

G.   1 Medium Can Evaporated Milk.

H.   1 Medium Can Full Cream Condensed Milk.

I.   1 Medium Can Separated Condensed Milk.

(1) Examine all samples both visually and for taste, colour, aroma etc.

(2) Re-constitute E, F, G, H and I to make 1 pint ($\frac{1}{2}$ litre) milk from each (check quantity required as given on cans).

(3) Examine re-constituted milks for colour, flavour, aroma.

(4) Using $\frac{1}{2}$ pint ($\frac{1}{4}$ litre) of each milk add a similar quantity to a cup of tea, sample for taste. (Do not add sugar).

(5) Using $\frac{1}{2}$ pint ($\frac{1}{4}$ litre) of each make up into a rice pudding. Sample for taste etc.

Butter Experiment

Take $\frac{1}{2}$ pint ($\frac{1}{4}$ litre) cream (double), whip with an electric mixer at high speed until a thick cream is formed, continue whipping and note the results. Weigh the mass formed.

The mass formed is butter — note its colour and flavour.

   Add yellow colouring to taste

   Add salt to taste — noting carefully the weight used.

   Taste the resultant product and note your findings.

   Work out the percentage salt used to obtain a good flavour.

Take a 1 $\frac{1}{2}$ oz (50g) sample of butter as supplied. Melt this in a beaker set in a pan of warm water. When melted place in the refrigerator to set — has any separation occured? — If so what do you find — check the weights of any items you can separate as carefully as possible.

Take 2 pt (1 litre) of fresh, full cream milk, add 10 drops of rennet. Whisk this in an electric mixer at high speed until butter is formed. Weigh the butter produced and calculate the proportion produced as a percentage of milk.

Examine all butter produced under the stereo-microscope.

Write a report on your findings.

Creaming Test

Take 3 $\frac{1}{2}$ oz (100g) butter. Place in mixer bowl. Using a cake beater beat 1 min. on slowest speed, scrape down, beat 1 min. on slowest. Scrape down, beat 4 mins. on Speed 6. Scrape down, beat a further 4 mins. on Speed 6. Empty into a glass beaker, level off. Measure the volume obtained. Repeat using different butters. Compare results.

Water Absorption Test

Return creamed butter to the bowl. Add cold water 0.105gill (15ml) at a time and beat in. Scrape down after each 0.315gill (45ml) added. Continue until the emulsion breaks. Record the amount of water added. Compare results.

From the last two tests determine which butter would give the best results in a cake mixing.

Cheese Experiment

Take a number of samples of different cheeses. Taste each and note your findings.

Grate each cheese and obtain a 1oz (25g) sample of each.

Place the sample on a piece of silicone paper which has been placed on a grill tray.

Set the grill at a medium heat, place the first sample under the grill and cook until it boils and the edges commence to brown. Record the times before and after cooking and note the cooking period required. Taste the cheese again.

Repeat the experiment exactly with each cheese.

Note the following observations:

(a) Which cheese cooks most quickly.

(b) Which cheese browns most quickly.

(c) Which cheese has a superior flavour and aroma:

    (1) Raw

    (2) Cooked

(d) Which cheese has the better eating quality

    (1) Warm

    (2) Cold

From these observations which cheese should be used for dishes such as Welsh Rarebit?

Repeat the experiment by heating the cheese in a frying pan in which $\frac{1}{4} - \frac{1}{2}$ oz (10g) butter has been melted.

Again note your observations.

Which is the best cheese for frying?

Eggs

Eggs are intended to be the first stage in the growth of birds. They are all, therefore, capable after incubation, of forming the body of the baby chick. They contain protein, fats, moisture, minerals and vitamins and are used by the caterer in many dishes. All types of birds' eggs contain approximately the same percentage of these items and can, therefore, be used in catering. It is usual in Great Britain to use only eggs from hens for most dishes with those of ducks being used in certain speciality dishes and a few wild birds' eggs used in some other dishes.

Hens' eggs are available in various sizes graded from 1 to 7. Size gradings are made as follows:

1. over 75g
2. 70 – 75g
3. 65 – 70g
4. 55 – 65g
5. 50 – 55g
6. 45 – 50g
7. under 45g

They may be fresh or preserved. Most hens' eggs in the fresh form are supplied by British farmers with a few being imported from near European countries. Processed eggs can be imported from countries further afield. As the caterer only makes use of one or two types of processed eggs, we propose to deal briefly with those which are little used in the industry and in greater detail with preserved shell eggs, dried eggs and frozen eggs which are the ones the caterer uses more often.

As we have said the egg contains in primitive form all the make-up of the young chick. The yolk contains the embryo which uses the remainder of the egg as its food during the incubation period. An important feature is that the shell is porous in order to allow the chick to breathe during the latter stages of incubation. This is the point which must be remembered in storage and processing and more will be made of the point in the latter stages of this section.

Fresh Eggs

Fresh eggs are supplied under two names — New Laid or Fresh.

These two terms are often confusing. There is no apparent legal definition of these two points, but it is generally accepted that New Laid Eggs are those which have been laid recently and Fresh Eggs are those which are still sound and have not undergone any preservation process.

A simple test is to place the egg in a solution of salt and water. If 4oz (100g) salt is added to 2 pints (1 litre) of water at 75°F (23.8°C) and stirred in this will produce a 10 per cent brine solution. If the egg is placed in this is a fresh egg, it will sink and an older egg will float. The egg packing stations employ a different method. The egg is passed over a strong light and skilled operatives can look at the egg and, by seeing the placement of the yolk, the size of the air sac and the colour can determine if the egg is fresh. At the same time any cracks in the shell or any other damaging features can be determined. This process is known as 'candling'.

After candling, the eggs are graded as required and any which do not pass the tests are rejected from the packing stream.

Sound eggs which are rejected because of faulty shells etc. are passed on to a freezing plant for use as processed eggs.

There are certain catering operations which require an egg of good quality. In these all eggs used must be fresh. Typical of these are boiling, poaching and frying. In each case it is important that the yolk of the egg remains in the centre of the white. If the white is weakened by age, then the yolk will sink and thus produce a finished product with an uneven appearance.

Remembering that the shell is porous is of the utmost importance. The longer the time between laying and delivery to the caterer's store, the greater the risk of contamination and the shorter the period in which the egg will remain usable. If stored in a refrigerator immediately after laying at 35 to 40°F (2 to 4.5°C), eggs will store for 100 days before they become unusable, but the strength of the white will be decreasing all the time. If left in normal kitchen storage conditions, life in store may well be shortened to 30 to 40 days (less in warm weather or surroundings). It is therefore important to store fresh shell eggs in cool conditions and to make sure that the eggs are used in rotation (oldest used first). Duck eggs require particular care because they often have a higher salmonella count.

Shell Colour

The colour of the shell varies according to the breed of the hen from white to a deep brown. Heavyweight hens produce a smaller number of eggs of a deep brown colour and lightweight breeds a larger number of eggs of a white colour. Cross-breeds and dual purpose breeds produce eggs which vary between the two shades.

Because of their lower egg production and their higher consumption of food per egg produced, the breeds producing the brown-shelled eggs cost more to keep so the producers generally have to charge more for brown-shelled eggs. It is most important for the caterer to realise that, once the shell is cracked, there is no difference between white or brown shelled eggs. Their food value is exactly the same and their efficiency in dishes does not vary. The tradition in Great Britain that a brown-shelled egg is superior is completely wrong. One point to be remembered though is that, if the client prefers a brown-shelled boiled egg, it may be worth paying a little more for brown eggs.

Processed Eggs

Eggs are processed to preserve them. Three major stages of preservation are employed.

A. To preserve the egg in its shell, these are often known as cooking eggs and can be used by the caterer in many dishes.

B. Dried egg — the moisture is taken out of the egg and the dry solids can be stored for a long period. Although useful for a few items these eggs lose much of their aeration qualities and are thus not often used in the kitchen.

C. Preserved liquid egg — the egg is cracked, mixed together and then subjected to one of a number of preservation methods in order to enable it to be kept. The most useful type of preserved liquid egg in the kitchen is Frozen Egg. This is of very good quality and can be used in many dishes.

A. Preserved shell eggs

The eggs are tested as already described for Fresh Eggs and then are processed.

(1) *Chilled eggs* The eggs are packed in trays, boxes etc. and placed in a refrigerator at a temperature of 37°F (3°C). They can be stored at this temperature for up to 100 days before they are unusable in foodstuffs. They must be transported at this temperature and must be used as quickly as possible after removal from the refrigerated store.

(2) *Waxed eggs* The eggs are dipped into molten wax. The wax sets on the shell sealing it and the eggs can then be stored in a cool, dry store for 3 months or longer. This type has the advantage that eggs can be used as required over the storage period and they do not need refrigerated storage.

(3) *Chemically preserved shell eggs* Fresh eggs are dipped into chemical solutions and, after the chemical has dried on the shell it seals it and prevents bacteria entering. The eggs will then keep in a cool store for up to 12 months before they become unusable.

Eggs preserved by the chemical method tend to become watery during storage but waxed eggs retain much of their original character and will give good results.

B. Dried eggs

The tested eggs are cracked, mixed together and then fed by spray into a warm room, the moisture evaporates off leaving behind the dried egg. This can then be packed and will keep in good condition in an unopened packet for 2 or 3 years. After the packet has been opened it is best to use it within 3 or 4 months although in good storage conditions this period can comfortably be exceeded.

Dried egg whites (Albumen)

Egg albumen is very widely used in all food production work where egg whites are required. By its use the caterer has no problem of using up egg yolks from the eggs and so can produce goods far more economically. In addition albumen produces an egg white of the highest quality and, furthermore, the strength can be adjusted for the work on hand. Egg albumen is available in crystal form, in ground form and as specially prepared products which will reconstitute immediately. The crystal form usually requires to stand overnight before use and the ground form has to stand an hour or so.

To reconstitute egg whites, $1\frac{1}{2}$ oz to 3 oz (37.5 – 75g) of albumen is added to 1 pt ($\frac{1}{2}$ litre) of cold water. 3oz (75g) produces a very strong white, 2oz a standard one and $1\frac{1}{2}$ oz (37.5g) a weaker one.

To reconstitute whole dried eggs 1lb ($\frac{1}{2}$ kg) of whole dried eggs is added to 3 pt ($1\frac{1}{2}$ kg) of cold water and whisked together. After standing for a few minutes the eggs are ready for use.

Dried yolks are also available but are not often used in the kitchen.

C. Processed Liquid Eggs

Frozen eggs

Frozen whole eggs, Frozen Egg Whites and Frozen Yolks are all available. Frozen whole egg is the more common with the frozen whites only being used where a larger quantity of whites is required.

The eggs are checked and either separated or mixed together according to the type to be produced. They are then packed into tins containing various weights 5, 10, 20 Kilogrammes and 7, 11, 14, 28 and 40lb being common sizes. They are then quick frozen and are stored in a deep freeze store at 0°F (– 20°C) until required. When they are required they should be allowed to defrost slowly and then used within 2 days, being stored in a refrigerator at no more than 40°F (4.5°C) until used up.

The storage problem, both before and after opening is the major problem with this type of egg, as there are only a restricted number of dishes that whole egg mixed together can be used in. The quality they give, however, is very good and equal to the best fresh shell eggs.

Preserved liquid eggs

Liquid eggs can be preserved by other means including by concentration as is done for evaporated milk or by adding sugar as is done for condensed milk. These types are only rarely used in the kitchen therefore we do not propose to dwell upon them here.

To close our section on eggs we would offer some basic facts and figures:

A normal egg (size 3 or 4) normally weighs 2oz (56.7g)

12 cracked eggs make up 1 pint ($\frac{1}{2}$ litre) of liquid egg

20 egg whites make 1 pint ($\frac{1}{2}$ litre) of egg whites

35 egg yolks make 1 pint ($\frac{1}{2}$ litre) of yolks.

The average egg has a composition as follows:

Shell and membrane	12%
White	58%
Yolk	30%

The Chemical composition of an egg is: –

	Whole egg less shell	White	Yolk
Moisture	73.5%	86.5%	50.5%
Protein	12.5%	12.5%	16%
Fats	12%	Nil	32%
Mineral Salts and Vitamins	1%	0.5%	0.75%

All figures to nearest .5%

Eggs contain calcium, phosphorous, iron, vitamin A, thiamine, riboflavin, vitamin D and niacin. They are low in calories and are easily digested so they are an important item in any diet.

CHAPTER 4

Meat, Poultry and Game

Meats are delivered to the catering establishment in various forms. For the purpose of this book we propose to assume that all the larger meats are delivered to the larder or kitchen from an abbatoir. Much poultry is now available in prepared form but we propose to give brief notes on stripping and the removal of entrails etc. Game is delivered in various ways according to type, so we will deal with each type as appropriate within its own notes.

We do not propose to make this a lesson in butchery or larder work so, although mentioning the various cuts and joints available for each type of meat, we propose to deal with them as the larder chef would present them to the kitchen and to advise upon the type of joint, fat layering etc. as the kitchen staff would see them.

Beef (*Boeuf*)

We have already mentioned in the dairy products chapter that the selection of the breed of the cow or steer is of prime importance in order to get the best carcase for use in the various beef dishes.

The type of meat required, whether very lean, with a small quantity of fat, or heavily fatted has changed over the past two or three decades and so the popularity of this type of meat selected by both the housewife and the caterer has influenced the farmer's choice in breeding. As this change may well continue we do not propose to stress too heavily our own present-day choice, but will try to define the present-day breeds and types as we see them.

There are many cross-breeds produced in order to obtain the type of beef most in demand and as these are varied to suit areas of growth and styles of farming it becomes impossible for us to advise upon these.

Popular breeds in use at the present time are:
Aberdeen Angus, Hereford, Sussex, Lincoln Red, South Devon, Charolais, Welsh Black.

The Charolais is a French breed which is much used in crossing to obtain a good beef animal and the Welsh Black is a breed which can do well upon the sparse conditions of the Welsh Mountain pastures. The Galloway is a Scottish breed which has similar characterisitics.

The various types of beef animals available are as follow:

Bobby calf A young calf of up to three weeks old, very little flesh and almost no fat.

Veal The next stage of growth, from 3 weeks upwards. They provide a whiter flesh than the older beef cattle and the flesh is very tender.

Heifer A female which has not produced young.

Cow A female which has produced young.

Steer or Bullock A castrated male animal which has not usually been used for breeding before castration.

Bull An entire male animal, usually used for breeding.

The Hanging of Beef

All types of beef should be hung after killing and before cutting into joints. The exact time of hanging must be regulated by the season of the year and the temperature the meat is hung in, as well as the type of carcase being hung.

The hanging is carried out to allow the muscles to relax and the meat thus to become more tender. The flavour also improves. In cool weather in a good store the beef carcase will be hung for a week or ten days. During this period the colour of the carcase will darken both in the flesh and the fat and the cut surface will dry out. A sign of the meat having been hung for too long will show if any cut surface starts becoming moist again.

In selecting a carcase the following points should be noted:
1. A good carcase will have uniform flesh throughout with the hindquarters being heavier than the forequarters.
2. Beef in prime condition should have a 'marbling' of fat, that is to say that little streaks of fat will be running through the lean. If pressure is applied by the finger the meat should spring back quickly. Old carcases will have a thick layer of gristle under the fat. Beef of too dark a colour with a deep yellow fat is considered to be of inferior quality.
3. The meat from the male carcase is considered to be superior to that of the female carcase.

The Various Cuts of Beef

With beef, and indeed various other animals, there are regional variations in the local names given to joints and differences in the joints themselves. The smaller caterer buying from the local butcher will have to appreciate these variations especially if he is working in an area away from that in which he trained. The cuts the butcher makes for the housewife may not be those which the caterer requires for any particular dish so he must take care that he and his butcher have a complete understanding

Side of Beef

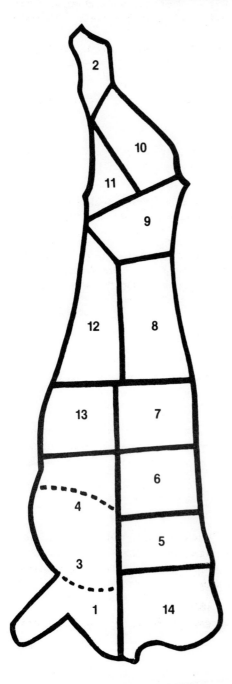

1 & 2 Shank

3 Leg of Mutton cut *(Reverse)*

4 Brisket

5 Chuck Ribs

6 Middle Ribs

7 Fore Ribs

8 Sirloin

9 Rump

10 Topside *(Reverse — Silverside)*

11 Thick Flank

12 Thin Flank

13 Plate

14 Sticking Piece

of what is required when placing the order. It is for this reason that many catering establishments prefer to butcher their own carcases as far as possible and that, of course, is the importance of the larder chef's work and why he is often considered to be one of the most important members of the kitchen staff.

The accompanying diagrams show the normal joints the English caterer will use and we refer to each one in turn:

Aitchbone (Culotte de boeuf)
This is between the rump and the buttock. After trimming it is roasted, braised or pickled.

Shank (Manche)
The shank is usually boned, may be trimmed of fat and is often used for boiling or in the make-up of various liquid stocks etc.

Heels (Pied de boeuf)
A traditional dish in Lancashire is tripe and cow heels, but in general use they are blanched and used to make stocks, soups and invalid foods.

Sirloin (Aloyau)
There are usually three cuts of sirloin, the *sirloin* (tête d'aloyau), the *middle cut* (milieu d'aloyau) and the *wing ribs* (côte d'aloyau). The sirloin is that part of the haunch up to the first rib together with its undercut of fillet.

Undercut (Faux-Filet)
This is the boned sirloin without the fillet.

Entrecôte Steak
This is a slice of steak cut from the contre-filet and weighs about $1 - 1\frac{1}{2}$ lb ($\frac{1}{2} - \frac{3}{4}$ kg).

Entrecôte Minute
A similar cut to the above but cut as thinly as possible, often less than $\frac{1}{2}''$ (2cm) and then flattened with a cutlet bat or some similar implement.

Sirloin Steak
Cut from the rib of beef between two ribs and weighs some 2 to 3lb (1kg). Served either grilled or braised. Also available boned.

Porter-house Steak
Another steak cut from the sirloin. This should be cut from the best part of the loin and includes the bone, loin and underloin. It is about 4cm thick and will weigh in the region of $1\frac{1}{2}$ to 2lb ($\frac{3}{4}$ to 1kg). Served as a grilled steak with a watercress dressing.

Fillet of Beef (Filet de boeuf) or **Tenderloin**
The fillet is a long muscle lying alongside the backbone. As it is not used

for any heavy work it is a very tender piece of meat. It will vary in weight between 3 and 9 lb and may be subdivided into:

Fillet steak Normally about 8oz (250g).

Chateaubriand Large steaks cut from the widest part of the fillet and weighing up to 2lb (900g).

Tournedos Taken from the narrow end of the middle part of the fillet and usually weighing about 5oz (150g).

Médaillon Similar to the Tournedos but slightly smaller and weighing about 4oz (120g).

Filet Mignon Taken from the point of the fillet and usually used for stroganoff.

Fore Ribs (Train de côtes)

This cut is taken in three parts.

The Fore Rib The best part of the joint and situated between the sirloin and the shoulder. It is a top quality roasting joint.

The Middle Cut A lower quality joint, usually used for stewing and braising.

The Chuck Ribs The lowest quality section, contains a section of gristle running round the flesh and so is used for stewing.

Brisket (Poitrine)

A popular, economically-priced joint which can be roasted, braised, stewed or pickled. It can be lean or fatty. If too much fat is present it can be cut off prior to cooking. May be offered with or without bone and the use to which it is to be put dictates which way it is ordered.

Shoulder of Beef (Macreuse)

The upper part of the foreleg weighing some 9lb (4kg) and used for stewing, braising or roasting.

Shin or Shank (Jarret)

This section of the forequarter is used for many purposes. Cut into cubes of about 1″ (2.5cm) it is used to make pies etc. Boiled and minced it makes meat patties etc. and minced before cooking it can be used in stocks, soups etc. and for pasta work. The better part of the joint can be used for braising.

Rump (Cimier)

This provides some of the best steaks for grilling or frying; cut into larger sections a very good roasting joint is produced. Weights 18 – 20 lb (9 – 10 kg).

Silverside (Gîte à la noix)

Also providing the Topside and Aitchbone cut. All are usually slow roasted or braised. Where the end of the joint merges into the Flank it can be cut as the Thick Flank, and may be grilled or fried. Weights 24 – 26 lb (12 – 13 kg).

Flank, Thick Flank, Thin Flank and Plate
These are cut from the stomach wall. It gives a coarser textured joint, which is usually used for cut meat, to be braised or stewed. Total Weight 40 − 44 lb (20 − 23 kg).

Sticking Piece or Neck
A coarse meat, usually used for cut meats which are to be minced for use in various dishes or in made-up meats. Weight 16 − 18 lb (8 − 9 kg).

Kidney (Rognon de boeuf)
The kidney provides certain essential nutrients and is useful in diets. It can be used with shin for steak and kidney pies and puddings, served as a separate dish for main course or in various mixed meat dishes and sautéed for use as a breakfast dish.

Ox Tail (Queue de boeuf)
Cut into sections. Trimmed of surplus fat and used to make ox tail soup. Can also be braised with or without the bone as a main course dish. Is often stuffed when it has been boned.

Ox Tongue (Langue de boeuf)
Can be served fresh, salted or pickled and either hot or cold. A very popular sandwich filler. When preparing, the base of the tongue must be cleaned before pickling.

Heart (Coeur de boeuf)
Is stuffed, braised and roasted

Brain (Cervelles)
Is boiled or fried and used in hors d'oeuvres

Liver (Foie)
Ox liver is considered the best and is served fried, sautéed, stewed or braised as a main dish or as a part of a mixed dish at most meals.

Sweetbread (Ris de boeuf)
The pancreas of the ox served fried, stewed, boiled or sautéed.

Tripe (Tripes de boeuf)
A popular dish in the north where it is served both raw and cooked and usually eaten with salt and vinegar. Tripe may be cooked in many ways and with many additives. The traditional way is to boil it in milk with onions, but it can also be stewed or sautéed in certain classical dishes.

Carcase Weights

It is very difficult to give precise weights of carcases as they vary with breed, age and method of feeding. In addition the amount of bone present can vary due to the same factors so each side must be considered

on its own. The following, however, may be taken as a general guide:
Hindquarter   170 to 190lb (75 to 95kg).
Forequarter   150 to 175lb (65 to 87kg).
The full side of beef will therefore weigh approximately 320 to 365lb (140 to 180kg).

Veal (*Veau*)

Veal is available at all seasons of the year both from home sources and from imported supplies. The main local supplies are during the months from May to September.

In selecting a veal carcase the following points should be noted:
1. The flesh should be of a clear, pink colour with a firm fat of a pinkish-white shade. The kidney should be hard and covered with a fatty layer. The veins are blue coloured.
2. The meat of the young bull calf is considered to be of a better quality than that of a female calf but if the requirements are for the whitest coloured meat then that of the cow calf should be chosen.
3. If the flesh is soft and has a bluish colouration then the meat is old and should be rejected.
4. Veal meat can only be kept for two or three days after slaughtering so should be ordered daily and used within 24 hours of delivery.

In addition to its use in certain speciality dishes veal meat is used in dietetic work due to its ease of digestion and can be mixed with pork in certain dishes.

The slaughtered carcase will vary in weight considerably due to age, breed, sex and feeding but the average veal carcase will be in the region of 180 to 250lb (80 to 115kg) giving sides of from 90 to 125lb (40 to 57kg). The major joints are:

1. **Neck** (Collet) used for braising, stewing and pies.

2. **The Best End** (Carré) used for roasting, grilling and frying, often in the form of cutlets. Weighs approximately $4 - 5$lb (2kg).

3. **The Loin** (Longe) provides chops, escalopes and similar cuts and is roasted, grilled or fried. Weighs $6 - 7$lb ($2\frac{1}{2}$ to $3\frac{1}{2}$ kg).

4. **Breast** (Poitrine) used for braising, stewing and in pies etc. Weighs $4 - 5$lb (2kg).

5. **Shoulder** (Épaule) can be stuffed, casseroled, roasted, braised, boiled, sautéed. Weighs $7 - 9$lb ($3 - 4$kg).

6. **Leg** (Cuissot) is usually cut into various smaller joints. The whole leg weighs $12 - 15$lb ($5 - 7$kg). When divided the following sections are obtained.

Shank used for braising and stewing.
Fillet used for Escalopes, roasting, frying and grilling.
Quasi used for roasting, braising and escalopes.
The carcase will also provide the following smaller pieces.

The Head (Tête)
Can be boiled whole, used in soup-making or sections cut off and fried. The whole head will normally weigh $7 - 10$lb ($3 - 4$kg).

Tongue (Langue)
Can be treated in exactly the same manner as ox tongue and pickled, boiled and served hot or cold with various meals. Normal weight in the region of $1\frac{1}{2}$ lb ($\frac{1}{2} - \frac{3}{4}$ kg).

Calves' Feet (Pied de Veau)
After trimming can be boiled and served as a dish in their own right, grilled or made into a jelly which is used as a invalid food. Usually weigh about $1\frac{1}{2}$ lb ($\frac{1}{2}$ kg).

Sweetbreads, (Ris) **Kidney,** (Rognon) **Liver** (Foie)
and Brains (Cervelles)
All of these may be used in a similar manner to beef offal. They often provide a more tender dish for the invalid where this is required. In some cases trimming may be required to remove excess fat. Normal weights are:
sweetbreads $1\frac{1}{2}$ lb ($\frac{1}{2}$ kg); kidney $1\frac{1}{2}$ lb ($\frac{1}{2}$ kg), liver up to 4lb ($1\frac{1}{2}$ kg); brains 6 to 8oz (175 to 230g).

Lamb (*Agneau*) and Mutton (*Mouton*)
Lamb

The lamb is, of course, the young sheep. Sheep have many uses in our civilisation. They produce wool which we use for clothing. The milk of the ewe is used in some areas as milk or as the provider of butter or cheese and the carcase is used as meat.

As with all other animals different breeds are used for different main purposes, — some produce lambs early in the season and are thus well thought of for this purpose. Others have a good milk yield and are the ones chosen where milk production is of importance, and other breeds are renowned for the production of long wool fleeces which are used in the weaving industry. The long wool breeds generally produce poor carcases, with mutton, which is coarse grained, and a greater amount of fat than do the other breeds. In attempts to provide all-round breeds a great deal of cross breeding has been done and a number of cross breeds have achieved considerable fame. The area in which the sheep are kept also has an influence upon the quality of the meat. Various breeds of hill sheep have, in their day, gained a high reputation for the quality of the meat they give. We also import a considerable amount of lamb principally from New Zealand where the rich pastures produce a very fine meat carcase and the New Zealand Canterbury lamb has rightly gained a high reputation for its good quality.

Typical of the sheep breed on the farms in Great Britain are the following:

Long Wool Breeds
Mainly for shearing: English Leicester, Lincoln Longwool, Wensleydale, Cotswold, Romney Marsh, Devon Longwool, South Devon, White-faced Dartmoor

Short Wool Breeds
Used mainly for their facility of producing early lambs: Devon Closewool, Dorset Horn, Dorset Down, Hampshire Down, Oxford Down, Southdown, Shropshire, Western

Mountain or Hill breeds
Produce the best flavoured mutton: Derbyshire Gritstone, Cheviot, Dales Breed, Exmoor ·Horn, Hardwick, Swaledale, Scottish Blackface, Shetland, Welsh Mountain

The choice of this large number of breeds, often bred for use under the climatic conditions of a particular area, gives a lambing season which can range from September to May, but the majority of home-produced lambs arrive in February, March and April. It is usual practice to allow the lambs to grow for at least 5 months before killing them so this gives us the greatest supply of home-grown lamb carcases during the months of June to September with early lambs bringing high prices during the early spring months. Some farmers allow the lambs to grow on longer and then offer them as hoggets at other seasons.

Types of Lamb available
Prime lamb — up to five months old.
Milk lamb — considered the best, has been fed on milk.
Grass lamb — fed on normal pastures
Canterbury lamb — imported from New Zealand. The better grades are very good quality meat, easily digested and of a good flavour. The grades are as follows:
New Zealand lamb is graded by letter and colour codings. There are three primary letters:
'P' A well-muscled carcase with an even but not excessive fat cover over the whole carcase.
'Y' A moderately fleshed slightly more elongated carcase with a light fat cover.
'O' Similar to the 'P' grade but with longer legs.

Carcass of Mutton

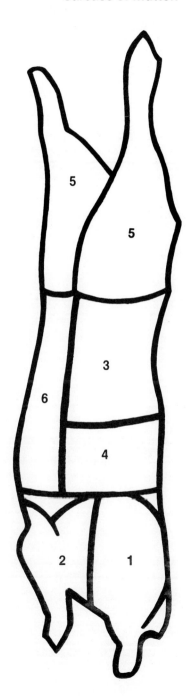

1 Neck

2 Shoulder

3 Saddle

4 Best End

5 Leg

6 Breast

A second letter is then introduced showing the weight range.

L being 17.5 to 27.5lb (8 – 12.5kg)

M being 28.5 to 35.5lb (13 – 16kg)

H being 36.5 to 56lb (16.5 – 25.5kg)

so a lamb coded PL would be a 'P' grade lamb of $17\frac{1}{2} - 27\frac{1}{2}$ lb (8 – 12.5kg). There is also an inspection stamp on all approved New Zealand lamb carcases and this provides an additional check, to show that the carcase has passed its inspection.

All New Zealand lamb is supplied frozen and can be stored in its frozen state at 14 to 18°C (6 to 0°F) for up to 12 months.

When selecting lamb, a carcase with a firm flesh of a light pinky colour should be selected. The loin should well-covered with flesh and the kidney firm with a light-coloured fat covering.

The main lamb joints are as follows:

The Neck (Cou) — Weighing 1 to $2\frac{1}{2}$ lb ($\frac{1}{2}$ to 1kg) usually used for boiling or stewing.

Shoulder (Épaule) — Weighs from 5 to 7lb (2 to 3kg). Can be roast or braised.

Saddle (Selle) — Weighing from 6 to 10lb ($2\frac{1}{2}$ to 4kg). Can be used whole or cut into various smaller pieces including chops, loin, or noisettes. Whole, the saddle can be roasted as a banquet dish. If cut into sections it can be roasted, braised, fried or grilled according to the dish to be produced.

Best End (Carré)
Weighs from 4 to 6lb ($1\frac{1}{2}$ to $2\frac{1}{2}$ kg). Can be used whole to produce a crown roast or cut into cutlets. Whole it is roasted. As cutlets it can be fried, grilled, braised or stewed.

Leg (Gigot)
Weighing approximately 5 to 8lb (2 to $3\frac{1}{2}$ kg). It can be roasted whole or as a half leg or cut into chops for frying or grilling.

Breast (Poitrine)
Weighs from 4 to 6lb (2 to $2\frac{1}{2}$ kg). Can be stuffed and roasted, stewed, braised or cut into riblets for frying.

Forequarter
A combination of the neck, foreleg, shoulder with part of the breast. Can be roasted or casseroled whole or boned and rolled for roasting. Will normally weigh from 10 to 12lb ($4\frac{1}{2}$ to $5\frac{1}{2}$ kg).

The kidneys, sweetbreads and liver can all be used in a similar way to other offal.

Mutton (Mouton)

Mutton is available both as home-grown and as imported carcases, many of the latter coming from New Zealand. The flesh can vary from a light pinky colour in young animals to a brick red colour in the more mature animal. To many tastes mutton should be more mature and an older animal which has a strong flavour is often preferred. The exact flavour, colour and general make-up of the carcase will vary according to breed, area of growth and method of feeding . Southdown mutton is considered to be the best of the English mutton and wethers (between the hogget and full mutton) to be the best for roasting. Cuts are similar to those listed for lamb with an appropriate increase in weight.

A whole mutton carcase will weigh from 45 to 80lb (21 to 36kg).

The forequarter about 14 to 17lb (6 to $7\frac{1}{2}$kg).

New Zealand hoggets, wethers and ewes are again graded by letter codings, but in these classifications the first letter, H, W or E indicates the major groupings with a second letter L, M, H, or X indicating weights.

Pork (*Porc*)

As with the other meat animals we have discussed, the pig has a number of different breeds. The choice of breed is broken down by two major factors. Firstly, as to what type of carcase is required i.e. Pork or a Bacon carcase; and secondly by the growth period.

Some breeds grow quickly and usually produce a smaller mature pig; others grow more slowly but will produce a larger carcase after killing. Different breeds have a variation in the fat and lean proportion and so this again affects the use to which the carcase is put. Cross breeding is again practised to gain the advantages of two or more breeds and, as the pig is kept for meat use in a great many areas of the world, then each area has its own breed as the one most suited to the existing climatic and housing conditions.

Typical examples are:

The Berkshire produces a good meat carcase and is popular in cross breeding. Early maturing.

The Large White (also known as the Yorkshire) — a good bacon pig, again popular in cross breeding. Late maturing.

The Tamworth — produces a carcase with lean flesh.

The Landrace — a Scandinavian pig which has an unusually long body and thus gives a good carcase. Used for both bacon and pork.

The Duroc — an American pig. An early maturer which gives a good-sized carcase.

The Hampshire — a medium maturing pig which puts on weight easily and so produces a good sized carcase.

The pig is used in various stages of maturity. Originally it was considered that it should not be used during the summer months (only used when there is an 'r' in the month) but with deep freeze and other preservation methods this is now a thing of the past.

Types of pig are:

Suckling (sucking) pig — five to six weeks old, often roasted whole for banqueting and similar functions.

Pork pig — usually six to eight weeks old but note must be taken of breed maturing times so this figure cannot be taken as absolutely accurate.

Bacon pig — fully matured, usually over 8 – 10 weeks old. Again note must be taken of breed for age of maturity.

Hog — a castrated young male pig. Will have put on additional flesh in relation to its age.

Gilt — a female which has not had a litter.

Stag — A castrated boar — an older, larger carcase than the hog.

Sow — a female which has had a litter.

Pork Joints

Head (Tête)
Can be boiled whole or the cheeks cut off. Usual use is for brawn and similar made up meats. Will weigh from 7 to 8lb (3 to $3\frac{1}{2}$kg).

Fore end or low cutlets (Basse-côte)
6 to 10lb ($2\frac{1}{2}$to 4kg). Used for roasting, braising and in pies and sausages.

Loin (Longe)
12 to 14lb (5 to 6kg). Can be roasted whole or cut into chops for grilling or frying. If boned can also be stuffed and roasted.

Belly (Poitrine)
6 to 8lb ($2\frac{1}{2} - 3\frac{1}{2}$kg). Normally a rather more fatty joint so is more often boiled or stewed, can also be salted, pickled or smoked.

Shoulder or Hand (Épaule)
12 to 14lb (5 – 6kg). Can be roasted or braised. It is also used for pies and sausages.

Leg (Jambe)
Can be roasted, salted or boiled. The leg often has the leanest meat and in the best quality pork pies leg meat is preferred. 20 to 25lb (9 – 11kg).

The weight of the joints will, of course, depend upon the carcase weight and the method of butchery used. In general, a pig will kill out at

Side of Pork

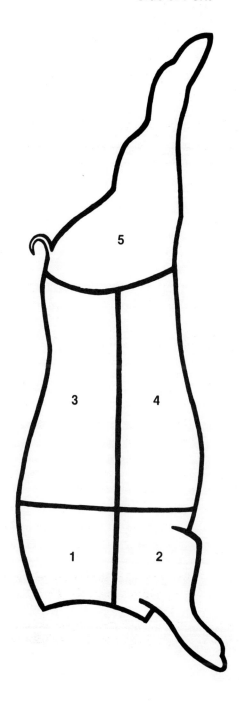

1 Spare Ribs *(Fore End)*

2 Shoulder

3 Loin

4 Belly

5 Leg

between 100 and 200lb (40 to 80kg). A 200lb carcase will produce two sides of approximately 60lb (16kg).

Bacon (*Lard*) and Ham (*Jambon*)

Bacon and Ham are produced by curing the pig carcase by immersing in or injecting with brine. There are two definite types — 'green' or 'smoked'. Tastes vary so that the caterer has to choose which he will serve.

Ham (Jambon)
Ham is the hind leg of the pig. Various methods of curing are used and as these are often associated with areas they are also associated with breeds of pig. York and Wiltshire hams are recognised as the best. These have a layer of firm white fat surrounding a solidly fleshed lean leg. York ham has the heavier weight and is thus favoured.

The ham may be sliced for service after frying or grilling or may be roasted, baked or boiled whole for service either hot or cold. Often Demerara sugar is sprinkled over the ham before roasting. Port wine and/or cloves may also be added to give a distinctive flavour — 13 to 15lb ($5 - 6\frac{1}{2}$ kg).

Gammon
This is an alternative name for sliced ham used for frying or grilling.

Belly (Poitrine)
Usually contains a rather larger proportion of fatty layers and is thus sold as a cheaper bacon cut. Often used for pickling and boiling as joints. The bones may be left in or removed; where the bones are still in they are usually removed before slicing or using as a joint — 10 to 14lb ($4 - 6$ kg).

Middle
The name varies in different cuts but this is the section from the centre of the back or from the top of the rear leg joint. In the Wiltshire cut the middle is the middle of the back and is a leaner piece than the belly. As well as slicing for use as frying or grilling bacon the cut can be used as a joint for roasting — 6 to 7lb ($2\frac{1}{2} - 3$ kg).

Back
This piece can vary in weight according to the cut. A similar type of meat to the middle described above. In some cuts it includes the middle cut. Used for frying, grilling and boiling. Weight will vary according to the cut from 7 to 14lb ($3 - 6$ kg).

Collar
The rear of the head above the fore hock. Can vary from being rather lean to rather fatty. Major use is as joints for boiling and for grilling. Often used in made up dishes. Weighs approximately 8lb ($3 - 3\frac{1}{2}$ kg).

Hock or Fore Hock
Usually used as a small joint, for boiling. Weighs some 6 to 7lb
$(2\frac{1}{2} - 3kg)$.

When selecting bacon or ham the caterer should look at the colour of
the flesh and fat. Unless a smoked joint is chosen the flesh should be a
deep pink in colour with the fat firm and free from any signs of yellowing.
It may have a pinkish tinge due to the salt solution passing from the flesh
into the fat. The flesh should always be attached to the bone. If the bacon
is stored too long and under poor conditions it will begin to smell strongly
and should therefore be rejected. Care must be taken with end pieces of a
side. If the side has been hung up with too much water present in it or too
much blood then the liquid will seep to the lower sections and leave these
tasting very salty. When using a side which has been hung it is always
better to inspect it closely for signs of this heavy salting which will often
show as salt crystals on the surface. The first slice should be used in stocks
etc. and not served as sliced bacon or ham.

Poultry

Poultry is the general term given to all the domestic birds which are bred
for eating or for egg laying.

Chickens and Hens (Volaille or Poulet)

As with all other animals bred for domestic use, breeds vary considerably.
We have seen in the section on eggs how both brown and white shelled
eggs are available. In general, the breeds which are bred to produce the
white shelled eggs are known as lightweight breeds. They have the ability
to produce a large number of eggs each year and have a very good
commercial record for their efficiency in this field. They do not, however,
produce good birds for use as meat owing to their light body weight.

The heavyweight breeds are mostly those which produce the brown
shelled eggs and most of them are used in a dual-purpose capacity. The
unwanted cockerels are fed to produce carcases for use in the various
meat dishes.

Various cross breedings are used, mostly for the purpose of either
increasing egg production or for helping in the specialist area of sexing
the day-old chicks. Many of the eggs we eat are infertile, as the hen does
not need to be fertilised before she can lay her eggs. As a result, many egg
producers keep hens only and the cockerel chicks are rejected by them as
day-olds. Those producers interested in meat production usually feed up
the heavyweight cockerels so there is a very definite advantage where the
sexes can be separated by a natural process. This is possible in the cross
breeding of some white feathered breeds with some dark feathered

breeds, Rhode Island Red and Light Sussex being typical examples. In these cases the female chick is of one colour and the male chick the other. If sex selection is not done by the breeding process then the services of highly skilled chick sexers are employed and this, of course, adds additional expense.

A further factor needs consideration. It is possible to caponise the male birds during their early days of life by either surgical or chemical means. Capons produce far more flesh than normal cockerels and birds can grow to the region of 6 to 10lb ($2\frac{1}{2}$ – 6kg).

We list below some of the breeds of poultry with their uses.

Lightweight Breeds
White Leghorn
Brown Leghorn
Black Leghorn
Ancona

Heavyweight Breeds
Rhode Island Red
Light Sussex
Buff Rock
Maran

Breeds especially favoured for cross breeding for meat production
Cornish Game
Indian Game

Birds are divided into various classes as follows:

Spring Chicken (Poussin) approx. 1lb ($\frac{1}{2}$ kg)
Roasting Chicken (Poulet) approx. $1\frac{1}{2}$– 4lb ($\frac{1}{2}$ – 2kg)
Boiling Chicken (Poularde) approx. 4 – 6lb (2 – 3kg)
Steam Roaster (normally older birds of 1 to 2 years age) approx. 5 – 7lb ($2\frac{1}{2}$ – $3\frac{1}{2}$ kg)
Boiling Fowl (Poule) approx. 6 – 8lb ($2\frac{1}{2}$ – $3\frac{1}{2}$ kg)
Capon (Chapon) approx. 6 – 9lb (3 – 4kg)

Many birds are available in an oven-ready state these days but to help those who select their birds at an earlier stage we suggest the following points should be noted.

Live Selection

A white feathered bird will have a lighter skin than a dark feathered bird and is therefore to be preferred.

Inspection of the vent will indicate if the bird has been laying eggs. There are two bones at the vent. If two fingers can be placed between these bones the bird has laid eggs within a recent period. If the vent is moist and open the bird is probably still in lay.

If the legs have small scales and small spurs the bird is young. If the scales are large, and the spurs long, in many breeds the bird is a mature one.

Dead Birds

The above will apply to birds offered with feathers on. Where they have been stripped of feathers, the following additional points should be looked for.
1.   The skin should be unbroken. If the bird has been cleaned out then this should have been done in a neat and tidy manner so that the cooked bird is not offered in a poor condition.
2.   The breast should be plump and the carcase weight suitable for the size of bird.
3.   The end of the breast bone nearest the vent should be pliable.

Cleaning Poultry

Most poultry will, as we have said, be supplied in a prepared state but we offer a few brief notes for the guidance of those wishing to purchase poultry in other stages.

It is presumed that the bird will be supplied killed.

If the bird still has its feathers on the easiest way to strip it is to use the hot water method. In this a large sink or similar container is filled with very hot water at about 180°F (85°C) or above. The bird is held by the legs and immersed in the hot water for about 1 minute. A gentle movement through the water will make certain that the feathers are thoroughly soaked. Lift the bird out and wipe the hand down from legs to head. The heat will have opened the ducts in the skin from which the feathers grow and, as a result, the feathers will wipe off cleanly. A further check to remove any remaining feathers and then a swift singe with a lighted taper to remove any hairs and the bird will be ready for cleaning out.

Draw the skin of the neck towards the body and cut off the head about 2" (4cm) away from the body. Now slit the skin of the neck a little towards the body, withdraw the windpipe and crop and free the entrails. Now turn to the vent, make a small slit to enlarge the vent and by inserting a finger withdraw the innards. Take care not to burst the gall bladder. Retain the heart, stomach and liver. Check that all internal organs have been removed and wipe out with a clean, damp cloth. The bird is now ready for preparation for cooking.

Duck (Canard)

As with hens, ducks are available in various breeds. Although duck eggs are not plentiful there are still those breeds kept for egg production and those kept for meat production.

The most popular breed for table use is the Aylesbury. According to age they can weigh from 2lb (1kg) to 7lb (3kg).

Other English breeds include the Pennine 6 to 7lb ($2\frac{1}{2}$ – 3kg) the White Table 5 to 9lb (2 – 4kg) and the White Campbell. The latter is often kept, along with the Khaki and Dark Campbell as a laying duck, but the White Campbell can be used as a dual-purpose breed, and the Muscovy, available in various feather colours and at weights from 5 to 14lb ($2 – 6\frac{1}{2}$ kg). The flesh is darker than the other ducks mentioned above but as it is a very close relative of the game duck it does taste rather similar, especially if hung, and can be used in Game Pie and similar game dishes.

Other breeds available include two French breeds the Nantes and the Rouen. Nantes is a smaller duck usually weighing in at $2\frac{1}{2}$ – 3lb ($1 – 1\frac{1}{2}$ kg) and the Rouen from $4\frac{1}{2}$ to 6lb (2 – 3kg). These are birds which offer a rather different flavour and are usually only used for specific dishes.

Ducks are available as ducklings (le caneton) and ducks (le canard) with the ducklings giving the smaller weights and ducks the larger ones. One danger is that the flesh can take on a distinctively 'fishy' taste if the duck has been fed upon fish scraps or fish meal. This should not occur with commercially-produced carcases but care should be taken when buying supplies.

Ducks contain quite a high proportion of fat and so tend to lose far more than hens during cooking. In addition the bone content is somewhat higher so a higher weight of raw carcase must be allocated for each portion. An average allowance for the oven ready bird is to expect to serve 20 to 22 per cent meat from raw carcase weight. If the bird is bought rough plucked and the entrails have to be removed this proportion goes down to about 15 per cent meat. Bought with feathers the proportion to be served will be even lower still at 11 to $12\frac{1}{2}$ per cent.

When selecting carcases the following points should be looked for:

1.   If the feathers are still on and they are dirty it shows that the bird has been on free range often with water and mud in the area. This will indicate the probability of a higher than normal salmonella count. If the feathers are clean the bird has probably been kept under more closely controlled conditions and the salmonella count will usually be lower.

2.   The feet and bill should be a bright yellow colour in most breeds.

3.   The web on the feet should be tender and break easily.

4.   The bill's upper portion should also be tender and break easily.

5.   Stripping and cleaning can be carried out as noted for Hens.

Goose (Oie)

The two principal breeds of geese are the Embden and the Toulouse. These have been inter-bred to produce a number of varieties of English table breeds which may be known by their own name or classified as Embden/Toulouse crosses. For this reason we do not list them separately.

The Embden weighs from 20 to 35lb ($9 - 15\frac{1}{2}$ kg) and the Toulouse from 20 to 30lb ($9 - 13\frac{1}{2}$ kg). Other breeds found include the Pilgrim or West of England 13 to 14lb ($6 - 6\frac{1}{2}$ kg), the Buff 15 to 20lb ($7 - 9$kg), The Chinese $10 - 12$lb ($4\frac{1}{2} - 5\frac{1}{2}$ kg) and the Roman $8 - 15$lb ($3\frac{1}{2} - 6\frac{1}{2}$ kg).

There is then, quite a wide range of weights, sufficient to enable the caterer to select a correctly weighted bird for any occasion.

When selecting geese the following points should be looked to:

1. A white bird will have a lighter skin with no dark feather stubble.
2. An old goose will have thick legs with harsh scales.
3. The bill on a young goose will be smooth and thinner round the nostrils than that of the older bird.

If the bird is ready dressed, check that the ribs are still whole. It is a method in some areas to make a faulty table bird look better by breaking or cutting the ribs in order to enable the tieing to push up the breast and make it look plumper. This practice can be applied to all table poultry.

Turkey (Dinde)

Once only used as a Christmas dish in the United Kingdom and as a Thanksgiving Day dish in the United States, the turkey has now become far more popular and is offered in many establishments at all times of the year.

The British Turkey Federation, the trade organisation of the turkey producers have developed, by advertising, an all the year round demand for turkeys for use in the domestic household and this, together with the increasing use of them by the catering trade, has resulted in turkey prices dropping in proportion to those charged for other meats.

In all poultry it is usual that the larger bird will give a greater proportion of usable meat so the turkey, being the largest used bird has this in its favour. Breeding has, however, also been designed to look after the interests of the housewife wanting the smaller bird so that there is now a very wide weight choice ranging from as low as 5lb (2kg) up to an immense 40 to 45lb ($18 - 20$kg). The larger birds may be caponised, the smaller ones may be young birds or birds from a smaller breed.

Lighter breeds are the Beltsville White, the Norfolk Black
Heavy breeds include Broadbreasted White, the Bronze, the White Holland.

As with all other poultry, cross breeding is common and many crosses are offered to the farmer under names or numbers given to them by the breeder.

Normally the turkey will lose some 25 per cent of its live weight in plucking and evisceration.

A white feathered bird will give a paler skin with less dark feather stubs on it than a bronze or black feathered bird.

The male is rather better for flesh/bone proportion and, if supplied rough plucked or unplucked can be determined quite easily by its rounder head, larger caruncles and spike. The male also has a chest tassel and a shorter neck than the female.

As turkeys are only kept for their meat production. There are no laying birds available for use as boiling fowl or the like.

Guinea Fowl (Pintade)

Not a commonly served fowl in Great Britain but available at times for speciality dishes. The meat is usually tender and has a game-like eating quality. Rather smaller than a chicken in weight they usually weigh in at about 2 to 3lb (approx. $1 - 1\frac{1}{2}$ kg). The flesh is rather darker than that of a chicken.

Pigeon (Pigeon)

There are two main sources of pigeons; the wild wood pigeon and culls from racing pigeon lofts or birds from lofts kept for flesh production only. The wild bird is often rather larger than the reared bird but may not be as plump. The flesh is a dark reddish colour. The wood pigeon is considered Game whilst the home reared bird is not. Normal weight from 10 to 15oz (approx. $\frac{1}{2}$ kg).

Game (*Gibier*)

Game is divided in three sections — furred, feathered and fish. We propose to deal with the game fish in the section dealing with fish and only to cover the furred and feathered game in this section.

Game meat is usually served after it has been allowed to hang long enough to become tender and develop flavour. The period of hanging differs for the various species and also varies a little with the wishes of the chef dealing with the dish. The age of the game, the area of storage and the storage temperature will also have its effect upon the aging of the meat. Generally speaking, the older the game the longer it will be hung. Venison and hare together with all game birds are hung before skinning or plucking. Most of the game birds are hung as shot complete with entrails; venison and hare are usually degutted before hanging. Rabbits are more often used as soon as they are killed and are not hung.

The area required to hang game should be a well ventilated, cold and dry storeroom. Care must be taken with hygiene so that there is a minimal danger of bacterial contamination to cause food poisoning.

Furred Game

Venison, hare and rabbit are covered in this section.

Venison (Venaison)

Venison is becoming more plentiful in recent years owing to some landowners making a commercial attempt to produce meat from the forest areas and moors which can successfully house the deer herds which once roamed this country. The normal type of carcase provided is from either young animals culled because of various factors or old animals which are culled from the herds so that the younger breeding stock can develop. It is available in full carcase form from the various estates at culling time and in joints from speciality butchers.

There are various species of deer and they can range considerably in size. The normal deer used is the roe deer but larger supplies of red and fallow deer have been finding their way onto the market in recent years. The flesh of the buck (the male) is considered superior to the flesh of the female and the best age for eating is between 18 months and 24 months old.

Good venison meat should be a dark red in colour, finely grained with a white, firm fat. The best cuts are the haunch, the loin and the fillet which are used for roasting, grilling and frying. The other cuts are used for stews, braising and in game pies.

Venison is at its best in the late autumn and early winter months but is available throughout the year as frozen meat.

Hare (Lièvre)

Hares weigh between 5 and 12lb $(2 - 5\frac{1}{2}\,\text{kg})$. They are usually stewed or roasted. The larger the carcase the older the hare is likely to be. The age can be tested in a hare which has not been skinned by inspection of the ears and the lip. If the ears tear easily the hare is a young one. If the hare lip is pronounced the hare is an old one. If the teeth are white the hare is young, if yellow the hare is an old one. If the claws are long the hare is old. If they are small and mostly covered by hair it is a young one.

The two main species of hare are the English or brown hare and the Scottish or blue hare. The brown hare is usually the larger of the two at the same age.

If the hare is bought as shot it will lose some 40 per cent of its weight when ready for cooking and will tend to shrink rather more than many other meats in the oven. Hares are considered at their peak in the later months of the year.

Careful inspection of any carcase should be made to check the amount of shot left in it. If the carcase is badly damaged by shot it should be rejected so that there will be no danger of the small pieces of shot missing a careful inspection and ending up on the plate.

Rabbit (Lapin)

Rabbits may be wild ones or those produced on a farm for meat production. The farmed rabbit is usually the more tender and will have more flesh on the carcase but the wild rabbit is often preferred for its more 'gamey' flavour. The wild rabbit will weigh in the region of 2 to $2\frac{1}{2}$ lb (1kg) but farmed rabbits of the larger breeds can weigh considerably more — often up to weights of 20lb (9kg) for the Flemish Giant, the largest of the farmed breeds. The larger rabbits do not dress out as well as their medium-sized brethren and so are only on offer as culls from breeding pens. As with many other meat-producing animals a great amount of cross breeding takes place in order to produce the type of carcase the buyer requires. Pure breeds listed at the moment include Flemish Giant, Belgian Hare — not a hare really but a large rabbit — New Zealand White and Californians, with New Zealand Whites as possibly the most popular.

Rabbits are often supplied in frozen form and in this case, of course, the buyer must rely upon his knowledge of the supplier. But where they can be purchased in skin the guides given for hare purchase, except the point about the hare lip, can be used.

Rabbits are traditionally eaten only when there is a 'R' in the month, that is when the breeding season is over, but as they are now imported in the frozen state from Australia, New Zealand and China this point can be disregarded with these supplies. However, older people may still prefer to keep this tradition. In addition, the myxomatosis epidemic some years ago reduced demand for this very pleasant dish and it is now up to the chef to use his ingenuity to build up the demand for it.

Feathered Game

Pheasant (Faisan)

They are in season from 1st October to 31st January, but at their best during the months of November, December and January. Pheasants are usually sold in braces giving two birds to deal with at a time although the caterer buying by the larger number will, of course, not be restricted in this manner. The young pheasant is the more tender and the female is preferred. Weight can range from 2lb to 4lb (1 – 2kg). The young bird has soft feet and lighter feathers than the older bird. The cock has a short pointed spur on his leg and has the larger and more colourful tail feathers. The young cockerel has a pointed feather on his wing tip which becomes rounded in the older bird. It is normal to hang the pheasant from 4 to 7 days according to age and storage conditions.

Partridge (Perdreau)

Various species of partridge are available in Great Britain. The two main species are the grey partridge and the red- legged partridge, the latter being found mainly in the counties on the north and east of London with the grey partridge being found in most parts of Great Britain and being especially plentiful in arable areas, such as East Anglia.

The partridge is in season from 1st September to 31st January with the birds being in prime condition in October and November. The birds are usually grilled, roasted or braised with the red-legged species being considered the more suitable for braising and the grey being more suitable for roasting or grilling. With both types the older birds can be braised or casseroled.

The young red-legged partridge can be recognised by the rounded tip of its first flight feathers and, the grey, by its yellow-brown feet. A young bird will weigh about 12 oz (320g) and an older, more mature bird, about $1\frac{1}{2}$ lb ($\frac{1}{2}$ kg). The best weight is considered to be about 1lb (450g) at which weight it should have a plump breast with soft bones.

Hanging partridges usually takes from two to five days depending upon choice and conditions of storage.

Grouse (Tétras)

The earliest of the major game birds and the start of grouse shooting is often referred to as 'The Glorious Twelfth', namely the 12th August. Although grouse is usually required to be hung there are great efforts made to bring the first grouse from the moors of northern England and Scotland to the major cities in order to be able to serve grouse for dinner on the 12th August. The season is from the 12th August until the 15th December. The birds are considered to be in prime condition from the 12th until the end of October, with the birds of that season's hatching preferred.

As with partridge and pheasants many grouse are reared in hatcheries and then released onto the shoots to be ready for the 12th. The young bird has soft, downy feathers on the breast and under the wings. The wing feathers are pointed.

Normally the grouse is hung from two days up to a week according to choice and conditions of the bird and the store. The birds will weigh from about 12oz (320g) to 1lb (450g).

Woodcock (Bécasse)

In season between 1st October and 31st January and at their best in November and December. The average woodcock will weigh about 12oz (320g). It is rather different from most birds in that the legs are considered better eating than the breast. When roasted they are prepared in a different way from most birds. The entrails are left in and the head is still on the body. Some chefs remove the eyes — others prefer them left in. They are usually presented roasted. The smaller bird is usually the younger one but where choice is available the condition of the carcase must be taken into account. A well-feathered bird will normally be younger than one whose feathers are showing signs of thinning.

Woodcock is normally left hanging for from two to four days depending upon condition of carcase and storage.

Quail (Caille)
Quail may be game or farm-bred with the wild bird being considered to have a superior flavour to the farm-bred bird. They are not hung but used immediately for roasting, braising or grilling. They may weigh from 2 − 6 oz (50 − 170g) and are usually dealt with by being plucked, drawn and trussed before roasting. The smaller birds are usually served two to a portion.

Plover (Pluvier)
Three species are known in Great Britain, although the use of both the bird and its eggs for culinary purposes has been claimed to reduce the number of some types to near danger levels with the result that egg collecting is now prohibited as is the shooting of the green plover. As this was considered to be the worst tasting of the three possibly its loss is not too great. The others are the grey and the golden plover with the latter being considered the best for eating. They are usually cooked undrawn and by roasting. The average bird weighs some 8oz (225g).

Wild duck (Canard Sauvage); Teal (Sarcelle), Pintail (Pilet), Mallard (Malard) and Wigeon (Canard Siffleur)
All the above are types of wild duck. They are available on the menu in some establishments either by the collective term of 'wild duck' (le canard sauvage) or by their individual names. Slight variations in feather colour or shapes do not affect the cooking quality of these birds so we deal with all five as one.

The shooting season for wild duck is from 1 September to 31 January with an extension in some areas to 20 February. Most wild water birds tend to have a fishy taste to their flesh. However, the wigeon, because it feeds more on grass than fish, is considered to have a superior flavour to that of its fellows. The time when each bird is considered to be at its best varies. The wigeon is favoured in October and November, the wild duck and mallard in November and December and the teal in late December.

Unlike the farm bred duck the wild duck does not have such fatty flesh. It is lean and requires the addition of fat during the cooking process. The birds are usually roasted or braised and will weigh some 2 − 3lb $(1 - 1\frac{1}{4}$ kg). It is usual to use duck without hanging.

Snipe (Bécassine)
In season from 12th August to 31st January snipe is at its best in its later season. It will vary in weight from 2oz (50g) to 10oz (225g). It may be served undrawn or drawn and may easily have its skin removed before cooking by cutting off the head and pulling the skin gently away from the legs or neck.

96

Black Game (also known as Black Grouse)
The black game is in season from mid-August to mid-December with the exact dates varying a little in different areas. It is rather larger than the grouse weighing from 1lb to 2lb (450 to 900gm). It is usually hung for six to seven days.

Wild goose
This is a similar bird to the farm bred goose, but has a more gamey flavour. The wild goose is rather leaner than the farm bred one and therefore requires fat to be added during the cooking process. Otherwise this goose can be used in the same way as we would the domesticated goose. It should have a slightly longer cooking period.

Meat Experiments

In the previous notes on meat, poultry and game we have mentioned on various occasions that the different joints of meat or different ages or types of birds are cooked in a different manner. It is useful to appreciate why this is so and the following experiment can be carried out with various types or cuts of meats to emphasise the point.

For the investigation the use of a stereo-microscope, so that the variations in fibre structures of the different meats and joints may be observed, will be useful. If one is not available the use of a powerful magnifying glass may help.

Take as many different samples of meats, poultry and game as possible. Note carefully the joint in a piece of meat and the source (beef, mutton, turkey etc.). First examine a cut slice of each meat under the stereo-microscope. Note that the traditionally tougher meats have a different fibre structure than that shown by the traditionally more tender meats. Note also the presence of any fatty layers in the meat.

Now take an equal weight of each sample, trying to make up each piece to be the same shape and size.

Experiment 1
Place one sample of each meat on a grill tray and place under the grill setting the heat at medium. Cook, cut, note the finished appearance and then weigh the piece to discover what weight loss there has been. Now taste the meat noting flavour, tenderness etc.
Repeat the experiment with the heat setting at High and then again with the heat setting at Low — do these variations affect the findings?

Experiment 2
Take an equal weight of each sample and cut into cubes of equal size. Add a measured quantity of seasoning and water to each sample and bring to the boil. When boiling turn down to simmer until tender. Repeat the weighing and testing.

97

Experiment 3

Take a larger sample of each meat (still making certain weights are equal). Prepare for roasting. Roast all in the same oven if possible and make certain that all are the same distance from any heat source. After cooking reweigh, check and test as before.

By a comparison of all the results it will become apparent that some meats can be cooked far better by one method than can others. Do these results tie in with the first observations of texture and fibre structure? Does the question of the heat setting during grilling affect the results?

The experiments may be extended in various ways but the above suggestions should be sufficient to give a guide as to how they may be carried out.

CHAPTER 5

Fish (*Poisson*)

Fish are divided into various classifications. These may vary according to
the interest of the person naming them. For instance, the angler is
interested in main divisions such as sea fish, fresh water fish and game
fish. The commercial fisherman would divide them into inland water fish
and deep water fish. The chef will often divide them into round fish, oily
fish and shell fish and give sub-divisions under each heading.

In recent years the overfishing of some species has resulted in the
danger of a considerable drop in their availability and in some countries
restricting fishing in their own waters. It seems probable, therefore, that
for many years the caterer will be meeting the problem of not being able
to obtain supplies of traditional fish and will be having to consider using
alternative species. For this reason we are including some unusual fish
which, at the moment, are not in frequent use in the catering industry but
which can still make up excellent meals when served with a little care.

Fresh Water Fish

Barbel (Barbeau)
A large fresh water fish which is found in many European rivers. It is in
season from July to the end of February. It has not been favoured in
catering because it has so many bones.

Bream (Brème)
Both fresh water and sea water types are available. The bream makes a
very tasty dish, especially when freshly caught. The fresh water type are in
season from September to March with the sea water type following the
same pattern but being available at other periods on occasion. A round
fish.

Carp (Carpe)
There are types of carp in both fresh and sea water but the principal one
used under the name is the fresh water type. Weights can rise to ten
pounds and considerably more but the smaller, younger fish is often
preferred. In season December to March.

Char (Ombre Chevalier)
A fresh water fish which is a member of the Salmon family and whose
flesh is very highly prized. It is a white-fleshed fish and there are a number

of varieties available. At one time the greatest delicacy was the arctic char, once found in large numbers in Lake Windemere and which was potted and sold in that area. Other varieties come from the Alps and North America.

Dace (Vandoise)
A small river fish in season from June to September and also during January and February.

Grayling (Ombre)
A fresh water game fish which has a high reputation when used quickly after catching. In season in July and August and is a relative of the trout and salmon.

Gudgeon (Goujon)
In season from October to June the gudgeon is one of the smallest of the river fishes to be used for human food. There are two species, the white and the silver and when served fried it is considered to be one of the best of all the smaller fish offered on the menu.

Loach (Loche)
A river fish rather like an eel in appearance but smaller, the flesh is very bony and has a sweetish taste.

Perch (Perche)
Found in inland waters. The small fish are fried after filleting, the larger ones stuffed to provide a classical dish. Is considered by some anglers as a game fish because of the fight it offers.

Pike (Brochet)
Another inland water game fish. As with many other fresh water fish the flavour of its flesh can be a reflection of the waters it has lived in, being at times a rather muddy flavour, but when caught from clear waters and roasted soon after catching is a much esteemed dish.

Tench (Tanche)
A fresh water fish which provides an oily flesh. Highly thought of when cooked shortly after catching. In season June to October.

Trout (Truite)
There are a number of varieties of trout. The two major ones being the brown trout and the rainbow trout. In the traditional French restaurant the trout are kept in a fresh water tank for the customer to choose a fish which is then caught and cooked as required. Unfortunately this practice is becoming less frequently used and the majority of the trout used in the industry are now frozen supplies from trout farms, often based overseas. Fresh trout are in season April to October and give their best results when cooked as soon after catching as possible, the reason for the practice described above.

Some fish are caught in both fresh and sea water. Salmon and salmon trout leave the sea and swim up the rivers to spawn. They are caught by both sea and river fishermen.

Eel also spawn in rivers and in Great Britain a large number of eels and elvers (the young eel) are caught and used in various dishes.

Salmon (Saumon)
A fish which lives in both the sea and the river but which are usually caught in the rivers. In season from May to September the flesh is a rosy pink in colour, oily and has a fine flavour.

Sea Trout (Truite Saumonée) — also known as **Salmon Trout**
This is a fish which can be caught in either the river or in coastal waters. It varies between the salmon and the river trout in size and has a pinky, oily flesh. Its habits are the same as the salmon, coming up numerous rivers in all parts of Great Britain to spawn. The fish range in weight from about 2lb (1kg) through the rather common weight of 4 to 5lb ($1\frac{1}{2}$ – 2kg) up to 7lb (3kg) for the large fish.

The sea trout is in season as fresh fish during a similar period to Salmon with some variation being given by water authorities in different parts of Great Britain. In actual fact the fish can be caught somewhere in Great Britain at any time between January 1st and October 31st with the best period being in late summer and autumn.

Smelt (Éperlan)
A member of the salmon family, it has a cucumber-like smell and is often served as a starter course through the winter months.

Sea Fish
Round White Fish

Bass (Bar)
A sea fish considered by anglers to be a game fish. It can grow to quite a good weight but usually presented at about 2lb (up to 1kg). In season the whole year. There are many dishes in the classical French menu using Bass.

Cod (Morue)
One of the most popular sea fish. In season from May to February and available as both young and mature specimens. Owing to recent international restrictions our supply of cod has decreased considerably in recent years and has also become far more expensive. Cod liver oil is a well known supplier of vitamins A and D but the fish itself is classified as a round fish.

Coley (Lieu noir)
This fish is becoming a popular replacement for the more expensive cod in many family diets. Coley provides a good eating flesh which is slightly darker than cod. At the time of writing it is priced at about one third the price of cod so its use as an economical alternative is something to be considered. In season the whole year round and a member of the White fish group.

Eel (Anguille)
There are a number of varieties of eel found in inland lakes and ponds, rivers and in the sea. Classed as an oily fish, the larger eels are in season all the year round, but the younger eels (elvers) have a restricted season. They have the ability to cross overland from one section of water to another so can be found in many unexpected areas. The common eel breeds in the rivers and then the young elvers cross thousands of miles of ocean to develop into adults. It is during their passage up and down rivers that many of them are caught. The largest — the conger eel — is a very large fish, which is caught in the sea areas around most of our coastal areas. It may weigh as much as $50-60$lb ($23-27$kg) and some even larger, have been caught. Conger eel steaks can provide a very satisfying dish. The smaller eel should, when possible, be purchased alive and killed by the poissonnier or the garde-manger in order to ensure that it is in the freshest possible state.

Gurnet or Gurnard (Grondin)
Three species of gurnet or gurnard are available — the yellow, the grey and the red. The red is one that is available in Great Britain with the yellow and grey coming from the Mediterranean. It is usually available during the summer months. The flesh is only moderate in flavour and requires the addition of spices or other seasoning to make it into a favoured dish.

Haddock (Aiglefin)
Best when small and available in all seasons of the year but especially good during the winter months. Another round fish.

Hake (Merluche)
One of the most highly favoured of the sea fishes, a round fish; in season through most of the winter months.

John Dory (Saint Pierre or Dorée)
Another sea fish which is not commonly used yet can provide a good meal. It has a flattish body with a large head and staring eyes and is at its best in the autumn and early winter months.

Pollack (Merlan Jaune)
A member of the cod family the pollack varies in size from two up to twenty pounds (1 to 8kg) with commercial fish weighing in at five to ten

pounds (2 to 4kg). It is used in a similar manner to cod although the flavour is often considered not quite up to that of the cod.

Sturgeon (Esturgeon)
Traditionally the royal fish. The flesh is not highly thought of, but the roe produces caviar. In season December to April.

Tunny; also called Tuna (Thon)
The tunny is one of the largest of the sea water game fishes. The world record is in the region of 1,000lb for a rod caught fish. Tunny are found in the North Sea area; Scarborough is the base of the Tunny Fishing Club of Great Britain. It is canned as tuna or may be used fresh in many ways.

Whiting (Merlan)
A sea fish of similar size to the herring but with a vastly different flavour. It is a member of the cod family and can be made into many very appetising dishes suitable for invalid cookery. It is available in fresh form at all seasons of the year with the fish possibly being at their best in the spring months.

Wolf Fish
Also sometimes known as 'Woof'. This is a type of catfish and is used in a very similar manner.

White Oily Fish

Anchovy (Anchois)
Fillets of anchovy are used as a decoration and flavouring in many dishes. They are usually purchased in tinned form.

Cat fish or Rock Turbot (Loup de Mer)
The catfish is found in both fresh and salt waters. It provides a coarse fibred, oily flesh, the flavour of which is not highly regarded. Owing to the housewives' dislike of purchasing catfish it is often named rock turbot in the fishmonger's displays. When correctly prepared it can provide an excellent meal at a very reasonable price. The sea fish is the one usually supplied. It is available at all seasons of the year.

Herring (Hareng)
An oily sea fish averaging some 10" (25cm) long. It is available in fresh form and smoked as kippers. When in good supply it is considered a cheap fish but owing to smaller catches, prices have risen considerably in recent times. Available as a whole fish, or as fillets or in various other ways. In season during winter and spring months.

Mackerel (Maquereau)
Called the scavenger of the sea, the mackerel has a red-coloured flesh and a green and silver coat. When used really fresh it provides an

Oily Fish

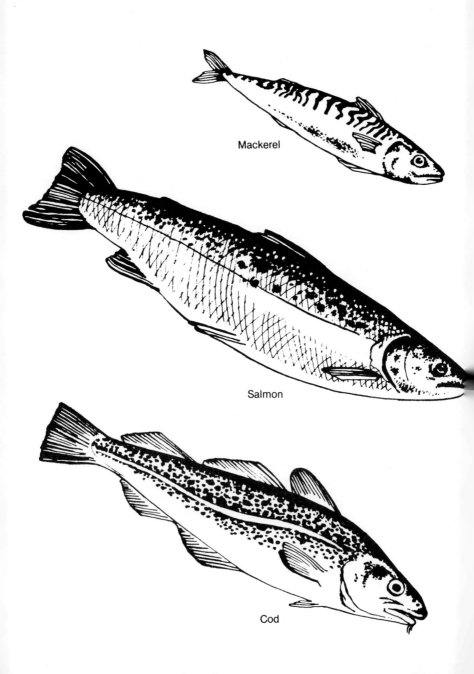

Mackerel

Salmon

Cod

excellent dish which, cooked correctly, cannot be beaten for taste or its low price. An oily fish, it is available during many months of the year. The mackerel shoals travel round the coasts of Great Britain from the northern Scottish waters in winter round to the Welsh waters in late summer and as they pass the eastern coast fishing ports they are caught and shipped to consumers.

Red Mullet (Rouget)
A red-coloured sea fish listed in the round fish classification. When fresh it provides an excellent dish but soon deteriorates on keeping.

Pilchard (Sardine)
A small version of the herring usually salted or canned in tomatoes or oil. The fresh fish is also used in various dishes. In season from mid summer to December.

Sardine (Sardine)
Can be used fresh but mainly used in the home in their tinned form where they are available in tomato sauce or oil. In season from January to June.

Sprat (Harenguet)
A small fish of the herring family and of a similar size to the sardine it is an oily fish and is in season during the winter months. As the sardine and pilchard it is available in preserved form, but can also be used fresh to make a number of interesting dishes.

Whitebait (Blanchaille)
A small young sea fish cooked whole and at its best during July and August but also available in frozen form at any period of the year.

Flat Fish- White

Brill (Barbue)
This is a fish which is akin to the turbot. Its skin is spotted with white.

Dab (Limande)
A small member of the flat fish family principally caught in inshore waters around the coasts of Great Britain. In season from August to November.

Halibut (Flétan)
A white flat fish available during the summer months. Has a dark flesh which tends to be soft.

Plaice (Carrelet)
A rather larger flat sea fish. In season throughout most of the year but considered to be at its best in the early months of the year.

Sole (Sole)
There are a number of species of the sole family. All are flat fish of

White Fish (*Flat*)

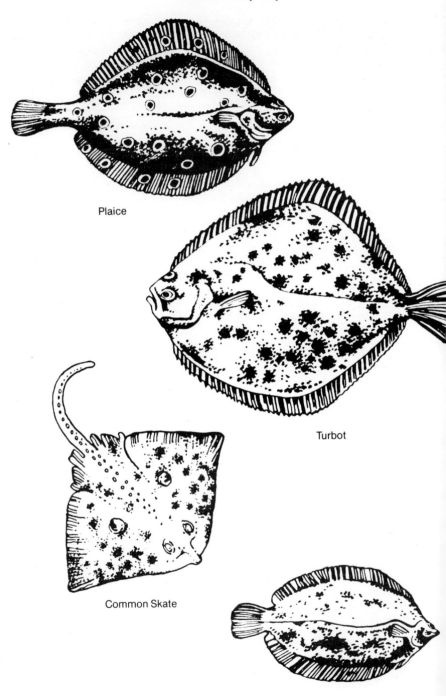

Plaice

Turbot

Common Skate

Lemon Sole

varying size and flavour and all are highly esteemed. They include the dover sole, the lemon sole and the Torbay sole. Each has a slightly different colouration but all are used in a similar manner in the kitchen.

Turbot (Turbot)
A large flat fish related to the brill. It is usually cooked in the traditional turbotière but many of the sole recipes can also be used to provide excellent dishes.

Flat Fish-Oily

Flounder (Flet)
Another of the flat fish grouping but rather larger than the dab.

Skate (Raie)
A large flat sea fish available in most months of the year. White fleshed, the main section eaten is taken from the 'wings'.

Shellfish

The shellfish are divided into two major groups — Crustaceans which include such fish as lobsters and crabs and the Molluscs which include the oysters and mussels.

Crustaceans (Crustacés)

Crab (Crabe)
In season during the summer months and a product of many of the waters surrounding our coasts with some areas having a much higher reputation for good quality crabs than others. The crab is largely a costal water creature and is often caught by fishermen in small boats setting traps of various types which they gather in daily. They are normally boiled alive and so should be purchased live if they are to be really fresh.

Crayfish (Écrevisse)
Both fresh and salt water crayfish are available. In season through the winter months. The fresh water crayfish is usually smaller than the salt water crayfish. The latter is the one most often used.

Crawfish (Langouste)
A type of lobster but of different body shape, having no claws and a larger body. In season during the summer months.

Lobster (Homard)
At their best during the summer months and the size preferred for top quality work is in the region of $1\frac{1}{2}$ to 2lb (700 to 900g), larger lobsters are available up to $4\frac{1}{2}$lb (2kg) but they tend to lose their eating quality at this weight. The male lobster is considered superior to the female as its flesh is

Shellfish *(Crustaceans)*

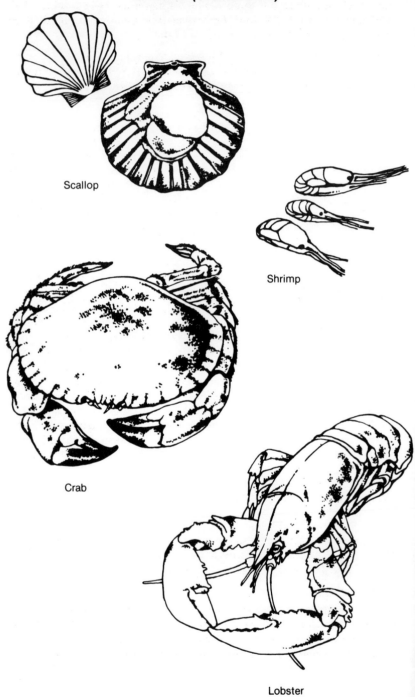

Scallop

Shrimp

Crab

Lobster

firmer and more tasty. It can easily be distinguished by its brighter shell and narrower tail. It should be remembered that lobsters are black when live and only turn red when boiled.

Norway Lobster, Dublin Bay Prawn or Scampi (Langoustines)
These are all different names for the same fish. They are a large prawn or small lobster and are used in a number of speciality shell fish dishes. In season at all periods of the year.

Prawn (Crevette Rose)
One of the few crustaceans which are always bought ready cooked and are often purchased ready shelled. The prawn is rather larger than the shrimp but is often used in exactly the same way. Indeed one often replaces the other where this can be done without too much difficulty. They are used both as a principal ingredient and as a garnish and are in season throughout the winter months and available in frozen form at other times of the year.

Shrimps (Crevette Grise)
As has already been stated these are a smaller version of the prawn and are used in a very similar manner. They are in season throughout the year and are again caught around the coast of Great Britain by inshore small boat fishermen. Both shrimps and prawns are often purchased ready for use but for those fortunate enough to be able to purchase them freshly boiled, the following notes on taking off the shell may be of use.

The shrimp or prawn is taken by the head between two fingers of one hand and by the tail by the first two fingers of the other hand. The body is then straightened out and then a gentle pull will take away the body shell leaving the edible portion attached to the head, a second pull of the head from the edible body portion will leave the shrimp or prawn ready for service. A little practice soon leaves the operative experienced enough to do this task quickly. Freshly boiled and shelled prawns or shrimps have a flavour and eating quality which far outweighs that of the frozen types on offer.

Molluscs (Mollusques)

Clam (Lucène)
Also known as the palourde in France. A popular mollusc in France and the USA. It is used in many dishes in the same way as oysters and can, like oysters, be eaten raw or cooked.

Mussel (Moule)
The smaller mussel is considered to be the better one to eat having a more delicate flavour and more tender flesh. Mussels are often bought live and should be inspected prior to boiling. Any shells found to be opened should be rejected as the occupant will be dead and may be diseased in

Shellfish *(Molluscs)*

Common Whelk

Common Cockle

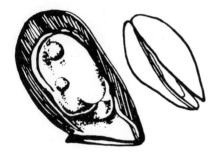

Edible Mussel

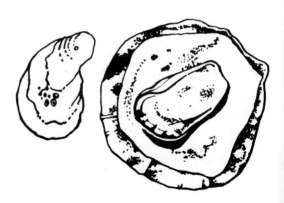

Oyster

some way. They should first be washed in two or three changes of water and left under a running tap in a sieve for some five minutes. This is to remove any dirt which may be on the shells. They are then placed in a pan, often seasoned with herbs and spices and may be either dealt with by covering with water or, in some cases, left to be heated without any water added. Cook until the shells open, then drain the pan and remove the mussels from their shells. Remove the beard and tongue and use as required.

Octopus (Poulpe)

The name often causes some discomfort to the uninitiated diner but when used in speciality dishes the octopus can provide a really excellent meal for the connoisseur. May be served hot or cold as well as in various seafood cocktails.

Oysters (Huîtres)

Oysters are at their prime when there is an 'R' in the name of the month. We have in Great Britain a number of areas famous for their oyster beds and these produce some very fine specimens. They may be eaten raw or cooked in any of a number of dishes, but traditionally eaten raw with brown bread. The oysters, together with many other shell fish, live in the estuaries of our rivers or in the sea just outside the area where the rivers empty into the sea. Because of this they may be contaminated by river polution. It is therefore essential that all shell fish gathered from such areas are relaid into pure water for at least 24 hours before using so that any such contamination can be removed. It is usual for the water to be chlorinated to assist in this work.

The chef may be required to open the oyster for presentation to the client so we give a brief note on this task. The same procedure is applied to opening raw mussels where this has to be done.

Take the oyster in the left hand in a clean cloth with the fat side uppermost, pierce under the hinge with a short wide-bladed kitchen knife (this need not be sharp) and push the knife in; a slight twisting jerk of the knife blade coupled with light pressure on the shell from the left hand will easily force the shell apart. This will now leave the oyster ready for presentation on ice as a cold dish or for use for cooking as required. (It is wise to check the appearance for purity — a dark-coloured flesh indicates that it has not been purified of any harmful bacteria and a quick search may even find a small pearl!)

Scallops (Coquille Saint-Jacques or Pétoncle)

They are also known as escallops. The scallop requires a warmer water than is offered in most of the coastal areas of Great Britain. However, it can be found in a few localities where, due to some unusual feature, the water is warmer than normally would be expected. It is available from September to April and mostly imported from France, where it is found on the Channel and Atlantic coastlines.

The tongue or ova is considered to be a great delicacy. The scallop is at its best when the flesh is white and the tongue full and bright orange in colour. It forms the basis of many speciality dishes.

Sea Urchin (Oursin)
Not often used as human food but some of the species of sea urchin can provide an attractive meal. They should be eaten as soon as gathered so are not a suitable proposition for those who cannot obtain fresh supplies. As there are, at the moment, no frozen supplies, they must remain a possible dish of the future.

Squid (Calamar)
Another member of the octopus family but much smaller in size. Available from speciality fishmongers throughout most of the year and used in certain speciality dishes.

Whelks and Cockles
Traditionally eaten by using a pin from a saucer after heavily seasoning with salt, pepper and vinegar. Cockles and whelks are not usually highly regarded in the classical kitchen. They do, however, provide a very nutritious meal for those who like them and can be used in various sea food mixtures such as sea food cocktail.

Purchase and Storage

Fresh fish should never be stored but purchased fresh daily. Any short periods of storage before use should be in a refrigerator at around $35 - 40°F$ ($1.5 - 4.5°C$). It must be remembered that fish can smell strongly and thus spoil other food so where any size of fish usage is intended it is wise to use a separate storage area for all fishes.

Selection

In the vast majority of cases the selection of the fish should be by taking account of its appearance. Fresh fish will have bright red-coloured gills, shining scales and bright eyes. As it becomes old the flesh will soften and become 'droopy'.

According to type of fish and the catching methods used, the fish may have its entrails still present, or may be cleaned but otherwise still be whole, or may be offered in cut pieces such as steaks etc. It may still have the bone in or it may be filleted.

The type purchased will, to some extent, depend upon the type of establishment, its staffing and the numbers of covers dealt with at each meal. The experience and skill of its staff will also have a bearing upon this factor, as each fish is dealt with individually, according to shape, requirements etc. We would suggest to any reader interested in learning more about the work of fishmongers in the larder that he seeks further instruction on the subject.

We have referred to the food value of many commodities as we have discussed them. The food value of all fish is of importance. They all supply good protein of high biological value and the sea fish have the additional advantage that they supply iodine which is essential for the action of the thyroid gland. The inclusion of sea fish is therefore essential in any balanced diet.

CHAPTER 6

Cereals

Botanically the cereals are the cultivated grasses; in catering the term is
widened to include sago, arrowroot and rice. As it is used in some cases for
the same purpose as some cereals we also will include potato starch in our
commentary.

Possibly the most important cereal in the western world is wheat. From
the wheat berry is produced our flour so we commence these notes with
the wheat berry and its products which are used in the kitchen.

Wheat

Wheat is grown in many areas of the world; its botanical name is
Triticum Vulgare and it can vary according to the type of seed wheat
used, the time of year the seed is sown, the area of the world the wheat is
grown in and the weather conditions during growth and harvesting. As
all of these have a great effect upon the flour produced, we should deal
with these first.

Wheats are known by various headings which indicate the type of
wheat which may be anticipated:

Hard wheats are those normally grown in hot, dry climates which experience cold winters.

Soft wheats are those grown in temperate climatic conditions.

Winter wheats are those sown in the autumn to weather in the soil during
the winter and are harvested in the following summer.

Spring wheats are those sown in the spring for harvesting the same year.
Wheats may be referred to by the colour of the skin; red, white, cream or
yellow are the normal colours found.

They may also be known by the country or area of growth and typical
examples are Manitoba (a Canadian province), 'Plate' (the area around
the River Plate in South America), Queensland (Australian), Western
Australia, English, French and Russian.

The wheat berry is composed of a starchy centre known as endosperm
which is surrounded by skins known as the bran and the germ of the
wheat. In the growing process the starch is moistened and changes into

Cereals

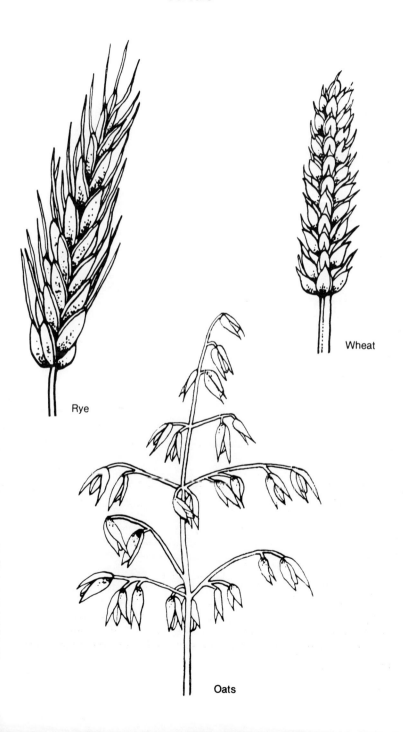

Rye

Wheat

Oats

malty sugars, the germ feeds upon these and sends up its shoots and produces roots.

The important factors for the caterer are the strength and colour of the flour.

The strength is determined by the amount of insoluble protein present in the flour, the colour by the amount of bran present in the flour. The amount of bran and the process he uses (described later in this section) is determined by the miller. The strength of the flour is determined by the amount of protein in the wheat berry used for milling into flour. Typical world figures are quoted in the table below. The strength is indicated as gluten content. The proteins combine when water is added to the flour to form gluten, a rubbery-like substance which stretches to give bread doughs and similar products their extensibility.

Area	Gluten content	Wheat characteristics
Britain	7 – 11%	Most British wheat is considered to be soft but there are steps being taken to improve the strength of British wheats in order to make stronger flours.
North America	11 – 15%	The stronger wheats from the North Americas are highly prized for the strength of flour they produce.
Eastern America (California, Oregon etc.)	8 – 10%	These are softer wheats grown in the more temperate climatic conditions of the Pacific coastal areas.
South America (Principally 'Plate')	10 – 11%	Medium strength wheats usually used as 'fillers'.
USSR	11 – 15%	Only available occasionally; these wheats produce a strong flour when they are of the better quality.
Asia (India and Iran)	10 – 12%	Usually poor quality wheat, not often exported so not usually used in this country.

It is not anticipated that catering students will normally require to study the various types of wheat sown. A knowledge of growing areas with an appreciation of the importance that a lack of supply from any such area owing to either natural conditions such as drought or man-made conditions, such as political changes, should be sufficient to enable them to appreciate any coming changes in market conditions.

The wheat known as 'durum' is the one favoured by most manufacturers of the Pasta products. This is actually a different wheat from that normally used in flour milling and has the botanical name *Triticum Durum*. It produces a flour of reasonable strength. A yellowish colour with a degree of sweetness, it has a protein content of about 13 per cent.

Flour Milling

There are two methods of flour milling, stone milling and roller milling.

116

The stone-milling process is the old-fashioned one which has been superseded in the vast majority of cases by the roller mill but it does produce a type of flour which is in demand by some people, particularly those who follow a 'natural' type of diet.

Stone Milling Process

The wheat is fed into the mill after cleaning and blending in the same manner as is done for the roller-milling process so we would ask the reader to look into this aspect whilst studying the roller process. The mill itself is composed of two stones, the bottom one being stationary whilst the upper one is revolved. The stones have grooved surfaces which move the wheat berry across from the centre to the outer edge; in this process the wheat is sheared open and then ground to a meal, the fineness of the meal depending upon the adjustment of the top stone. This meal is composed of the whole of the wheat berry and is known as wholemeal flour. Some of the larger particles of the bran can be removed by sieving but this is not usually practised.

The Roller-Milling Process

In selecting the wheat to be used for his mill the flour miller has to consider a number of factors,

(a) the price of the wheats available to him
(b) the strength of the wheat
(c) the availability of the wheat.

As the different areas of production harvest their wheats at different times then the supply situation can change at different times of the year. The miller attempts to produce flour of the same strength at all times so that his customers can always rely upon using the same recipe and the same process. In order to do this, he blends the various wheats available to produce a flour of a standard strength and character. This blend is known as his 'grist.'

The wheat is often purchased in the area of growth and shipped as required to the miller. As it may have travelled thousands of miles by many methods of transport it requires cleaning and then its moisture content must be adjusted by a process known as 'conditioning'. The various wheats are then blended to form the grist to produce the type of flour required.

The roller mill is composed of various rollers. The first are known as the 'break rollers.' In this, grooved rollers revolve at different speeds shearing the grain apart and allowing the centre of the endosperm to fallout. After this, the wheat is passed over sieves. The endosperm which has fallen out is separated from the rest of the wheat berry which is then passed on to the next break roller. The endosperm separated is now known as 'semolina'. Sets of sieves now separate the semolina into various sizes and it is at this stage that the semolina to be used is taken off. The remaining semolina is then passed on to reduction rollers. These are smooth rollers revolving at the same speed which break down the semolina into smaller sizes. After passing each set of reduction rollers, the product goes through another set of sieves, and the flour which has reached the required size is taken out and the remainder passed on to the next set of rollers. In many mills there are as many as twenty sets of reduction rollers, each followed by a set of sieves known as plan sifters.

The remainder of the wheat berry has, meanwhile, been passed on to the next break roller and goes through the same process. There are usually five sets of break rollers.

Any parts of the wheat berry such as the bran and germ, which will not pass through the sieves after the last set of break rollers are either extracted for use in various feeding stuffs such as breakfast cereals, or used to blend back with the white flour to produce brown flours or they are sold, to be used in animal feeds.

The flour, after having passed through the plan sifter is often bleached. This has two effects, firstly to whiten the flour to produce whiter coloured goods and secondly as an ageing process to allow its use within a few days of being milled. Flour which has not had this ageing process should be kept for a period of up to 6 to 8 weeks before it reaches its best quality.

In addition it is, at the time of writing, the law in Great Britain that all flour, other than wholemeal must have added to it calcium, iron and vitamins in the following proportions:

Creta Preperata (Chalk) 14oz (397g) per 280lb flour (127kg)

Iron 1.60mg per 100g flour

Vitamin B1 0.24mg per 100g flour

Nicotinic Acid 1.60mg per 100g flour

As has been mentioned the correct proportion of bran and germ may be added back to the white flour after milling to produce a wholemeal flour or wheatmeal flour.

The amount of flour produced from the wheat is known as the 'extraction rate'. If the extraction rate is known then the probable whiteness of the flour can be estimated — wholemeal flour will have an extraction rate of 100 per cent, a wheatmeal flour is likely to have an extraction rate of between 95 and 98 per cent. White flours will vary, from between 25 and 30 per cent for the best white flours which are produced solely from the first break roller, to 70 per cent when the production from all the break rollers is blended. The 25 – 30 per cent extraction flour will be known as a top patent flour and will be stronger than the 70 per cent extraction rate flour which will be known as straight run flour.

Uses of Flour

Flour is used as a recipe ingredient in many dishes produced by the caterer. The highest usage is probably in the area of work covered by the pastry cook where it is used as a major ingredient in most breads, cakes, pastries and many dessert dishes. In general kitchen work it is used as a thickener, a gelling agent, or as a part of batters. The batters are both used as dishes in their own right such as Yorkshire puddings and as coverings for deep frying or as a coating when shallow frying.

It is essential for the student chef to appreciate fully the uses of all cereals in these dishes and to choose from them the one best suited to the work he is doing. For this reason our experimental notes are divided into two sections for this work. The first section shows how the selection of the correct flour can easily be determined. The comparison of the use which can be made of flour and of other cereals is dealt with in the experimental notes at the end of this section.

Flour Experiments

These are designed to select the best flour for:
(a) colour
(b) strength
(c) water absorption properties

To test the colour of three samples of flours

The Pekar Test
Take a palette knife with a 10" (25cm) blade.

Place a sample of the flour on the end to cover about $1\frac{1}{2}$" (3.5cm) of the blade, smooth off with another palette knife and trim off the edge nearest the handle. Place samples of the other two flours next in line and trim off and smooth down again, leaving the knife with a smooth, even coating of flour.

Compare the colours of the flours and note the results. Now take a 12" mixing bowl and fill it with cold water. Immerse the flour covered portion of the knife and leave for about 10 seconds. Remove the blade and allow to stand for about one minute and compare colours again. The whiter flours will be easily seen in this test. Any flour containing branny particles will be seen to have a creamier or darker colour or may even be seen to have brown coloured specks.

Gluten test for strength, and water absorption test

These tests can be made from a single operation.

1. Take an even weight of each flour — the weighing must be as accurate as possible and a good weight to use is 2lb (1kg) but any suitable weight can be used.

2. Add to each flour the same weight of salt calculated on the basis of 1 of salt to 50 of flour so for the kilo of flour use $\frac{3}{4}$ – 1oz (20g) of salt. Sieve the flour and salt to mix thoroughly.

3. Now take a measured quantity of cold water. Mix the flour/salt mixture into a dough taking care that each mixture produces a dough of the same consistency. Measure any water remaining and calculate the amount of water required to produce the dough. It would be ideal if the dough was of the consistency suitable for making a common product such as bread. If possible the use of three small mixing machines fitted with a dough hook and operating at the same time would eradicate human error which could occur if the doughs were mixed by hand. All doughs should have been mixed for the same period of time.

A typical result would be shown as follows:

Flour A 2lb (1kg) required 580ml water

Flour B 2lb (1kg) required 550ml water

Flour C 2lb (1kg) required 595ml water

From this it would be determined that Flour C had the higher water absorption property and would thus, other factors being equal, be the flour with the greater profit potentiality.

After this test take an equal proportion of the doughs produced. One tenth of the kilo experiment would be suitable and this would give approximately 158g, 155g, and 159.5g respectively.

Place each dough in a separate bowl of cold water and allow to stand for 20 mins. If the dough is now worked in the hand under water it will be seen that the water becomes cloudy. This is the starch content of the flour which is being washed out. After a few minutes working the water will have become very thick with the starch and should be poured off and a fresh bowl of cold water prepared and the dough left to rest for some 10 mins. before working again. Repeat this until the water remains clear. Weigh the rubbery substance remaining. This is gluten, the protein content of the flour. The weight produced will indicate which flour has the higher gluten content. The gluten can now be examined for its strength by testing between the fingers. A good quality gluten present in a strong or hard flour will have a good deal of elasticity and will spring back into shape when stretched. A weak or soft flour will have a smaller quantity of gluten which will break easily.

On considering the results obtained it should be possible to determine quickly which flour would be the best to use to make bread, rolls, puff pastry etc. and which would be the best to use for puddings, short pastry, cakes etc.

Rice

Rice is the oldest known cultivated cereal. Records have been found of its cultivation in China some 7,000 years ago.

It is the principal food of over half of the world's population and used by many of the remainder.

Rice requires a tropical-type climate and its cultivation is traditionally done in paddy fields where the river waters are allowed to flood the growing areas during its early growing period.

The main countries of production are China, Japan, and other Far Eastern countries, North and South America and some Mediterranean countries principally Italy, Spain and Egypt. Many countries do not export their rice crops but use their entire production for feeding their own population. This does mean, of course, that if there is any crop failure in these areas then they must make a demand upon the world market and thus reduce the supplies available and force the price up.

There are various types of rice available to the caterer. It has been said that there are some 7,000 varieties of rice grown in the world. The three major types are:

1. Long grain rice
In this variety the length of the rice grain is four or five times its width. The grains are clear with very little chalkiness. They have the characteristic of remaining separate after cooking and so are the type used to prepare rice for curry and similar dishes.

The type name given to many of these is 'Patna' and rice for use in the curry style dishes is often ordered by that name.

2. Medium grain rice
The length of the grain is about three times the width. This type does not remain as distinct after cooking as the Patna rice but does not easily break down into a creamy mass so it is not often used in the kitchen. It is generally rather cheaper to buy than the other two main varieties.

3. Short grain rice
The length of the grain is only one and a half to two times the width and after cooking the grains stick together, with continued cooking they form a creamy mass. This is the type used to make dishes such as rice puddings. The general name given to this type is Carolina.

There are various kinds of rice products available to the caterer. The most important of these are as follows:-

Brown Rice
It still retains the bran layers and germ. It is becoming increasingly popular in 'natural food' types of diet because it retains most of the vitamin and mineral content of the rice grain and provides roughage in the diet.

Milled or White Rice
This is the rice grain which has been treated to remove the hulls, germ and branny layers and is then polished. It is the normal type of rice used.

Pre-Cooked Rice
This is milled rice which has been cooked and then had its water content removed. It only requires the water adding back and a short cooking period before it can be served.

Rice Bran
The bran of rice which is removed in the milling process is mainly used as animal feeding staffs.

Rice Polish
The final layers removed from the rice kernel during the polishing process. It has a high fat and carbohydrate content. It is used in some foods and also for animal feeding.

Rice Oil
Oil may be extracted from the bran and polish. This can then be used to manufacture margarines, and cooking fats and is also used as cooking oil and as a salad oil.

Ground Rice
This is milled rice which has been ground down to a granular powder. It is used for dusting and coating in certain dishes and for making milk puddings.

Rice Flour
This is a flour produced by grinding milled rice. It is a granular powder which is much favoured in the manufacture of crusty rolls because it has no gluten content and therefore any flour adhering to the rolls during the baking process cannot make the crust tough. It may also be used to weaken wheat flours where this is required for a particular product. The use of 1 or 2oz (25 – 50g) of rice flour in the place of wheat flour in every 1lb ($\frac{1}{2}$ kg) of wheat flour in the recipe will change a strong flour into a medium or weak flour. Rice flour is used also as a filler in some meat pies and, as all other cereals, as a thickener for soups.

Preserved Rice
Rice is also available in tins as prepared rice puddings and similar dishes for use as a convenience food.

Rice Paper
This is a thin, edible paper made from rice which can be used to place such items as Macaroons on during the baking process. Any paper left sticking to the food may be eaten with it.

Oats

Oats are a hardy cereal, probably the one easiest to grow in the harder climatic areas of the world. They are traditionally the principal cereal crop of the Scottish countryside and therefore an equally traditional part of the Scotsman's diet, usually taken in the form of porridge.

Oats require a cool, temperate climate and grow well in the higher areas. The major cropping areas in the United Kingdom are Scotland, Wales and the Pennine areas of Northern England and in many of these areas oats or oatmeal form an important part of the local dishes. In addition to porridge there are the oatcakes and havercakes of Derbyshire, Lancashire & Yorkshire and parkins of these areas.

Oats are available in various forms.

Rolled Oats
The cereal is milled by passing between rollers which flatten the berry. Good quality rolled oats should have a minimum of floury dust.

Patent Rolled Oats
These are rolled oats which have been heat treated in order to reduce the cooking time required; typical of these are the domestic packs of 'Quick Quaker' and similar products, the use of which enable porridge to be made in a few minutes instead of the overnight methods originally used with rolled oats.

Oatmeals

These are available in various sizes.

Pinhead Oatmeal
The milling breaks the oat berry down into pieces about the size of the normal pinhead. There should be little or no dust present. When pinhead oatmeal is used care must be taken to allow sufficient time for either the water present in the recipe to soak into the pinhead oatmeal to soften it or a long enough cooking period.

Coarse Oatmeal, Medium Oatmeal and Fine Oatmeals
These are, as their names indicate, various sizes of oatmeal. Each is used for its own particular purpose in the kitchen. These include use as a coating before cooking, use in various recipes and in making porridge. Again, the coarser the oatmeal the longer the cooking period required.

Groats
Not often seen these days, groats are the oat berry after the removal of the hulls and were originally used to make porridge.

Scotch Oats
These are groats which have been cut into pieces by steel rollers.

Oat Flour
This is finely-ground oats. It is used for making oat biscuits and similar products.

Sussex Ground Oats
A very finely ground oatmeal very similar to oat flour used in some speciality dishes.

Oats contain the highest proportion of fat in all the normal cereals and have a high protein content. For this reason they are highly nutritious food. The protein, unlike that of wheat, will not form gluten so they cannot be used to manufacture normal breads, etc. without the addition of wheat flour or some other glutinous substance.

Maize

Maize is used in catering as both a vegetable and a cereal. It is our purpose in this section to deal with the cereal aspects of its use only. Use as a vegetable will be considered in the appropriate section.

Maize is a native plant of the Americas but is now widely cultivated in other warm, temperate and sub-tropical climatic areas. In the United Kingdom it is cultivated mainly in East Anglia and the South Coast areas. The major use of maize as a cereal is in the form of its flour, cornflour. Cornflour is almost pure starch having very little protein content. The fat content of the original cereal is removed to provide maize oil (see Oils and Fats).

Cornflour is used as a thickening agent in soups and sauces and is the main ingredient in Custard and Blancmange powders. It is also used as an ingredient in certain types of cakes. As with rice it may be used as a flour weakener should this be required.

Barley

The principal use of Barley which is of importance in catering is its use as the producer of malt for the brewing industry. Barley, as gathered, is soaked and then allowed to commence growing on a 'malting floor'. After it has produced short roots and the leaf shoots show, the growth is stopped. At this stage the starch in the endosperm has been converted to malt sugars which, if growth were continued would be used to feed the plant. After the removal of the roots and leaf shoots the barley is known as Green malt. This may be then roasted to reduce various grades and types of malt. At first a malt flour is produced by a milling process and from this can be produced the sticky malt extract known to most people. Both of these may be used as a yeast food in fermented items and many specialist producers of crusty rolls use malt flour or malt extract to help them produce the type of crust required in these goods.

The whole barley kernel is used in catering as an ingredient in some soups and stews. There are two types, Pearl barley, the more popular variety which is the whole kernel which has had the husk removed and is then polished, and Scotch barley which still retains some of the husk layers.

Pearl Barley is milled into a flour which is known as *Crème d'orge* and is used as a thickening agent.

Pearl Barley is also used to make Barley Water, a good drink for invalids.

Sago

This is produced from the pitch of the Sago Palm which is principally grown in Malaya, Borneo, the Philippines and the Indian sub-continent. After being scooped out of the tree the pitch is pulped with water and then strained. The starch settles and this is then washed, drained and dried. The flour is granulated by being sieved and the grains are roasted for a period to produce the hard grains of sago. These are subdivided by size into small, medium and large sizes.

Tapioca

A very similar product to Sago. Tapioca is the starch produced from the underground stem of the Cassava plant. The rhizomes are dug up, washed, scraped and pulped; the juice pressed out of the pulp is boiled to concentrate it and then washed. After standing the starch settles and can be drawn off. After drying and roasting Flake and Seed tapioca is produced.

The cassava plant is grown in many areas of the world and used as local food so export from these areas is not frequent. The major British supplies come from Africa and China.

Both Sago and Tapioca have the same uses, as a garnish and in the making of milk puddings.

Arrowroot

Arrowroot is derived from the roots of the Maranta plant which is grown in the Caribbean, the tropical regions of Africa, and America.

The starch is separated out in a similar manner to that described for tapioca and after the separation the liquid is dried off in large copper pans. Two types are available — granular and pulverised. The pulverised form is in the form of a flour which is used in some cakes and puddings and can be used as a thickening agent. Arrowroot has a particular use in dietetic cookery as it is very easy to digest.

Potato Flour

Although not a cereal Potato Flour is used for similar purposes in the kitchen so we refer to it here.

It is prepared from the normal potato and is used as a thickening agent in soups and sauces. It must not be confused with the fine type of dried potato which is an entirely different product.

Rye

Rye is the only cereal, other than wheat, which has a protein content capable of forming gluten. The gluten formed is not as strong as that formed by wheat flour and enzymic action during fermentation results in goods using all rye flour being much smaller in volume than those made from the same weight of wheat flour. It is principally used in breads and rolls but can also be used in many other catering dishes in the place of wheat flour where this is required by diet or other considerations. In general use it is normal in Britain to use at least 25 per cent of strong wheat flour with rye flour in all fermented goods.

The types available are wholemeal (usually known as coarse rye meal), flour which has had the coarser particles of bran removed and is often known as a medium meal, and white rye flour, a flour made in a similar manner to white wheat flour with much of the bran removed. White rye flour can be used to make white rye breads and rolls and the browner flours produce coarser, darker products.

Cereals and their Food Values

Much is made in certain articles and books on slimming of the high carbohydrate values of many of the cereals we have discussed. The original cereal, as processed, may have a rather high carbohydrate value, but when it is made up with water and other ingredients into the dishes we prepare, the carbohydrate values are considerably reduced. Another very important point is that our cereals provide many essential nutrients in the form of vitamins and mineral salts. We list below the average food values of the more common cereals:

White Breadmaking Flour
14% protein, 2% fat, 75% carbohydrate (CHO) sodium, potassium, calcium, magnesium, iron, copper, potassium, and chlorine. Vitamins: thiamine, riboflavin, nicotinic acid, biotin, B_6, folic acid

Wholemeal Flour
13% protein, 2.5% fat, 69% CHO, vitamins and minerals present as listed above.

Cakemaking Flour
8.5% protein, 1.5% fat, 79% CHO, vitamins and minerals present as listed above.

Note
The wholemeal flour has a different amount of the listed vitamins and minerals from an unfortified white flour but where fortification has taken place the amounts of calcium, iron and certain vitamins are equal in white and wholemeal flours.

Rice (Polished)
6% Protein, 1% fat, 86% CHO, minerals as listed for flour plus sulphur. Vitamins as for flour with increased amounts of B_6 and biotin and lesser amounts of others.

Sago
0.2% protein, 0.2% Fat, 94% CHO, with most nutrients as listed for rice but in much smaller quantities.

Tapioca
0.4% protein, 0.1% fat, 95% CHO, minerals as for sago.

Storage

We propose to deal with the storage of all cereals in one item as the requirements for each are basically the same.

All cereals are suitable homes for insect life, and when storing them this must be borne in mind. They are also a very suitable food for vermin such as rats and mice.

The storage given must therefore be such as to exclude these pests, and a sealed metal container has been found to be the most suitable. As most of the cereals arrive in stores in paper packages the best way of dealing with them is to remove them from the delivery package and place them in a clean metal bin or other suitable container. The store itself should be cool and dry, with suitable ventilation. In order to prevent any dirt or other foreign bodies entering the store, it is preferable to have at least two similar containers, one in use in the working area and a second one holding the reserve stock in the store. When the container in use is emptied it can be thoroughly washed, dried and then returned to the main store for refilling whilst the second container can be brought out for daily use. An alternative is to have a smaller container in the store. In every case the important factors are that all must be washed out, dried and then refilled so that no old stocks remain in the base of the container to contaminate new stocks.

Kept in this way, most cereals have a reasonable storage life of two months or so. Flours, especially brown flours, have a shorter storage life than this and should be used within some 4 weeks of delivery.

Orders must therefore be placed with the daily or weekly usage in mind so as not to exceed these periods.

Cereals — Experiments

All the cereals discussed are used as setting or thickening agents. The chef has to determine which cereal is the best one to use for each item of work he has to undertake. In our experiment we test an equal quantity of each cereal as a setting/thickening agent. It is important that all weights, temperatures and cooking times are the same, so all cooking should be done in a double-jacketed pan with the heat set at a standard mark.

It is useful if a suitable microscope is available to examine cells of each cereal. This will show the size and shape of each starch cell, and also whether there are any, or a large number of, broken cells in the sample.

Setting properties

Take a 1 oz (25 gm) portion of each cereal, together with 1 pint ($\frac{1}{2}$ litre) of cold water for each. Let the cereal down with 5 oz (125 cc) of the cold water and mix into a thin cream; boil the remaining water. Pour the boiling water onto the cream and stir well. Remove a measured sample of the mixture. 1 oz (25 gm) or a level dessertspoonful would be suitable.

Pour the remaining mixture into the double-jacketed pan (the water in the outer pan must be boiling) and place the pan on the heat. Cook for 10 minutes, stirring constantly. Remove a measured sample every minute and then remove the remainder from the heat and allow to cool.

Make notes on the appearance and condition of each sample. Then allow it to cool for 5 minutes and repeat the observations. Again compare and note down any points noticed.

Particular items of interest would be:
    A.   The colour of the mixture
    B.   The clarity of the mixture
    C.   The consistency of the mixture
    D.   The taste of the mixture
    E.   Has the 5 minutes' standing produced any changes?

From these determine which could be the most suitable cereal to use for each catering purpose and which, if any, would be a suitable cereal for general use in all catering purposes.

The final choice as to which cereal to use must, of course, also allow for factors such as the cost of the various cereals, whether any of them requires a particular skill in use, and whether they produce goods of the type required in particular establishment. If microscopic examination has been possible it may be useful to see if any conclusion can be drawn from the size of each cereal, and if any had damaged or broken elements present.

CHAPTER 7

Oils and Fats

Oils and fats occur throughout the world, and for the caterer may be of animal, vegetable or marine origin. A fourth area, shale (mineral) oil must not be confused with edible oils for these have no value as a food and are prohibited under the Food and Drugs Act.

For our purpose 'fats' and 'oils' are terms used in their generally accepted sense — a fat being solid and an oil liquid at normal room temperatures. This does not mean, however, that a fat will behave as an oil when heated nor will an oil behave as a fat when cooled as we shall see later.

The table below lists the main fats and oils used by edible oil producers.

Animal	Vegetable	Marine
Lard	Groundnut	Pilchard
Tallow	Cottonseed	Whale
	Coconut	Herring
	Palm	Anchovy
	Palm Kernel	Meahaden
	Soya Bean	
	Rapeseed	
	Sunflower Seed	

Source of Oils and Fats

The supply of the refined oils and the products made from them can vary according to the price and availability of the original plant or animal from which the oil was produced. Factors such as the weather conditions in the areas of growth, political changes which effect the availability, labour problems which cut down or prevent the supply of the oil or its source all have their effect upon the price and supply of the product used by the caterer. The wise caterer will, then, try to be well informed on these factors so as to be able to forecast how any of these points may affect him during any forthcoming period. For this reason we list the major sources of oils and fats used in the food manufacturing industries.

Animal Oil and Fats
Lard

The lard used in our kitchens mainly comes from either local supplies or from the USA with some supplies coming from other European countries. American Lard is classified as follows:

Neutral Lard no. 1.
The top quality lard rendered from leaf pig fat at a temperature below 110°F (433°C).

Neutral Lard no. 2.
Second quality but still very good lard produced by rendering the fat from the back of the pig.

Leaf Lard
Produced by steam rendering the residue left after the production of neutral lard no. 1. A lower quality which has been rendered at higher temperature.

Kettle Rendered Lard
Produced by rendering the residue from neutral lard no. 2. in a high pressure steam kettle; again lower in quality.

Prime Steam Lard
The lowest quality lard, produced from trimmings and other fatty parts of the pig, may have a poor colour and flavour.

Tallow

Rendered from the fatty sections of beef or mutton carcases in a similar manner to lard. The first rendering gives *premier jus*, often used to make high quality margarines. The second rendering produces a harder fat with a higher melting point called stearine.

Vegetable Oils

Coconut Oil
Produced from the coconut grown in the islands off the Asian and Australian continents.

Coconut Seed Oil
Produced from cotton seed grown in East Africa, China and America.

Ground Nut Oil
Produced from the ground nut grown in South and West Africa and India.

130

Refining Oil from Seeds and Nuts

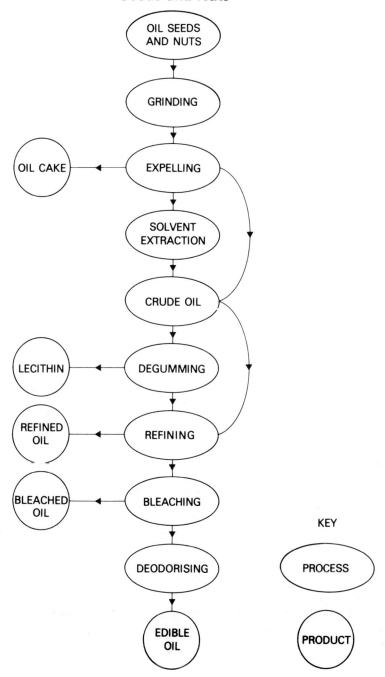

OIL SEEDS AND NUTS

GRINDING

EXPELLING → OIL CAKE

SOLVENT EXTRACTION

CRUDE OIL

DEGUMMING → LECITHIN

REFINING → REFINED OIL

BLEACHING → BLEACHED OIL

DEODORISING

EDIBLE OIL

KEY

PROCESS

PRODUCT

Rapeseed Oil
Attempts are being made to grow rape as a commercial crop in Great Britain, imported supplies come from China and other Asian countries and Canada.

Sunflower Seed Oil
The sunflower can be grown in Great Britain and some commercial cropping is practised, imported supplies come from Asia and the Americas with some South European countries offering small supplies.

Soya Bean Oil
Principal area for growing the soya bean is America but owing to its high food value attempts are being made to grow it in various other parts of the world.

Marine Oils

Many of the sources of marine oils have been sadly depleted by over fishing and this has resulted in conservation areas being set up and some of the fish are at the moment protected. We list those used in the recent past for supplies of marine oils in the hope that this situation will be improved in future years and the supply position return to normal.

Anchovy
Main fishing area is the Pacific Ocean off the South American coastline.

Herring
Supplies of oil from herring are now affected by protection orders and poor catches. The main areas for herring fishing are the North Sea, the Baltic and the Atlantic ocean round Britain and Norway. Another area is the Pacific Ocean off the North American coastline.

Pilchard
Main supply of pilchard for use in oil production comes from the South Atlantic, other areas producing smaller supplies.

Menhaden
A type of herring found in the Atlantic Ocean off the coasts of the USA and the West Indies.

Whale
Not in use much now owing to protection orders. The main supply came from the Antartic Ocean.

Although they may appear dissimilar, oils and fats are chemically one family, being compounds of glycerine plus fatty acids and as such are known as triglycerides, which in turn are compounds of carbon, hydrogen and oxygen.

There are many such fatty acids found in edible fats and oil, but the most frequently occuring are the following:

Stearic $C_{18}H_{36}O_2$
Palmitic $C_{16}H_{32}O_2$
Oleic $C_{18}H_{34}O_2$
Linoleic $C_{18}H_{32}O_2$
Glycerine $C_3H_8O_3$

All triglycerides have different properties. The most important of these for the caterer is, firstly, the melting point.

As all oils and fats in the natural state are a mixture of various trygly-cerides the amount of each and its melting point determine the degree of hardness of the fat. Notice, for instance, the plasticity of lard and the brittleness of suet as but one example, and this is repeated throughout the whole range of fats and oils.

The hardness in suet comes from the high proportion of tristearin present, whose melting point is 164°F (73.3°C). At the opposite end of the scale some of the frying oils in use today contain a high proportion of trilinalein whose melting point is only 8°F (− 13.3°C). That is to say, 24°F below the freezing point of water. Between these two extremes we have a full range of oils, plastic fats and very hard fats.

Secondly, there is a difference between the ratios of carbon to hydrogen in the chemical make up. Stearic and palmitic fatty acids contain twice as many hydrogen as carbon atoms. Oleic, however, contains two less hydrogen atoms whilst linoleic has four hydrogen atoms less that stearic.

The triglycerides made from the first two (stearic and palmitic) are said to be 'saturated' whilst oleic and linoleic are 'unsaturated'. It is possible, however, to 'add' hydrogen atoms to give a degree of 'saturation' and thereby hardness. This process is known as hydrogenation and will be discussed later.

The third and final consideration is that an 'unsaturated' triglyceride besides having the ability to combine hydrogen atoms can also combine oxygen atoms from the surrounding air. This form of oxidisation produces compounds which are responsible for rancidity. At normal temperatures this is quite slow, but as most frying oils belong to the unsaturated group, high temperatures are expected and therefore a speeding up of the oxidisation process takes place and the more unsaturated the product, the faster occurs oxidisation.

Production of Fats from Oils

Most, if not all, oils entering this country do so in the raw state, that is they contain many impurities which must be removed by the manu-

Processing of Fats and Oils

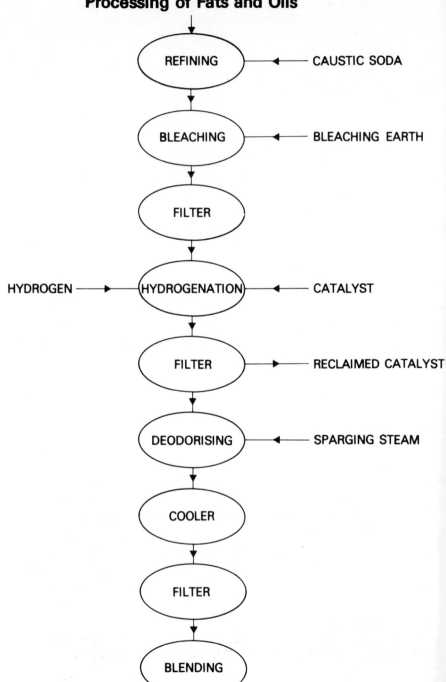

facturer before being processed into 'shortenings'. In the case of ground nuts and soya beans, the oil must be separated from the protein which is a valuable product in its own right. For instance, groundnut extraction is 50 per cent oil and 30 per cent protein. This oil is then subjected to a continuous refining process which results in a pure white fat which provides the base for such items as margarine. This process is as follows:

1. Neutralising

This is intended to remove a number of impurities, in particular the 'free fatty acids'. These are fatty acids which are not combined with glycerine. These usually occur at the rate of $2 - 3$ per cent and can be removed by the addition of an alkali such as sodium carbonate or hydroxide solution. These alkalis act upon the fatty acids to form crude soap, which being heavier than the oil separates out and can then be removed by centrifuging and washing. Repeated centrifuging and washing leaves an oil of high purity. This method, besides removing the free fatty acids also removes proteins, gases, carbohydrates and some colour.

2. Bleaching

Most fats and oils have a natural colour which must be removed. This is done in a 'bleaching kettle' — a large vessel where the oil is activated with paddles. While being activated carbon or Fullers earth is passed into it. Both these ingredients have the ability to take up colour by 'absorption'. This bleaching earth is then removed by passing the contents of the vessel through filter presses; the resulting clear oil is then passed into storage tanks.

3. Hydrogenation

The oils destined to be 'hardened' by the addition of hydrogen are then moved from the storage tanks to the reaction vessel. Shortenings and margarine must contain about 20 per cent solid and 80 per cent liquid to have the right consistency. It is possible to achieve this by mixing stearic (tallow) and oleic (oils) together, but this depends upon the availability of these on a world market. It is much easier to work on the understanding that what is available can be used.

The oils are heated to a high temperature by internal steam pipes then a stream of hydrogen gas is passed through the heated oil. A catalyst, nickel, in powder form, is added to make the process move at a reasonable rate. Samples are taken continuously for testing and the process stopped when the degree of hardness is achieved. The catalyst (nickel) is removed by filter presses. The hydrogenated oil is now placed in storage to await final treatment whilst the reclaimed catalyst is ready for the next batch.

4. Deodorisation

Even though the fats and oils have undergone such a process, they could still contain undesirable flavours. Oils used for the production of margarine for instance must be completely bland, so that there will be no interference with the flavour of margarine.

The oils, therefore, must be deodorised. To do this the oil is again heated to a high temperature (400°F or 204.4°C), but under a vacuum. Steam is then blown through the heated oil. As colour and flavour compounds are more volatile than oils and fats they will come off with the steam. This method is known as sparging and takes several hours after which the oil is cooled down.

Oils which are to be used as oils and therefore have not been through the hydrogenation process, but have been transferred from bleaching to deodorisation are now ready for use by the consumer and are, therefore, packed into their respective containers — bottles for the housewife's kitchen, gallon and five gallon drums for the industry.

The oils which have been hydrogenised do, however, have further treatment depending on the projected end product.

5. Shortenings — Plasticising and Packing
The deodorised oil is now chilled to bring about crystallisation of these tryglycerides which are solid at room temperature. This chilling takes place in a heat exchanger which has scraper blades fitted to the inside of the tubes through which the oil passes; as it solidifies the oil is removed by these blades. At the same time air is injected into the resultant fat to produce a smooth white creamy fat, ready for packaging and distribution.

6. Manufacture of Margarine
Margarine is an emulsion, which is to say that it is a blend of oils and water with the addition of salt, flavour agents and vitamins.

From the very beginning of the margarine industry, milk has been used as a means of flavouring the product in the same way in which milk (as cream) flavours butter.

Milk powder is reconstituted with water, which makes up the disperse phase of the margarine emulsion, and is then pasteurised. After that salt is added. Flavours are added and the whole solution given a thorough mixing.

Flavour in margarine is crucial to give that 'true butter taste'. The best results are achieved in the same manner as in the manufacture of butter, namely by the use of milk which has been soured or ripened under controlled conditions. Ripening is the addition of carefully selected bacterial organisms which lead to the development of the butter flavour.

The next stage in the process is to blend together the oil and the ripened milk in the correct proportions. The legal requirements are that these should be a maximum of 16 per cent water. This is done on a continuous process. The liquid emulsion which results is about 120°F (49°C) at this stage. It is then pumped into a scraped surface heat exchanger and treated in a similar manner as shortenings. The finished margarine leaves the machine as a semi-soft fat at about 60°F (15.5°C) which can then be packed and stored ready for delivery.

High Ratio Shortenings

At this point it would be, we feel, convenient to discuss a fat, with very different properties, which is also produced. Most fats and margarines used for the production of pastries, cakes and sweets are of a type with which we are familiar — that is to say, they use the normal formulae and recipe construction. High ratio fats, however, differ in so far that they are produced from blends of pure edible oils into which monoglycerides as emulsifiers are co-plasticised. This results in a fat which is capable of taking up a greater amount of liquid and sugar than ordinary fats. Because of this, normal recipes are not suitable for these types of fats (hereinafter called super-glycerinated fats). Also such fats cost more to produce than normal fats and whilst this cost is offset by the recipe change necessary for them, when used in catering to produce standard pastries etc. the cost becomes prohibitive.

One of the difficulties confronting the catering student is the appreciation of the number of ways in which fats and oils are used, their suitability for certain tasks and the properties required to carry these out. It is in fact more useful to consider the function of the oil or fat rather than the product in which they are used. These functions are:

1. Shortening Value
This is the ability of a fat to make a product more friable and into this area fall butter, margarine, white shortening and lard. Each of these will easily coat the flour particles and thereby localise the development of gluten leading to the production of tender goods.

2. Plasticity and Malleability
This refers to those fats which are produced for the production of puff pastry. As such they must be capable of standing repeated rolling and folding without permeating the dough layer to give a perfect laminar structure.

3. Creaming Quality
The character of cakes is determined by the ability of the fat to take up and hold air during beating. Butter, margarine and white shortening are excellent examples. Lard and puff pastry margarine do not 'cream' at all.

4. Emulsification
This is the ability of a fat or oil to take up and hold liquid to give a smooth unbroken texture. This property is, for the caterer, closely linked to creaming for the two often go together in the same product, i.e. in making good quality cakes. Not only do we require good creaming pro-

137

perties to give an even texture throughout, but we require good emulsification to inhibit staleing and give a moist product.

5. Frying Quality

Today this usually applies to oils and not fats and as such is not one factor but many. In the first place there are two methods of frying:

(a) *Shallow pan*

Here the function of the oil is to prevent food from sticking to the pan and to achieve this the oil is usually brought to a high temperature before the food is introduced into the pan. It is important therefore that the oil does not mask the flavour of the food in any way, nor must it penetrate into the food. Its sole purpose is to seal and lubricate.

(b) *Deep frying*

In this the oil performs three functions. Firstly it conveys heat to the food, secondly it adds flavour and thirdly some of the oil penetrates the food so adding texture and nutritional properties. Temperature is very important in deep frying large pieces being cooked at lower temperatures than small items, to allow complete cooking before external browning takes place. For example, chicken joints should be fried 325°F – 350°F (163 – 177°C) whilst potato chips need 359°F – 370°F (182 – 188°C).

It is therefore obvious that the quality of the oil used in frying is important not only for its effect upon the food, but also upon its tolerance to withstand high temperature without serious breakdown.

N.B. When there is a breakdown of the oil, three things occur:

(1) The oil becomes darker — affecting the food colour.

(2) Burnt flavour develops and is transmitted to the food.

(3) Free fatty acids are formed causing heavy smoking.

CHAPTER 8

Sugar (*Sucre*)

All plants have a sugar content but in only three is there sufficient sugar to make its commercial development practical. These are the maple tree, the sugar cane and the sugar beet.

The Maple Tree

This is grown in Canada. In the spring when the sap is flowing up the trunk the bark is pierced with a tube and the sap allowed to flow into a container. Sap is collected from the plantation at regular intervals, cleansed and boiled to concentrate it to produce maple syrup.

Unlike the sugar of the cane and beet, maple sugar will not easily crystallise so it is only available as this syrup. It is widely used in the Americas and often served in Great Britain as an accompaniment to flapjacks and some similar dishes.

Sugar Cane

The sugar cane is a large grass looking rather like bamboo and growing to a height of some 12 feet (3.5 – 4m) or more at harvesting period. The leaves fall off leaving behind a tube of hard rind — some 1" to 2" (2.5 – 5cm) diameter which is filled with a soft fibre containing the sugar.

The canes are harvested either by hand or machine, cut into lengths of approximately 4′ (122cm) and taken to the factory. At this stage they contain some 14 to 17 per cent sugar.

At the factory they are crushed to extract the fibre. The crushed cane is washed in a number of changes of water to remove the sugar. After the washing out is complete the dried residue of the cane is used either as boiler fuel in the factory, or, in a few cases, to make building boards.

The syrup resulting from this washing process is now purified by filtering, and by treatment with lime while being heated. This removes organic and nitrogenous matter. The syrup is then heated to remove any surplus liquor and the sugar allowed to crystallise out. This produces raw sugar which is then transported to the consuming countries where it is refined. Any surplus syrup is further treated to produce sugar of a darker colour and the residue used to produce rum.

Sugar Refining Process

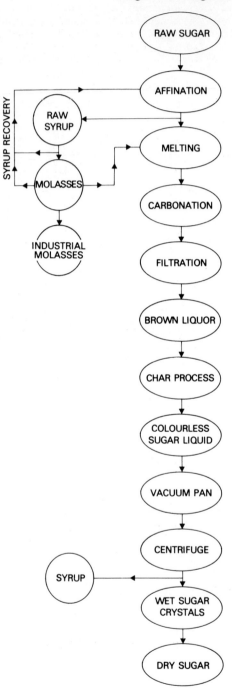

Sugar Beet

The sugar beet plant is grown in the temperate areas of the world. When harvested it is taken to factories where it is first tested for sugar content, then washed, then cut into small sections known as cossets. These are washed with warm water to remove the sugar content. After filtration and some purification this can then be allowed to crystallise as was done with the cane sugars or can proceed straight to the refinery section of the factory. It may, at this stage, be mixed with raw cane sugar.

The Refining Process

The raw sugars are dissolved in hot water, then passed through various processes to remove colour, flavour and any impurities. These include carbonation where the syrup is mixed with milk of lime. Carbon dioxide gas is pumped through and 'chalk' formed which settles out taking any gums and waxes with it. The liquid then passes on to a carbon filter where it is allowed to run through carbon which removes the brown colour. The clear, colourless liquid is then passed on to the vacuum pans where it is boiled under reduced pressure to remove some of the water. After a time sugar crystals are formed and the mass is transferred into a centrifugal separator which spins it at high speed. This removes the surplus water leaving behind the sugar crystals. This sugar is then passed into a granulator where it is dried and cooled ready for packaging. The liquid spun off is passed back for further treatment and to produce a lower grade of sugar. After the second boiling, the process is repeated a third and a fourth time and light brown sugars are produced. These are referred to under 'brown sugars'. The liquid left over after the fourth grade sugar has been produced is known as molasses. Some is used in the sugar refining process, some sold to yeast factories for the production of yeast. Some is sold to mix with animal feeding stuffs and some is used to produce treacles (see below).

Types and Grades of Sugar

Sugar is available in various types and grades. The following list gives a summary of most of these. It is most important that the caterer should realise that all sugars, whether produced from sugar cane, sugar beet, or from a mixture of both are exactly the same. There is no colour, or other physical difference between them nor is there any chemical difference between the sugar of the same type or grade.

Granulated Sugar
Available in fine, medium and coarse grades. Used for most kitchen purposes and for table use.

Castor Sugar (also spelt Caster)
Available in fine and standard grades. Fine castor sugar is produced by

141

milling granulated sugar and then sieving it. The finest of the sugars produced is castor. Used for many kitchen purposes, an especially favoured sugar for table use and for dusting prepared items prior to service.

Pulverised Sugar
This is granulated sugar which is in a large crystal form. It is a speciality sugar used to make water icing of a special type and can be used for sugar boiling work.

Nib Sugar (Coffee Crystals)
Basically the same type of sugar. Nibs are usually white. Coffee crystals brown — although a special type of coffee crystal is available in assorted colours such as red, yellow, blue etc. Sugar nibs are used as a decoration which may be applied before or after cooking. The crystal size is large enough not to be fully dissolved during the cooking or mixing processes and thus remains whole in the finished product.

Cube Sugars
Fine grain sugars which are pressed while still moist into a block and then cut into even sizes, square or oblong. They are used at table and in sugar boiling work. They are available wrapped in singles or doubles with the caterer's name or brand mark printed on the wrapper. This means that clean cubes are always on offer and portion control can be easily introduced where required.

Preserving Sugar
Large pieces of crystals separated during the process. It is a pure white sugar and will not easily clog when used in boiling work. It is therefore ideal for making up syrups, jams etc. in preservation work.

Icing Sugar
Preserving sugar is passed through a mill to produce a fine white powder. Calcium phosphate at a rate of up to 1.5 per cent may be added to help maintain quality. It is used for decorative work.

An alternative to water icing made from icing sugar is fondant. This is produced by boiling good quality sugar crystals and water to 240°F (115°C), adding glucose, and when ready pouring onto a cool marble slab and stirring until a mass of fine white crystals are formed. It is usually bought in a prepared state by the caterer in suitably sized blocks of 14 or 28lb (6.4 or 12.7kg). When required for use a suitable amount is cut from the block, placed in a double-jacketed saucepan and heated gently to 105°F (38°C). A small amount of sugar syrup may be added if required. The fondant is then used as a decorative medium for dipped Genoese fancies, cakes, pastries, etc.

Brown Sugars
These come from two sources. In the original preparation of raw cane sugars some of the syrup left, after the raw sugar is made, is reboiled to

give a brown sugar with some impurities in it. This sugar is often known by the name of the area of production. It is used in goods where the colour and flavour will be of advantage to the end product such as Christmas pudding and cakes, mincemeat etc. Typical of these sugars are: Demerara, Trinidad, Barbados, — Demerara is a large, crystallised, brown sugar often used in fillings for pastries such as eccles cakes and for service with coffee. Trinidad and Barbados are almost black sugars with a soft crystal used in a similar manner.

Third and fourth grade sugars produced by the refining of cane sugars are a soft brown sugar, called by various names in different parts of Great Britain. Fourths, soft brown and pieces are common names. The remaining syrup is known as molasses.

Treacles and Syrups
The molasses is passed through further refining processes to produce the various grades of treacle, the darker the treacle the stronger the flavour. Golden syrup is a mixture of refined molasses and glucose syrup.

Sweetness

There are suggestions that sugars vary in sweetness. This is false but what does occur is that the size and solubility of the grain influences the taste. If the grain dissolves quickly on the tongue then all of the sweet taste becomes available almost immediately. If it takes some time to fully dissolve then the sweetness become available over a longer period and the sugar therefore tastes less sweet.

Other Sugars

We have been referring to the sugar of the sugar cane and sugar beet plant as sugar in all our remarks so far. It is important to emphasise that this is only one type of sugar, known as sucrose. There are sugars in many other items of food and these are chemically different from sucrose.

All carbodydrates have a basic make up of molecules known as saccharides. These saccharides can contain a varying proportion of water.

The simplest sugars are known as monosaccharides and have a chemical formula of $C_6H_{12}O_6$. Typical of these are dextrose or grape sugar and laevulose or fruit sugar.

When two of these simple molecules are joined together with the loss of one molecule of water they become a disaccharide, with a forumula of $C_{12}H_{22}O_{11}$. Sugar produced from the cane and beet plants is in this grouping along with lactose (milk sugar) and maltose (malt sugar).

The final grouping is known as the polysaccharides. This is a complex grouping of the base molecule with a variable number of water molecules present and the formula is usually quoted as $(C_6H_{10}O_5)_n$, indicating this. Amongst the polysaccharides are wheat starch, dextrin and glycogen. In the digestive system the body causes the breakdown of the polysaccharide molecule and adds water molecules to form monosaccharides.

Each of these sugars has a different degree of sweetness.

The following table indicates those of most importance to the caterer. Cane and beet sugar (sucrose) is taken as the standard at 100

Sucrose	100
Laevulose	150
Dextrose	50
Maltose	50
Invert Sugar	85

(Invert sugar is a mixture of sugars found in ripe fruits)

Glucose

Glucose is not a sugar but is used with sugars in certain catering situations, particularly in sugar boiling work.

It is produced from starches such as potato or maize starch by the action of dilute acids upon the starches. It is available in both liquid and powdered forms, the liquid is a clear viscous substance, the powder is a fine white powder. The particular point about glucose is that it is non-crystalline and helps sugars to remain non-crystalline after boiling and can thus provide clear boiled sugar coverings for coating and similar purposes. It is largely composed of Dextrose and Maltose with some dextrin. The liquid type contains some 15 per cent water.

Honey

Honey, produced by bees, is largely composed of dextrose and laevulose. It is available in various types; some from bees which have been hived in areas where one type of plant is predominant, is sold as heather honey, clover honey, etc. This has a distinctive flavour and is especially favoured for this feature. Commercial honey may be thick or clear. The thick honey is usually the honey collected from the bee hives and prepared with very little processing. The clear honey often has had glucose added to it and has had some certain refining treatment given. Pure honey is some 70 per cent invert sugar (dextrose and laevulose). According to the proportion of each it will be a little more sweet or a little less sweet than sugar.

Sugar Boiling

Although this is a practical item we would briefly refer to sugar boiling here to explain what happens in certain aspects of cookery.

If sugar and water are mixed together and heated they will boil, and the temperature at which the mixture boils will vary with the amounts of each. If boiling is continued and water driven off by evaporation then the sugar contents of the syrup will increase. As the temperature rises then the syrup will react in a different manner. This can be tested either by thermometer or by the hand. In order to test by hand great care is required but the task is simple once fully understood. A bowl of cold water is placed alongside the sugar pan, the fingers are dipped into the cold water, wetting them thoroughly and then dipped into the sugar and removed back to the cold water immediately. The syrup is worked between the fingers and the sugar forms certain shapes, the shapes or types will be seen in the following list alongside the appropriate temperature:

215°F	(101.5°C)	Sugar and water boils.
225°F	(107°C)	Thread degree.
230°F	(110°C)	Pearl degree.
235°F	(112°C)	Blow degree.
240°F	(115.5°C)	Feather degree.
245°F	(118.3°C)	Soft ball degree.
250°F	(121°C)	Hard ball degree.
280°F	(137.5°C)	Soft crack degree.
315°F	(157°C)	Hard crack degree.
320°F	(160°C)	Start of caramelisation; the boiling sugar will start to turn an amber colour and as the temperature rises will become darker until
350°F	(176.6°C)	Caramel degree.

Uses of Sugar

It is important to remember that sugars have a number of uses in catering work, particularly in the pastry section.

In addition to the sweetness they give to goods in which they are used they encourage goods to take on more colour during the cooking process because of the fact that they caramelise when heated. They are a food for yeast and so their use in bread, rolls etc. speeds the fermentation period required. They act as a moistening agent, when used in mixings. They reduce the amount of moisture which is required to be added and after cooking they help to keep the goods moist and fresh and they have an aeration property. If sugar is used in a cake or pudding mixture for instance it lightens the item, if too much is used then the cake or pudding 'boils over' leaving behind a thick, sugary crust and often a sunken centre.

In selecting which of the many types of sugar is to be used in any particular task the following points should be remembered.

When the sugar is required to stay whole for a period during mixing or during the whole process, a hard, large grained sugar should be used, where the sugar is required to dissolve quickly then a fine or soft grained sugar should be used. The brown sugars will give colour and flavour to goods and should, therefore only be used where this colour and flavour can either be of advantage to the item or where the colour or flavour will be hidden by other ingredients in the make up of the dish (e.g. in ginger puddings where the colour is brown and the ginger will hide any flavours in the sugar).

CHAPTER 9

Herbs, Spices, Salt and Vinegar

These are the flavouring agents added to recipes and used as condiments. They are an essential part of the recipe in that they give the flavour to many of our dishes. The choice of the correct flavouring agent is of great importance as is quantity used.

The difference between a normal dish and one which is regarded as a great one is often the choice of the flavours the chef adds to his recipe. It is for this reason that we believe that a comprehensive knowledge of the herbs, spices and other flavours is needed by catering students.

There is some difficulty in determining which is a herb, which is a spice and how to regard a strongly flavoured ingredient which can also be used in another manner.

For the purposes of this section we shall suggest that the herbs are grown in the northern hemisphere whilst the spices are usually grown in the southern hemisphere.

Where a strongly flavoured ingredient is also used in other ways we shall make reference under both headings in the different sections of the book.

Herbs (*Herbes*)

Herbs comprise the leaves, flowers, stems, seeds or roots of various plants. The herb is a seed plant which does not develop woody stems. They are usually available in either fresh or dried form with some becoming available in a frozen form. Where a suitable supply is available it is possible for the kitchen to freeze chopped herb leaves in small blocks and store in the deep freeze until required. They are added to soups and stews, often during the last hour or so of the cooking period, to roasts by sprinkling on to the joint towards the end of the cooking period, to meat mixtures such as meat loaves, patés etc during mixing, to stuffings in the mixing stage and to vegetables, sauces etc in the initial cooking stage.

They may be added to salad dressings when mixing and may be made into sauces of their own flavour such as mint and horseradish sauce.

The principal herbs and their countries of origin are:

Angelica (Angélique)
This is a tall plant which grows wild in Great Britain and many parts of Europe and is cultivated as a decorative and flavouring material. The

stems are preserved by using a candying process similar to that described for candied peels and the seeds and roots are used for flavouring wines and liqueurs. The stem after it has been candied is offered as a green stem from $\frac{1}{2}$ to 1″ (1 − 2.5cm) thick which can be chopped up into small pieces and mixed into dishes as flavouring agents (cabinet pudding) or cut into strips as a decorative medium which also gives its flavour to the dish.

Aniseed (Anis)
The principal area of growth is the North African Mediterranean coastal region and South Eastern Europe with some supplies being available from India.

The major use is in flavouring various alcoholic drinks such as Pernod. The leaves or dried seeds are also used in a number of fish and fruit dishes.

Balm (Baume)
Lemon balm is produced in the Mediterranean countries. The dried leaves are used in various mixtures of herbs.

Basil (Basilic)
There are various types of the basil plant. The one usually used in cookery is the sweet basil, the others have a weaker or inferior flavour and are mainly used as decoration.

The areas of production are India and the Mediterranean countries. Its principal use is in conjunction with tomatoes and salads.

Bay Leaves (Laurier)
The bay tree is grown in the Mediterranean areas and is one of the popular leaves used in catering.

They may be used fresh or dried and are a principal ingredient in the make up of a bouquet garni. They are also used to flavour many meat dishes.

Bergamot (Bergamote)
This is grown in the North Americas. The flower is used in green salad dishes.

Borage (Bourrache)
Both the flowers and leaves of this herb, once grown mainly in the Middle Eastern areas but now common in most European countries, can be used. The leaves are the more popular and can be used fresh in salads or dried as a flavouring agent. The flowers may be candied when they are used as a decoration for cakes, trifles etc.

Chervil (Cerfeuil)
A native of Eastern Europe this herb is now available in many European areas. Rather similar to parsley in appearance the leaves have a spicy

taste. They may be used both fresh in salads and dishes and dried in a number of dishes.

Chives (Ciboulette)
There are mainly used as a fresh vegetable and reference is made to them in the section on green vegetables.

Chicory (Chicorée)
Chicory is used in its dried form in coffee mixtures (see Beverages) but is also an important salad vegetable and may be offered as a vegetable when the roots are boiled and eaten like parsnips.

Dill (Aneth)
Both the leaves and the seeds of the dill plant are used. It is a native of Southern Europe and Western Asia. It is used as a flavouring agent in pickling.

Fennel (Fenouil)
Fennel is one of the older herbs and is grown in most European countries. Seed, leaves and stalk are all edible and it can be used fresh or dried in a great many different culinary situations.

Garlic (Ail)
The bulbous root is used to provide the flavour in many dishes. It grows in both wild and cultivated form in Great Britain and many other Western European countries.

Horseradish (Raifort)
Principally known for the sauce of the same name, horseradish is grown in Britain and other European countries. The root is used to make the sauce.

Marjoram (Marjolaine)
A sweet herb related to the mints but with a flavour characteristic of the thyme family. Grown originally in the mediterranean areas some types are now naturalised in Britain. Rather more delicate than many other herbs it is more usual to add it late in the cooking process so that the flavour is not destroyed by the heat. It is used fresh in salads and dried in soups, sauces, stews and stuffings.

Mint (Menthe)
There are some ten varieties of mint grown in Great Britain. The two mostly used in catering are the common or garden mint and peppermint with spearmint a commonly used flavouring for sweets.

The leaf can be used fresh or dried. It is added to vegetables such as new potatoes and garden peas during the cooking process and used to make mint sauce and mint jelly for use with lamb dishes.

Oregano (Origan)
Grown in the colder areas of the Mediterranean, oregano is widely used in Italian cookery and Italian based dishes. To obtain the best flavour the leaves must be dried whilst young and be freshly gathered. Care must be taken when purchasing this herb so as to obtain the best flavoured variety.

Parsley (Persil)
Now a common British grown herb, parsley was originally introduced from Sardinia. Widely used for garnishing and flavouring it may be used fresh as a garnishing agent or dried as a flavouring agent. The drying process must not be allowed to turn the leaves brown as this indicates a loss of flavour.

Rosemary (Romarin)
Grown principally in the Mediterranean and in California; the leaves may be used fresh or dried for flavouring sauces, soups, stews and salads.

Saffron (Safran)
Saffron is obtained from the stigma of a crocus. British produced saffron comes from Cornwall and imported supplies come from Spain and Portugal. The stigma are dried and a powder produced which can be used as it is or made into saffron tea. An infusion of $\frac{1}{2}$ to 1oz $(14g - 28.35g)$ saffron in 1 pint ($\frac{1}{2}$ litre) of boiling water will produce a very strongly coloured and flavoured yellow liquid. Either the liquid, or the powder can be added to dishes to colour and flavour them. Care must be taken in its use as it is very strong. Typical uses are in colouring rice for oriental dishes and in making special breads and cakes.

Sage (Sauge)
Grown in this country and imported from southern Europe this is a strong bitter herb which has the ability to help the digestive system and is therefore used to make stuffings for fatty meat dishes such as pork, goose and duck.

Savory (Sarriette)
Grown in the Mediterranean area there are a number of varieties of this herb. The two principal ones used are summer savory and winter savory. Summer savory is the popular one. The leaf is dried and used to make stuffings for poultry and to add to various meat or egg dishes and also in salads.

Sorrel (Oseille)
It is grown mainly in France and can be used fresh or dried. The fresh young leaves are used in salads or can be boiled and made into a purée when they may be served with veal, pork, fish or egg dishes.

Tarragon (Estragon)
A native of Siberia but now available from France and Yugoslavia this

herb has a bright green leaf which is a popular decorative medium for chaud-froid dishes. Dried it is used in sauces, egg, fish and meat dishes or used in salads.

Thyme (Thym)
There are a number of different thymes, most of them used either in cookery or in the preparation of foods. The common thyme is grown in Britain and imported from Spain, France and Portugal. It is available as either fresh leaf or dried. It is used in flavouring soups, sauces and stews and as a major flavouring agent in stuffings such as parsley and thyme. It is also used in a number of other dishes and in bouquet garni.

Lemon Thyme
This type has a distinctly different flavour and is therefore used in different dishes, and also in pickling.

Tansy (Tanaisie)
A strongly scented herb grown in Europe and Northern America and used to flavour and garnish dishes. It is used both fresh and dried.

Herb Mixtures
In concluding this short section on the herbs we should mention that many are used as parts of mixtures of herbs. This practice has already been mentioned in parsley and thyme and bouquet garni. Another common use is in fine herbs (fines-herbes). This is a mixture of fresh herbs, usually chervil, parsley and tarragon and is referred to as fine herbs in many classical recipes.

Spices

Ajowan
A spice produced mainly in the Indian sub-continent and used in many Indian dishes.

It has a resemblance to Thyme in its flavour.

Allspice — see Pimento

Capsicum and Chillies (Piment)
We list these together as they are both from the same family. They are the bright red pods of bushes grown in the tropics, mainly the East Indies and Southern Africa. If the capsicum is ground to a powder it is known as a red pepper (see Peppers). Chilli powder is used in spicing various dishes. Both can be used either as pods or in the ground form. Capsicum is not as hot as chilli.

Caraway (Carvi)
Caraway seeds are one of the few spices grown in Europe, principally in

Flavourings and Spices

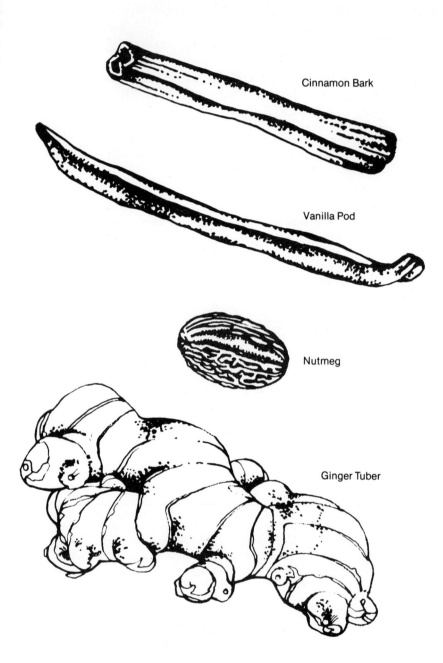

Cinnamon Bark

Vanilla Pod

Nutmeg

Ginger Tuber

Holland. The seeds are used as a decorative and flavouring medium, in seed cake.

Coriander (Coriandre)
The seed of a plant grown in Morocco, and the Caucasus. It has a warm, pungent flavour and is used in curry powder, mixed spice and as a flavouring in speciality breads, cakes and alcoholic liqueurs.

Cinnamon (Cannelle)
The bark of a laurel grown mainly in Sri Lanka. It may be used as a stick or as a ground powder. It has a wide use in puddings and cakes, is added to pears when stewing and can be mixed with the sugar used to dust doughnuts after cooking when it is claimed to reduce any 'fatty' taste. Many other dishes benefit from dusting with cinnamon or by adding a little cinnamon to them.

Cloves (Girofle)
These are the unopened flower buds of a small tree grown in the tropical areas of America and Africa. The buds are gathered green and used in a few dishes in this manner, but the more usual way is to smoke them over a wood fire and dry them in the sun. The whole clove is used both as a flavouring and a decoration in dishes such as *oignon piqué* and in apples and pears. Cloves may be added to dishes such as stewed apples for flavouring, and when ground used as an ingredient in some mixed spices.

Curry Powder (Poudre de kari)
A mixture of spices and herbs which may be bought ready-prepared or made up in the kitchen. As with all mixtures it can vary considerably both in flavour and in how hot it is according to the wishes of the blender. Suppliers take great care to keep their blends exact so that they may be used with confidence to repeat the same flavour. Typical of the spices and herbs used are: bayleaves, chilli, cardamom, cumin, carraway, cloves, cinnamon, fenugreek, garlic, ginger, mustard, nutmeg, pimento, pepper, saffron, all in more or less equal proportions with larger quantities of coriander and tumeric.

Cumin (Curmin)
Available from numerous areas in the southern Mediterranean and Far East, the seed is used as a spice in many dishes. It is also available in a ground form.

Celery Seed (Graine de Céleri)
Principally used in celery salt to give a celery flavour in dishes where it is unsuitable to use fresh celery or where the fresh vegetable is not obtainable.

Fenugreek (Fenugrec)
This is made from the seeds of a plant of the clover family. The main use

of this spice is in curry powder as mentioned above. The plant is grown principally in Morocco and Tunisia.

Ginger (Gingembre)
The root of a plant grown mainly in the Far East, India and Jamaica. It is used in its original fresh form, as dried ginger root, and as a powder. The fresh root can be candied and then added in pieces or in a crushed form to various dishes when it both gives flavour and a rather unique eating quality. Various grades of the fresh root are available, so care must be taken when purchasing to see that they are not too coarse. Dried ground ginger is used in a great many dishes and is also served at the table with dishes such as fresh melon slices. Dried ginger root is used in pickling.

Juniper Berry (Baie de genièvre)
Grown in Southern Europe and North Africa, the juniper tree yields berries which are used to flavour gin and are also used in various game dishes and mixed in with stuffings for poultry dishes.

Mace — see Nutmeg

Mixed Spice
A blend of spices, usually approximately equal parts of allspice, cloves, cinnamon and coriander with smaller parts of ground nutmeg and ginger. Used in puddings, cakes etc. and added to many savoury dishes.

Mustard (Moutarde)
There are two types of mustard available, black and white. Most mustards comprise a mixture of the two. The white mustard usually has a milder flavour than the black and so is traditionally favoured in this country. Manufacturers of prepared mustards blend varying proportions of black and white mustards with herbs and other spices to produce mustards claimed to represent the tastes required in various other countries.

As well as its use as a condiment mustard is used in sauces and as an additive to various dishes, a typical example being welsh rarebit.

Nutmeg (Noix de Muscade) **and Mace** (Macis)
These are both produced from the same tree. Mace is the product of the outer casing of the shell and nutmeg is the kernel.

Mace has a milder flavour than nutmeg, and is used in sauces, meat and fish dishes. The tree grows in the Far East and Grenada.

Nutmeg is available in two forms, as the original kernel and in its ground form. In the ground form it soon loses its flavour if it is not stored in an airtight container so in the type of unit where very little is used the whole dried kernel is often popular. Its principal use is in sweet puddings both as a flavouring ingredient and as a flavouring/decorative medium when a small quantity is sprinkled on to the top of dishes such as rice puddings and baked custards. It may also be used in fatty meat mixtures.

Pepper, Paprika, Cayenne Pepper (Poivre)
As all these are closely related spices we can deal with them together.

Pepper is grown over most of tropical Asia. If the berries are gathered at the stage when they are green and starting to turn red then black pepper is produced, if allowed to ripen more fully and are fully red when gathered then white pepper is produced.

White pepper is the one normally used for table purposes and the quality varies according to the quality of the original peppercorns and the treatment they have received. Ground white pepper should be a creamy colour going to a greyish shade as the quality depreciates. A better flavour is obtained when the pepper is freshly ground and this is done in many establishments by the use of pepper mills both on the table and in the kitchen.

The peppercorn can be used whole in some dishes, in others the ground pepper is added as required.

Paprika
This is a sweet red pepper prepared from a different plant — the capsicum. It is used to garnish and flavour dishes such as stews, gravies, etc. and is also used for its flavour in various dishes. It has a reputation of having a high vitamin C content in its fresh form.

Cayenne Pepper
This is prepared by grinding together capsicum and chillies, as was mentioned earlier. In addition to flavour is also adds red colouring to goods in which it is used. It has a hot flavour and its main use is in savoury dishes and cheese straws.

Pimento (Piment)
This has a similar flavour to mixed spice but is rather hotter.

Blue Poppy or Maw Seed (Pavot)
Grown mainly in Asia the blue poppy seed is used as a decorative medium of various Jewish breads and rolls and has developed from these to be used as a decoration on other fermented goods. It can also be used crushed in other mixtures.

Turmeric (Curcuma)
Grown in India and other Asian countries the root of the plant has the ability to give a strong yellow colour to goods in which it is used. The roots are ground to a powder which is added to various dishes which it is required to colour, a common use being in curry powder.

It has no strong flavour.

Vanilla (Vanille)
The whole pods are simmered in custards and other sweet sauces to enhance the flavour, removed, dried and re-used. They can also be stored in dry sugar which absorbs the vanilla flavour (see p. 160).

Spice Salts
Mention must be made at this stage of the numerous spice salts which are

available. It is possible to purchase specially prepared salts to which an amount of the spice has been added. By using these it is possible to add small quantities of the spice when cooking dishes for small numbers. They also, of course, offer a large variety of spices for only a small cash outlay and therefore are an asset to the kitchen accounts.

Salt (*Sel*)

Common salt is an important part of the diet. We are fortunate in this country in that there are large beds of underground salt in various parts of Great Britain. The main area of production is on the Cheshire Plains with other areas in the north east and the south west. In Cheshire the underground salt is brought to the surface by using pipes which pass hot water down into the salt beds and the brine solution is then forced to the surface up a return pipe. This salt is then allowed to settle, cleansed, dried and packaged ready for distribution. It is usually guaranteed to be 99.9 per cent pure.

The salt is available in various grades. Rock salt (only used for special work) is in large lumps. Dried salt or kitchen salt is in a fairly coarse granular powder which will easily go damp and form into hard lumps. Table salt has a powder (usually calcium carbonate) added to it to keep it free flowing so that it may be used in salt cellars and similar utensils.

Some salt has potassium iodide added to it in order to prevent or reduce troubles which can be caused if the iodine content of the diet is low. Iodine is required for the proper function of the thyroid gland, malfunction of which can cause goitre. This salt is known as iodised table salt.

In addition to its uses as a flavouring agent salt is also used as a preservative and mention will be made of this function in other areas of this study.

Vinegar (*Vinaigre*)

Various types of vinegar are available. Malt vinegar is considered to give the best flavour of the normal vinegar varieties. Malt vinegar is made by fermenting malted barley (See Cereals). During the fermentation process bacteria are added which convert the alcohol produced to acetic acid. Artificial non-brewed vinegars are made from acetic acid to which colouring is added; they tend to be sharper in flavour than the malt vinegar.

Spirit Vinegars can be produced by fermenting starch products such as potatoes but these have not as good a flavour as Malt Vinegar.

Wine Vinegars are used in some speciality dishes and by some high class establishments. These are made in France mostly from low quality red or white wines.

Fruit Vinegars are available, usually for special use only, typical examples are Raspberry Vinegar and Apple Cider Vinegar.

Distilled Vinegar is made from either malt vinegar or wine vinegars by distilling the appropriate vinegar. The product is a clear colourless liquid consisting mainly of acetic acid and water with a few of the aromatic volatile bodies from the original vinegar. It is known in Scotland as crystal vinegar.

Vinegar is used as a condiment in its own right, as an additive to various sauces and dressings and as a preservative for various pickles (see under appropriate item). It is used in marinades to tenderise various meats before cooking and in the cooking of some shellfish dishes.

Herb-flavoured vinegars can be produced by placing the appropriate herb in a glass container, covering with a good quality vinegar, sealing tightly and storing for at least two weeks before use.

Typical of these types is tarragon vinegar used to make sauce Béarnaise.

Storage

Herbs and spices are used in cookery principally for their flavour and aroma so storage must be arranged so that these are not lost whilst the goods are in store.

Fresh herbs and spices deteriorate rapidly and must therefore be used within a short period of delivery — normally within 2 to 3 days.

Dried herbs and spices must be stored in airtight containers in order to retain their flavours. Glass or metal containers are preferable so that the container will not affect the items.

As the total usage of these goods is in very small amounts the quantity ordered should be such as would allow usage during a reasonably short period. Large quantities may be cheaper to buy but both the capital outlay required and the gradual deterioration which can occur over a long period both indicate against this being a practical proposition. Wherever possible we would suggest that a total storage life of no more than one year should be contemplated.

As the heat of the kitchen will encourage loss of flavours it is a good point to allow only small containers to be kept in the working area with the larger stocks retained in the cool dry store.

Salt is hygroscopic, that is to say it will attract moisture. For this reason it must be stored in a dry area to prevent it becoming damp and going lumpy. Again it is a good idea to have a suitable container for kitchen use which can be refilled as required, the wooden salt box is ideal for the purpose.

Vinegar, as had been stated, is an acid and must not be stored in metal containers. Glass is ideal and many firms are now using plastic containers holding one gallon or more. Plastics, where the correct plastic is used, are good, they cannot easily be broken and are usually not returnable so do not require capital outlay by the user. It is important, however, that only a suitable plastic is used. Some plastic containers made for use with items such as detergents and drinks are not suitable for the storage of acid-containing items. Care must therefore be taken only to use the correct plastic container for such items as vinegar. Failure to keep to this rule could lead to a chemical action taking place between the acid content of the vinegar and the container. Some such actions in the past have caused food poisoning illnesses.

CHAPTER 10

Colours and Flavours

The major users of colours and flavours in the kitchen are probably the chef patissier, the boulanger, the confiseur and the glacier but, as in many kitchens these tasks are performed by non-specialist members of staff, we would suggest that study of these important ingredients is valuable.

Colours and flavours may be from natural sources, they may be of synthetic origin, or they may be a mixture of the two.

In the past many items have been used for these purposes and some of them have proved to be harmful to the consumer so many countries have passed laws to prevent the use of some colours and flavours in food. These laws are different in almost every country so we feel that it would be impossible to give in this short survey sufficient details to guide our readers on these details.

However, as these items are almost always obtained from one of the many caterers suppliers, it is usual for the caterer to rely upon these traders to supply only items which are within the law. For those using reasonably large quantities of these items, or those wanting special supplies there are a number of manufacturers and importers who will be happy to be of assistance to those who ask.

An important point to remember is that if any export trade is dealt with (and this can include supplying food to aircraft, shipping lines etc.), then care must be taken that the legal requirements of the countries where calls are made are also met.

Colours

Colours are available in liquid, paste and powder form. Each of these can be obtained in different strengths but usually the liquid colour is the weakest and the powder the strongest. Care must be taken in their use, a reasonable quality colour is often recommended to be used at 2 or 3oz per hundredweight of total mix (1.1 to 1.65g per kg).

Colours are often supplied for use in one specific situation (ice cream making, sugar boiling, cake making, decoration etc.) Some colours are very susceptible to temperatures and may fade, become stronger or even change colour if subjected to a different temperature range than that for which they are intended. It has been known for a supposed raspberry gateaux base to come out of the oven a light brown colour instead of raspberry red when an ice cream colour instead of a baking colour has been used.

It is always important to measure the amount to be used accurately, especially when the dish is to be repeated at regular intervals.

It must be remembered that colours do not actually add flavour, although to many people a colour indicates the type of flavour to be anticipated. Never strongly colour an item which is only intended to have a mild flavour or vice versa.

Flavours

The best quality flavours are the essential oils extracted from the original source. Cheaper supplies are a blend of essential oils and synthetic flavours with the fully synthetic flavour coming still lower down the price range. Again manufacturers often recommend quantities to use and in a strong essence or flavour these can be in ounces per hundredweight again (gms per kilogramme).

The chef can obtain a few of the flavours from natural sources. The main ones of these are vanilla, lemon and orange, vanilla flavour comes from the vanilla bean. Vanilla beans are in a long thin pod. If the pods are crushed and mixed with a food the flavour is dispersed through the food. An alternative method is to place one or two pods in a sealed tin with 21b or 1kg of sugar. After some 16 days an ounce (28.35g) of sugar added to any cake or ice-cream mixing will give a fine vanilla flavour.

Citrus fruits have their essential oils in small sacs in the skin. If the skin is ruptured the essential oil will be released. This process is used in certain dishes where a zester is used to release this essential oil and it then is incorporated in the dish. As with colours, flavours and essences can vary in their ultimate strength according to the use to which they are put. It should be remembered that almost all of them are alcohol based. This means that if the flavour, essence, or the dish they are incorporated into are left lying about in the kitchen then the strength of flavour will be lowered. All flavours must be stored in tightly corked bottles and any dishes which are to be cooked should be cooked as quickly as possible after preparation.

Combined Colour and Flavour Compounds

A very useful product, especially for the less experienced worker are the combined colour and flavour compounds. These may be in paste or liquid form and are so blended that when they are added to a white or lightly coloured mixture, the depth of colour will indicate the strength of flavour given. They usually are not as strong as the colours and flavours are when used independently and therefore can be added rather more generously than would be done if using the individual products.

Purchase, Storage and Use

As we have already pointed out, these products are produced by certain specialist firms. The buyer would be wise to contact such a firm and, once their products have proved to be of the quality required and at a suitable price, have that firm to supply their needs. When ordering it should be made clear to the firm or its representative how the product will be used and the containers inspected upon delivery to check the type, quality and recommendations for use.

Where large quarterly production is undertaken the use of a graduated measuring glass for each colour and flavour will reduce any mistakes and some suitable calculator of the amounts to be used in each recipe is essential.

Where only small quantities are used a dropper is very useful. One should be obtained for each different colour or flavour. Where no such instrument is available the liquid colour or flavour may be measured into the cap of the bottle before adding to the mixing. Never try to add two or three drops directly from the bottle. It is far too easy to pour in an ounce instead of a drop and so ruin the whole mixing.

Colours and flavours can be purchased in bottles of $\frac{1}{4}$pt (150g), 1lb (450g), 1pint ($\frac{1}{2}$litre), 7lb (3$\frac{1}{4}$Kilo), 1gallon (4.5litres), and 5 gallons (22.5litres) with the pastes and powders in tubes or jars of similar capacities. Colours, if correctly sealed, can be stored for years but once a flavour or essence container has its seal broken then the quality will slowly be lowered even when the container is well sealed and stored in a suitable cool store. The answer is obviously then to order only sufficient for a six-month period of use. This will, of course also assist with storage problems and the cash involvement in heavy stocks of little-used products.

When using these products their strength makes it necessary to take care. Any colour or flavour spilled on to the hands or on to any equipment can be difficult to remove and can mean that other dishes produced afterwards may be coloured or flavoured by this spillage.

Colours and flavours of all types can be used in the production of many dishes but it must be remembered that they are not able to cover up the use of inferior quality materials in the dish. To make the perfect finished dish requires careful selection of good quality commodities. Flavours and colours should be used to supplement, not replace this quality.

Typical examples of colours, flavours and colour/flavour compounds are as follows:

Colours

Caramel A dark brown colour made from burnt sugar.
Cochineal A red colour obtained from an insect *dactylopius coccus.*
Saffron A yellow colour obtained from the stigma of the *crocus sativus*
grown in Cornwall or imported from France and Spain.
Lemon Yellow A chemically based colour using tartrazine.
Aramanth A raspberry-coloured chemical colour.
Indigo carmine A blue chemical colour.
Guinea green B A bright green chemical colour.

Flavours and Essence

Vanilla essences or extract Produced from the vanilla bean
Essence of lemon and oil of lemon Produced from lemon peel
Orange essence and oil of orange Produced from orange peel
Almond essence Prepared from bitter almonds
Almond flavour A synthetic flavour containing benzaldomydo
Butter flavour A synthetic flavour made from diacetyl
Pear flavour Made from amyl acetate
Raspberry flavour Made from ethyl benzolate
Rum flavour Made from ethyl formate

CHAPTER 11

Gels and Gelling Agents, Jams and Jellies

To understand fully the nature of Jellies it is necessary firstly to define five situations. These are:

1. There is a difference between liquids in their ability to pass through a semi-permeable membrane; those which do not pass through or only very slowly are called colloids from the Greek *Kolla* (gums and glue).
2. The solid element of a colloidal solution is called a gel or gelling agent and is often in crystal form.
3. Should a gel contain all its liquid component and set upon cooling it is termed a jelly.
4. The small particles of gel when in solution are the 'dispersed phase.'
5. The liquid in which these particles are dispersed is known as the 'continuous phase.'

These five situations therefore make up the character of colloidal systems, which depends upon the large surface area of the dispersed phase. All the particles are separate from each other when in the continuous phase and present a very large surface area.

Gels such as gelatine, agar or pectin in dry form are elastic by nature and are capable of taking up very large amounts of water (which becomes the continuous phase). As an example, gelatine placed in water will take up six times its own weight in water.

All colloidal systems, and gels are no exception, are unstable and will often break down; usually this takes place in two sucessive stages:

1. The gel structure tends to shrink allowing the water to 'weep out'. This is known as Syneresis.
2. Being now short of some of its liquid content the gel element will crystallise out.

Edible gums used by the catering and allied food industries as gelling agents are to be found throughout the whole world and they can be divided into four main categories.

(A) Animal

Under this heading we have gelatine, casein and albumen, of which gelatine is the one in greatest use by the caterer.

Casein predominates in milk and is the basis of cheese, whilst albumen is found in greatest quantities in egg whites and accounts for the whipping, setting, and gelling properties of the egg.

Gelatine is produced from the bones and hides of animals. These are soaked in water with lime to remove all undesirable matter such as hair and blood, after which the lime itself is removed by sulphur dioxide which at the same time bleaches the stock and reduces the alkalinity. After this, hot water is used to remove the gelatine in successive stages.

The highest grade of gelatine is produced in the first extract having better colour and gelling power than subsequent extractions.

These extracts are then clarified from which a firm jelly results. This is dried to give sheet or flake gelatine, which in turn can be ground to produce powdered gelatine.

The grade of gelatine depends upon colour flavour, smell and gelling power, but good edible gelatine should be almost clear of colour and almost free of flavour and should make up into a bright, clear gel.

(B) Vegetable Gums

These can be sub-divided into two sections:

(1) *Exudates*

As the name implies these are in the main products of trees or large plants where the gum oozes out either naturally or is helped by incision being made in the bark. These latter forms of exudation are due to infection at the site of damage.

There are four such gums in common use. These are:-

a) Gum Tragacanth
This comes from the astragalus shrub which grows in most deserts. It is usually pulverised into a white powder. Although this powder does not completely dissolve in water it does swell to form a mucillage which makes a very strong gel. Its main use is to produce pastillage (gum paste) for modelling and moulding and as a glaze.

b) Gum Arabic
This is an exudation from the acacia trees which forms into 'tears' so called from the shape of exudation. It is to be found throughout the world between the two tropics.

The best quality is almost white with the lower grades becoming dark in colour with an astringent flavour. The parent form is known as Senegal gum. Its uses in food are in fruit gums, as a glaze and as an emulsifier.

This gum is sometimes known by other names. These are Turkey, Senegal, Sudan, East Indian, wattle and scent gum.

c) Gum Karaya
This comes from the sterculia uresis tree and is tapped much in the same way as a rubber tree would be. The best quality is white and the lower

grades dark to brown. It is often used as a substitute for the more expensive tragacanth and arabic gums.

d) Gum Ghatti
This comes from the anogeissus natifalia tree which grows in India and Ceylon which forms globular tears. While it is not completely soluble in water, it does, however, swell in the same manner as tragacanth and when heated under pressure forms a viscous mucillage. Its main use is in emulsions for use with baked products.

(2) *Seed Gums*

a) Caral Seed
The seeds of the caral fruit are separated from the pulp. They are then roasted at 304°F (150°C) until they become golden brown, after which they are placed in boiling water. This forms a viscous extract which is filtered and evaporated to a paste, and finally dried and crushed to a powder.

Its uses are mainly as a fat extender and as a substitute for more expensive gums. It also has quite high emulsifying powers.

b) Quince Seed
These are the seed of an apple-like fruit. The seeds, thirty to seventy five per fruit are dried and sold in this form. Extraction of the gum is costly in terms of time and wastage, the seeds being agitated in water for a period of time, after which the hulls are strained off. The extract results in a viscous mucillage.

This gum is often used as a stabiliser in ice cream — being more effective than gelatine at low temperatures.

(C) Marine Gums

Marine Gums are all closely related and are to be found in seaweed and algae round the shores of Great Britain, USA and Japan.

a) Agar Agar
This is produced from red algae and the modern method is to clean and cook the seaweed under pressure after which it is clarified, by the Accelerator Freeze Drying method (AFD) which gives a very good grade of gum. A good jelly can be obtained with $\frac{1}{2}$ per cent solution. This jelly is used in the production of jellies, sweets, water ices, marshmallow and in the production of Neuchatel cream cheese. Agar possesses eight times the setting power of gelatine and is capable of setting without refrigeration. It is also known as Chinese and Japanese vegetable kanten and seaweed iserylars.

b) Irish Moss

From seaweed collected from the Atlantic seaboard of both Great Britain and USA. It is treated in a similar manner to agar. Its use, however, is in the production of non-settling drinks such as chocolate.

c) Alginates

This is a more recently produced class of gum than the agar agar and Irish moss types. This form of seaweed grows upon the sea bed and has to be brought up by mechanical means.

A gelatinous mass is formed by the actions of firstly hydrochloric acid and secondly caustic soda, after which, clarification with calcium chloride produces alginic acid through calcium alginate which is then converted to sodium alginate by sodium carbonate additives. This gives a commercial gum with wide ranging uses but predominantly as a stabiliser within the food industry.

(D) Synthetic Gums

These are gums which were first produced about 1900 from cellulose derived from wood pulp. The pulp is treated with various chemicals to leave a 'pure' form of cellulose which possesses very high emulsifying and stabilising properties. As such they can be used in very many foodstuffs. In sauces they may act as thickeners, or in commercial mayonnaise as stabilisers. As pure cellulose has no nutritional value they are non-poisonous and non-putrefactive, which makes them an ideal gelling agent emulsifier or stabiliser.

Jams and Jellies (Preserves)

Not so very long ago the inclusion of preserves into a work upon commodities would have been a simple classification of various jams, jellies and marmalades available to the caterer.

Today, however, due to technology, we understand a great deal about the actual composition of food, the interactions which take place and the changes which occur. This section therefore does not deal with jams as such, but with pectin, a soluble carbohydrate found in nearly all fruits.

Today this pectin can be isolated from fruits and used in the manufacture of jams and jellies for specialised purposes.

On the face of it jam-making is a simple operation of boiling together fruit and sugar to a point where on cooling it sets. This ability to set is brought about by pectin. Fruit which has a high percentage of pectin sets well into good firm jam. Low pectin fruits do not. Therefore, in the past blackberry jam was difficult to make due to the low amount of pectin in the fruit. Apples however are high in pectin and these would often be used to bring about the setting hence blackberry and apple jam.

Today the extraction of pectins from apples and citrus fruits is a commercial proposition and they are available to industry in powder or liquid form. This has meant that jams, jellies and marmalades can be made for specific purposes and uses. It also means that the caterer has a range of 'new' commodities which are tailor-made for certain tasks. We therefore feel that some understanding of this product is essential for today's caterers especially those using extremes of heat, i.e. high frequency cooking and blast freezing which would destroy conventional jams.

1. Pectin is a natural carbohydrate found in fruit. It is a colloid which under correct conditions will form a gel. Commercial pectin is produced from apples and citrus fruits.

2. The grade of pectin is determined by the number of grams of sugar which one gram of pectin is capable of turning into a gel.

3. The setting properties of pectin are affected by two factors:

   (a) *Acidity* — jams and jellies require a pH of about 3.

   (b) *Soluble solids* — in this case these are the types of sugar present.

4. Although apple and citrus pectins are often interchangeable, under some conditions there could be a difference in clarity and colour depending upon what is being produced.

5. Whilst pectins are available in many forms, two in particular stand out.

These are:

   (a) *Rapid set pectins*, are as the name implies quick setting. These are capable of setting at high temperatures and when used with pre-baked flans etc. prevent the absorption of the gel into the walls of the flan or sponge.

   (b) *Slow set pectins*. The use of these is usually confined to the range of products commercially produced, i.e. jellied fruits where machines deposit the liquid into moulds. Slow setting properties are therefore essential to complete the batch process.

6. Flan jellies. This is a pre-packed syrup containing sugar and pectin, but with a relatively low acid factor (pH 4.0). At this point the jelly will not set. The caterer has only to add a small amount of fruit acid — usually citric — to bring about gel formation within a few minutes. These can be obtained either as hot or cold set.

7. Other uses for pectins are stabilisers for mayonnaise and similar sauces, fruit syrups for squashes, ice creams and in the pre-prepared pie fillings.

Commercial pectins are often sold to the catering industry with a buffer present in the form of sodium citrate, potassium citrate or various phosphates. These are necessary additions to ensure that the batch does not set until the correct acidity has been achieved. These buffers can sometimes cause a precipitation which forms as a scum on the surface of the hot gel. This must be skimmed off before the gel is used or it will affect the appearance of the finished article.

We have discussed above the technical aspects of jellies, gelling agents and jams but, in these days, a great many catering establishments buy their jams and jellies ready for use. What, then, are the differences between the various products on the market and how should they be used?

Jellies

These may be purchased as crystals, or as the familiar cubes which are available on the domestic market, or in a liquid form. The crystals and cubes are usually flavoured and coloured and are ready for immediate use. The required weight to be used with 1pint ($\frac{1}{2}$litre), 2pints (1litre), or 1gallon (4litres) of water is stated on the packet and all that is usually required is to weigh that amount out and pour on the required quantity of boiling water. Sometimes half the water only is used as boiling water with the remainder added as cold water in order to speed up the setting time.

One danger to watch out for with many of these is when fresh or preserved fruits are being used in the jelly or the jelly is being used as a glaze with such fruits. Most fruits have an acidic content which will alter the pH value of the jelly. As we have mentioned this can be critical for setting, so where an acid fruit is used, a rather stronger solution of the jelly may be required to ensure correct setting.

The liquid type of jelly is one in which an often colourless liquid is supplied in a container with a setting agent in another container. The resultant jelly may be unsweetened and so available for use with savoury products as well as being of use in making up covering jelly for flans etc. Quantities used should be as directed by the suppliers. Where an accurate measurement of both liquids can be made this is very useful for making up small quantities of jelly for glazing flans etc. As it is not required to be heated the jelly cannot have any effect upon fruits or casing.

Jams and Other Preserves

There are a number of well-established manufacturers of these products and all of them can supply very good quality items. We have found, however, that while one manufacturer excels in one type of preserve another will excel in another product. Where it is possible to purchase Messrs 'A's lemon curd and Messrs 'B's strawberry jam one is able to get the highest quality products. It is unwise to expect a low priced jam to give the same flavour to an item, whether it be used as a main filling as in a jam tart, or as a supplementary filling as in a cream sponge or a jam sponge pudding. Our recommendation would always be to purchase the highest quality product possible at all times. Another important point in purchasing is the use to which the preserve is to be put. Some very good quality jams or fruit curds are not intended for cooking so if used in such items as a jam tart or in the base of a jam sponge pudding they will boil too vigorously and thus be unsuitable for cooking. This is something which can only be found by trial and error. There is no easy way in which the matter can be determined without a test bake.

Storage of Preserves

Unopened tins or jars of preserves will store well for many months in a cool dry store but, once opened, they should be used reasonably quickly. Storage, particularly in a warm kitchen, will lead to a drying out of the surface and sugar crystals will develop. Another danger with opened tins or jars is the entry into them of flour, cake crumbs etc. These provide, with the preserve, an ideal home for bacteria and can easily start the preserve fermenting. Any fermenting preserve should be thrown out and not used. A final point, if the preserve is watered down to use as a brush-on masking base, the watered down preserve must not be added back to the main stock, a dilution of the preserve will again help fermentation to develop.

CHAPTER 12

Preservation and Preservatives

We have endeavoured to mention in each section what preservation methods are used for each commodity and where a particular point must, in our opinion, be made, we have given these in some detail. There are, however, other points to consider. We have referred to commodities available on the market today and how they are offered as preserved foods. While we were writing this book a further method of preservation of an item was introduced and so we added this to our notes after the original section was written up. We mention this to show that the suppliers of our commodities are continuously researching into ways and means of improving the supply of foods to the catering and other food industries. This improvement may take the form of a different type of food to use and TVP is a recent example of this. It may take the form of a different method of preservation or a change in an old method which will enable them to offer a better or different type of that food. AFD is an example of this. It may be a method which will improve the quality of the food or enable it to be preserved by a means not suitable before: the freezing of complete foods ready for presentation is something into which we have also researched.

All of these seem to us to suggest that if our readers are to study the supply of commodities to the catering industry correctly then they should be aware of some of the technicalities involved in preservation so that they can appreciate how to use any present food as well as to be able to adapt their methods of use to any new methods of preservation or any food introduced in another form on to the market.

What then is preservation? It is a process whereby the food may be preserved for a longer period than would be possible if no such work was done to it. This preservation must be done in such a manner that the food will remain as attractive as it was in its original state, or, by its preservation, offer a new line of food use. It must remain perfectly harmless when it is consumed and it must fill a need in the normal food use area.

Food decay is caused by micro-organisms present in the food, i.e. moulds, yeasts and bacteria. There is also a natural decay and ageing process proceeding which is caused by oxidation of the food. This process is catalysed by enzymes present in the food. Preservation then follows one of two lines, it either destroys the micro-organisms or enzymes which cause the decay or offers a condition in which they cannot develop. Some micro-organisms cause food poisoning diseases. Others cause the development in food of unsuitable conditions which are not poisonous but which make the food unsuitable for human consumption.

Micro-organisms need certain conditions in which to grow. Most require food, warmth, moisture and oxygen. A few will grow without oxygen and are known as anaerobic. The micro-organism, associated with foods are divided into two major sections:

1. The commensals, those which are harmless to man and are often used in food preparation. Yeast is an example of these.

2. The pathogens, those which are harmful to man. The pathogens can be subdivided into those which cause food poisoning and those which cause disease. The salmonella in eggs are an example of the first and the tuberculosis bacteria present in some milks are an example of the latter.

If we can deprive the micro-organisms of one of their conditions required for growth then we will stop them growing and thus prevent both food poisoning symptoms developing and prevent the food deteriorating in quality. The important point which must be appreciated is that this does not kill the micro-organisms and they will commence to grow again when that condition is restored. Thus dried food will not allow food micro-organisms to develop but when the food is reconstituted any mico-organism present will start to develop and the food must be treated in the same way as fresh food.

The normal way of killing micro-organisms is by the application of heat. Most micro-organisms cannot live at a temperature above 180°F (85°C) so if the food is heated to this temperature and kept at it for a short time these micro-organisms will be killed. Some, however, have the capacity to sporulate — that is that they form spores which are able to resist the heat and will recreate micro-organisms when the temperature drops. The most common of this type of micro-organism in food is clostridium perfingens, previously known as clostridium welchii which requires cooking at the boiling point of water for 5 hours before its spores are killed off. However, if the temperature of cooking is raised then these micro-organisms are killed off more quickly and this is the principle used in the sterilisation of milk and similar foods.

Another method used is to destroy the micro-organism by the use of sugar or salt as the preserving medium. If a strong solution of sugar or salt is used with the food then a process known as osmosis takes place. Osmosis is the passage of liquid from the centre of a cell to dilute a strong mixture outside the cell, with the resultant collapse of the cell itself. Foods preserved by sugar such as fruit in jams, or by salt such as bacon and salted meats have this action taking place within them and any new micro-organism attempting to settle on them is dealt with in a similar manner, so they can be preserved for quite a period.

Alternatively the goods may be placed in a solution in which the micro-organisms cannot develop. Pickling is a typical example of this. Most micro-organisms require a neutral type of condition in which to develop. If the food is pickled in vinegar the pH of the food is altered to one in which the micro-organisms cannot develop so the food is preserved.

We now consider the major methods of preservation we have referred to in the text. Most of them have attempted to remove one of the essential items for micro-organism growth.

All of the drying processes have removed the water naturally present in the food and have so stopped the development of micro-organisms. The one major exception to this is the dried fruits where not all of the moisture has been removed but where, by a partial drying process, the fruit juices have become strong enough to add to the partial drying factor that of sugar preservation.

The freezing of food removes the warmth factor and preserves the food at a temperature below which micro-organisms can develop so no such development takes place.

Canning and bottling processes normally use two factors. The foods are often part-cooked and so the micro-organisms present in them may be destroyed by this factor. They are then sealed so no oxygen can come into contact with the food with the result that many micro-organisms cannot develop. There is, however, one point which should be noted in this. Botulinum, a disease producing micro-organisms can be present in incorrectly treated bottled and canned foods and warnings have been given as to the risk home preservers take in this type of work. The food must be thoroughly sterilised in the process.

The addition of sugar and salt to foods is a part of the preserving process in many of our foods. Jams and similar preserves rely mainly upon the preserving capabilities of sugar. Bacon and other salted meats rely upon the salt introduced into them in the process. Associated with salting is smoking. This is a partial drying which reduces some of the moisture content. A partial heating can kill off some micro-organism and the smoke itself kills off other micro-organisms by excluding oxygen. The smoke also contains chemicals which condense onto the food and act as bacteriocides and anti-oxidants thus giving further preservation factors.

Increasing use is now being made of irradiation to kill off the spoilage organisms. The food is subjected to various forms of radiation which destroy the damaging micro-organisms. It can then be sealed and stored.

Finally, gas can be used. Some foods can be stored in a gas-filled chamber. This again removes the oxygen micro-organisms need and so helps in the preservation of the food. It is often used as a delaying of the maturing process and a typical example is in apples where the date of ripening can be delayed by a number of months if sound apples are stored in a cold chamber filled with carbon dioxide gas. This allows the apples to come on the market at a period of the year when that variety would not normally be available.

CHAPTER 13

Aeration

As a subject, aeration is more closely linked to the work of the patissier, than general cooking. It is the means whereby volume and texture are given to a product such as doughs, batters, cakes and pastries. This aeration or 'lift' as it is sometimes called can be achieved in one of four distinct ways.

1. Chemical Aeration

In its simplest form this is the heating of a chemical to give off carbon dioxide. The most important chemical to do so is sodium bicarbonate which, when heated, gives off carbon dioxide and leaves a non-poisonous residue of sodium carbonate.

$$2NaHCO_3 + heat = Na_2CO_3 + CO_2 + H_2O$$

(sodium bicarbonate)   (sodium carbonate)   (carbon dioxide)   (water)

By itself sodium bicarbonate is not an ideal aerating agent for:

(a) It leaves behind an unpleasant taste due to the residue of sodium carbonate.

(b) Not all the available carbon dioxide is released.

As sodium bicarbonate is an alkali the introduction of an acid would neutralise this strong alkali taste. Also when it is combined with a suitable acid double the amount of carbon dioxide is released. Therefore, with the introduction of one other chemical (acid) both drawbacks to sodium bicarbonate are removed. As a result the reaction of these two chemicals under heat is the basic principle upon which all modern baking powders are based.

As sodium bicarbonate commences to 'gas' when first moistened it is essential that the acid should also be in dry form otherwise the reaction would commence whilst in store. One of the first acids to be used in this way was tartaric acid, which is in dry powder form. Unfortunately, however, it does react under cold moist conditions and some carbon dioxide would be lost before the goods reached the oven.

Baking Powder (Poudre à lever)

A good baking powder should not react very readily when moistened with cold liquids but should produce its greatest volume of gas when the goods reach the oven. Therefore a good acid to use in conjunction with sodium bicarbonate is one which only reacts when moistened and heated.

Such an acid is potassium hydrogen tartrate commonly called 'cream of tartar' and is used in the proportion of 1 part by weight of sodium bicarbonate to $2\frac{1}{4}$ parts by weight of cream of tartar

$KHC_4H_4O_6$	+ $NaHCO_3$	= $KNaC_4H_4O_6$	+ CO_2	+ H_2
potassium	+ sodium	= potassium	+ carbon	+ water
hydrogen	bicarbonate	sodium	dioxide	
tartrate		tartrate		

This baking powder produces only a small amount of carbon dioxide during the cake-making process, but produces it slowly and evenly during baking.

Another acid in salt form often used is acid calcium phosphate which has the formula $CaH_4P_2O_8$. This substance is usually referred to as ACP and whilst it has the disadvantage of reacting when cold, it can be effectively 'aerated' with a second chemical such as potassium salts to prevent this cold reaction.

Whilst it is possible to use many other acids to give differing reactions, the caterer would be well advised to purchase one of the many proprietary brands of baking powder. Only one other requires mention and this is ammonia.

This substance is often known as 'vol' and can be either ammonium carbonate, or ammonium bicarbonate. On heating, these substances completely volatilise leaving no residue.

$(NH_4)2CO_2$	= $2NH_3$	+ H_2O	+ CO_2
ammonium	= ammonia	+ water	+ carbon
carbonate			dioxide

The objection to their use is that in large sized goods there might be insufficient heat to drive off all the ammonia — leaving an unpleasant taste. In small items however, usually biscuits, this does not apply. Also as no reaction takes place in the cold and as biscuit dough can take some time to prepare and work, vol makes an ideal aerating agent.

2. Biological Aeration

Yeasts (Levure) belong to that group of living organisms which are unicellular, that is being of only one cell. One such yeast, called *Saccharomyces Cerevisiae,* is used to bring about changes in doughs and batters by the process of fermentation.

Fermentation is the result of the normal life cycle of the yeast cell. As with all living things yeast has certain nutritional requirements which are:

(1) Carbohydrates — usually in the form of glucose, sucrose and maltose.

(2) Nitrogen, in the form of simple amino-acids.

(3) Sulphur and phosphorus, as sulphates and phosphates.

(4) Potassium, magnesium, calcium and iron.

For fermentation it is necessary for these four items to be present with the yeast in a warm-moist environment, such as in a bread dough where the first two items are supplied by the flour and the remaining two by the water used to make the dough. The process of fermentation is a very complex but natural situation. In other words the yeast, given a perfect medium of warmth, moisture, food and oxygen, will reproduce itself rapidly and in doing so will 'give off' carbon dioxide and alcohol.

Yeast should be purchased fresh, stored in a refrigerator at $35-40°F$ (2 to 4.5°C) and used within seven days. It can, however, be purchased as dried or flaked yeast. The supplier normally indicates usage methods on the packet. Dried yeast does not normally give as good results as fresh yeast. Carbon dioxide and alcohol are by-products of the living yeast, in aeration. The baker requires the former but not the latter. The wine maker requires the latter but not the former, and whilst it is not possible to suppress fully one or the other it is possible to increase the production of carbon dioxide and decrease the production of alcohol and vice versa with the simple use of oxygen.

Yeast with a supply of oxygen, as in a dough, will give off more carbon dioxide than alcohol due to rapid reproduction.

This is the fundamental requirement of the caterer — to aerate goods by the use of yeast.

The wine producer works upon the opposite side — the fermentation vessel is sealed to exclude the intake of air (oxygen). When the available oxygen in the medium has been used up, the yeast will cease to reproduce and give off carbon dioxide, but will instead convert all available sugars directly to alcohol.

Biological aeration then is the use of yeast given a perfect medium of warmth, moisture food and oxygen to produce carbon dioxide gas as a means of lifting and giving volume to goods.

3. Mechanical Aeration

This covers the whole area of whisking, beating, etc. which traps air bubbles in a mixture.

The simplest way to illustrate this is to observe the manufacture of meringue from egg whites and sugar.

Egg whites when whisked in a fat-free situation are capable of taking air into themselves as 'air bubbles'. If sugar is added it produces a very light foamy meringue. If this foam is baked at a low temperature the egg whites coagulate, setting the structure into rigid form.

Mechanical aeration then is the introduction of air cells into a mixture before the goods enter the oven, not as with the other methods of aeration which aerate during baking.

This method of aeration can be applied to several different commodities.

(a) Cream can be 'whipped' to increase volume and stability.

(b) Whipping of egg and sugar for the production of sponges.

(c) Beating of certain fats and sugar as in the sugar batter method of cake making.

(d) Beating of fats and flour as in the flour batter process of cake making.

With the exception of (a) the principle involved in the rest is the same, namely that air cells beaten or whisked into a mixture will give lightness and volume to that mixture. On baking these air cells will expand slightly due to heat. This same heat will also at the same time coagulate the protein present in the mixture (eggs and flour) to set the structure.

4. Lamination

By definition this only applies to puff and danish pastries but the principle behind it affects all baked goods.

Puff pastry is the layering of a fat between layers of dough. On heating, the water in the dough changes to steam. As one part of water by volume will convert into something like one and a half thousand parts of steam, this causes considerable internal pressure. The layers of fat prevent this steam from permeating through the puff pastry, and the resultant pressure build-up causes the pastry to rise. It is a fallacy to believe that puff pastry rises from 'air trapped inside'. Tests show that there is very little, if any, air within the pastry.

It is this same pressure from water being changed to steam, which operates within most baked goods, for if water is present in the recipe and if the internal temperature of the goods being baked rises high enough, then some aeration will be brought about by this method.

Aeration of anything is seldom brought about by the use of only one method; most goods are a combination of several. As an example a cake made by the sugar batter method and using self-raising flour will use chemical, mechanical and lamination methods, three out of the four methods of aeration.

Experiments
Chemical Aeration

(a) 1. Weigh up 6g sodium bicarbonate.
    2. Place into 50cc cold water — observe.

3. Stand in a water bath (at 200°F) and observe.
4. When all action ceases — leave at one side.
5. Weigh up 10g tartaric acid.
6. Place into 50cc cold water — observe.
7. Place into water bath (at 200°F) and observe.
8. Add the tartaric acid solution to the spent sodium bicarbonate solution — observe.
(b) Repeat this experiment using
   1. Cream powders
   2. A.C.P.
   3. Fumeric acid.
(c) Make up in dry form several baking powders using sodium bicarbonate and differing acids. Place each into cold water — note any reaction. Slowly heat the water up to boiling point. Note when each 'baking powder' gives its gas off.

Biological Aeration

Yeast will be killed if brought into direct contact with sugar — due to osmatic pressure-or into a liquid which has a high concentration of sugar or salt, due to the same reason.
1. Prepare three flasks each containing 200g of water and stand in a water bath at 90°F (32°C).
   Flask (a) — add 15g yeast only.
   Flask (b) — add 15g yeast plus 5g sugar.
   Flask (c) — add 15g yeast plus 5g salt.
   Observe a — b — c for 15 mins.
2. Add 5g sugar to (a) and (c).
   Add 5g salt to (b) — observe.

Mechanical Aeration

Using a standard recipe of

Margarine	100g	@75°F (24°C)
Caster Sugar	100g	@75°F (24°C)
Eggs	125g	@75°F (24°C)
Soft Flour	100g	@75°F (24°C)

1. Cream the fat and sugar on middle speed of a Hobart or similar machine for one minute.
2. Cream in the eggs over one minute.
3. Fold in flour on 1st speed.
4. Place into 8" (20cm) dia. sandwich pan and bake at 360°F (182°C).

Repeat, increasing creaming times by 30 secs.
i.e. $1\frac{1}{2}$ minutes
       2 minutes
       $2\frac{1}{2}$ minutes etc.
Observe volume of resulting cakes.

CHAPTER 14

Water

Water is essential to all food preparation processes, in the make up of many dishes, as a cooking agent and in the cleansing work associated with the cooking and service of the food.

It is rather surprising then that so many caterers consider water as of no consequence to their work.

We would decry this attitude and suggest that the water supplied to any catering establishment requires the closest consideration.

Water is classified as 'hard' or 'soft' because of any mineral salts which may be dissolved in it during the period it is falling as rain or while it is being collected in the streams feeding the reservoirs.

In cities the lower air layer is contaminated by all the fumes of civilisation and while every attempt is often being made to reduce these, they still cause us to have air polluted by industrial smoke and chemicals, by traffic fumes and by all the fumes of the normal household. This means that rain falling onto a town or city has to fall through this contaminated air, collecting chemicals on the way, onto the roofs on which fumes have deposited chemicals and down the gutter into the drain. This water would be completely unsuitable for use in any food process so our water catchment areas must be in the cleaner surroundings of the countryside, usually high in the mountains. There the rain falls onto clean ground and runs through it into streams which are fed into the reservoirs. Even here though, the type of soil upon which the rain falls and the streams run through to the reservoirs is of great importance. If the ground is largely peat then the water going into the reservoir will be 'soft'. If it has an amount of chalk or lime then the water will dissolve this and be known as 'hard' water.

An additional feature in causing hard water is that in falling as rain, the water absorbs carbon dioxide from the air it passes through. This causes a reaction with the limestone and causes the absorption of calcium carbonate.

Hard water is of two types — temporary hard water and permanent hard water. The temporary type is one which deposits the calcium in the form of fur on pans, kettles, central heating boilers, hot water pipes etc. These can in time become clogged up and cause a blockage. In the interim period they cause difficulties including a lowering of pressure in the pipes, a lower heat in the central heating systems and a need for a higher heat to be used on pans etc. which are furred up.

Permanent hardness is usually caused by calcium and magnesium salts dissolved in a similar manner. Permanent hard water does not deposit its salt content on heating but it will not lather when used for washing up etc. The salts react with the soap used causing a scum to collect upon the salt surface which often remains on plates etc. after washing. This also means that the supply of soap used must be increased to allow for the chemical action and then leave sufficient soap to perform the usual washing process.

Water can be softened by chemical means. If there is no option but to base the establishment in a hard water area then the system may be fitted with any of a number of water-softening plants.

The type used will vary according to the amount of hardness in the water and according to the amount of water used. It is usual to soften the water required for industrial use but to leave the water to be used as drinking water hard as the minerals present can often be beneficial to the consumer.

A process used in both homes and industries is the Permutit process. In this a cylinder of Permutit, consisting mainly of sodium aluminium silicate, is introduced into the water supply system and as the water passes through it there is an exchange of ions. The calcium and magnesium ions in the water are exchanged for sodium ions in the Permutit. The resin can be regenerated by flushing with a strong solution of common salt (sodium chloride). This may be done on site with the cartridge used in the system being replaced by a new one and the old one thrown away in the case of small users, or the cartridge replaced by a new one and the old one regenerated by the supplier. In the case of the larger unit, a similar process is performed by a chemical known as Zeolite.

Hard water is an advantage in a few situations — in beer-making the hard water districts are traditional for brewing good beer and in other areas. Some breweries sink their own wells in order to obtain suitable water. As has already been mentioned the calcium content of hard water is useful in the diet and increases the calcium intake of the person drinking it.

Soft water can have a chemical reaction when passing through lead piping and although this type of piping for water supplies is fast disappearing it should be noted.

Hard water makes far greater difficulty in washing up. This will be shown in the accompanying experiments.

Water Tests and Experiments

Try to obtain a supply of water from four different sources, ideally a well water, a spring water, one from a known soft water area and one from a known hard water area.

If water from a hard water area is difficult to obtain, sodium bicarbonate and/or magnesium bicarbonate can be made into a solution with water and added at varying rates to give different degree of hardness to pure water.

1. Obtain, or produce a soap solution — a simple solution can be made by adding 100ml of liquid soap to 1litre of distilled water.

2. Add a measured quantity of the soap solution to an equal quantity of each of the waters under test.

3. Shake the vessels for a similar time and measure the lather produced, allow to stand 3 minutes, measure any lather left and repeat the experiment.

4. Observe and note the lather measurements and any scum formed.

5. The water with the greatest lathering capacity and the least scum is the softer water.

Now repeat the tests with the local water and compare its hardness. This is rather similar to a test for water hardness which produces a measured scale of degrees of hardness in the water and which can be used to determine how the water in any area will react when used for washing up.

Hard water is measured either in degrees of hardness or in parts of the chemical producing hardness per million (ppm).

For example much of the water in some areas of London is hard water and is quoted as having 300 ppm. hardness. Manchester's water is particularly soft and is quoted as 15 ppm.

In degrees the measurement is 1g. of calcium carbonate (or any other chemical producing hardness) to 100 litres of water. As 1 litre contains 1,000 grams of water then this is 1 part per 100,000 or 10 ppm. 1 degree of hardness is therefore equal to 10 parts per million of hardness. This test must be performed with pure soap. Chemical detergents have a different reaction on hard water.

CHAPTER 15

Beverages

Coffee (*Café*)

Coffee was possibly first discovered in Ethiopia in the third
century — legend has it that a goatherd in the land of Yemen noticed
that his goats became more lively after eating the berries of a shrub. He
gathered them, took them back to his employers who eventually used
them and discovered the first coffee drink. The new drink was found to be
invigorating and so was given the name 'kahven' which eventually
became 'coffee'.

Coffee drinking spread throughout the Middle East and was eventually introduced into London in 1652 by travellers from the Levant. It
quickly gained popularity and the London Coffee Houses which are mentioned in many writings of the 18th century were developed.

Coffee is the berry of the evergreen shrub *Caffea Arabica* and is grown
in many countries in the tropics. Some of the large exporters of coffee to
this country are Central and South America, the West and East Indies,
Africa and India.

Coffee is available in various forms:

As 'green' coffee beans, as roasted beans, as ground coffee, as coffee
with chicory or other items added, as instant coffee and coffee
mixtures, as liquid coffee or coffee mixtures.

Green Beans

These are the beans as gathered. They are mainly used in the speciality
coffee houses which offer a large variety of blends both for sale as coffee to
be consumed on the premises and also offer to the customer the opportunity to have coffee beans blended and roasted to his or her taste.

The green beans will keep in good condition in a dry store for a good
period but they can easily take in other flavours so care must be taken
with storage.

Roasted Beans

These are the green beans which have been roasted. They may be beans
from a single area or a pre-determined blend of beans. The amount of
roasting given has a considerable effect upon the final cup of coffee.

a) *Light Roasting* will give a delicate flavour and aroma and is used
particularly with the milder types of green beans. It is traditional to roast
only lightly beans to be used for morning coffee and breakfast coffee.

b) *Medium Roasting* gives a stronger coffee and is usually used for those beans which have a stronger flavour.

c) *Full Roast* gives a still stronger flavoured bean.

d) *Continental Roast* is a very well roasted coffee. Any milder flavours in the bean are destroyed so a cheaper and stronger flavoured bean than that used for light or medium roasting should be used. This is the traditional roast used for black coffee and after-dinner coffee.

The roasted bean, unless kept in an airtight tin, loses its flavour very quickly so it is normal practice to roast daily or every other day. This has an advantage that, if the smell of the roasting can be allowed to spread outside the establishment, very often more customers are attracted.

Ground Coffee

After roasting the coffee is ground to a powder. The size of the granule should be adjusted to relate to the type of coffee required and the method of brewing used. A very floury coffee will result in a murky appearance in the final cup of coffee. This is considered correct in Turkish or Greek coffee but not in other types of coffee. It has the advantage that the finer the grind the more coffee can be obtained and the quicker it can be brewed.

Very fine grind is usually used where a filtration process is used in the making of the coffee. Any murkiness is removed by the filtration process.

Fine grind, giving granules about the size of a grain of sugar, is used for coffee made by the vacuum and Italian methods.

Medium grind is used in many percolators and in pan production methods.

Coffee with Additives

Chicory is the common additive to the ground coffee but there are many others used. Small amounts of various spices can be added at the roasting stage. The spices used include cloves (1 per cup), cinnamon, ginger, nutmeg, cardamom and fennel (all in smaller quantities). Their main use is to add a distinctive flavour to the resultant coffee whereas the main use of chicory is to cheapen the mixture. Chicory is ground to the same size as the coffee grounds and mixed with the coffee, often in quite large quantities. By law all such mixtures must be sold as coffee and chicory mixtures and must not exceed 49 per cent chicory. The chicory gives a strong coffee colour to the liquid produced and adds a slightly bitter flavour but has no other flavour or aroma. Its usual proportion of use is in the region of 80 per cent coffee to 20 per cent chicory.

Another addition to coffee is dried figs, used to produce a coffee known as Viennese coffee which is quite popular in some areas.

Instant Coffee and Coffee Mixtures

Instant Coffee was introduced into Great Britian in the late 1930s and has consistently gained popularity since that time. Development was

182

restricted by the war years and the times of shortage afterwards but as soon as it became possible, a number of firms were offering various types of instant coffee. Some of these have faded away whilst others have become very popular. In the manufacturing process the coffee or coffee mixture is made up from the original ground mixture and then dried either by using a freeze drying process or by spray drying. The freeze dried coffee is usually presented in granular form whilst the spray dried coffee is presented in a powdered form. The advantage is that the user can place the amount of coffee or coffee mixture required in a cup or pot, pour on boiling water and produce a good quality cup of coffee without any further bother and without the use of specialised instruments such as percolators, etc. Instant coffee can also be used for adding to many dishes to add coffee colour and flavour. It will be instantly dissolved in any liquid used.

Liquid Coffee and Coffee Mixtures

These were the pre-runners of instant powdered coffee and coffee mixtures. They fell out of favour while the development of the instant coffees was proceeding but at the time of writing they appear to be making a come-back. They are made up in a similar manner to the instant coffees by adding a spoonful of the liquid extract or essence to the cup and pouring on boiling water. Some of the mixtures are pure coffee, most are a mixture of coffee and chicory and almost all have sugar added in the manufacturing process.

Coffee Experiments

Obtain as many samples of the various types of coffee as possible. Where green beans can be obtained, roast and grind these in the various ways described to illustrate the variations which can be obtained by these factors.

Brew a specific weight of each coffee by a single method using an exact weight of the coffee, coffee mixture and chicory. Taste each brew after a set time, allow to stand again and taste again. A suitable timing could be immediately after brewing and then every two minutes. Note down the flavours of the coffee at each point and compare them afterwards. Draw up a conclusion from the results gained.

Take various types of raw coffee bean, (Kenya, Brazil, Mocha, Java, Jamaican, Blue Mountain etc.)

Examine a sample of each type and note any differences in the beans.

Take 100g of each bean and place in the coffee roaster. Turn on and roast the beans taking out a 20g sample after 1 min, then a further 20g sample every minute until none is left in the roaster (5 samples produced).

Pass each sample through a suitable coffee grinder. Make up the following blends:

(a) 2.5g of samples A, B, C, D, and E at each roasting stage.

(b) 5g of each A and B   Light Roast (1)
(c) 5g of each C and D   Medium Roast (2)
(d) 5g of each A and B   Heavy Medium (3)
(e) 5g of C and D   Heavy Roast (4)
(f) 5g of each A Medium Roast (2) with 5g of E Medium Roast (2)
(g) 5g of each E Heavy Medium Roast (3) with 5g of D Heavy Medium
     Roast (3)

Place 10g of each of the samples (a) to (g) in a coffee pot.

Place 10g of any remaining simple blends in coffee pots. Pour on 150ml of
boiling water.

Allow to stand for 3 mins. Pour a 50ml sample off.

Stand a further 3 mins. Pour another 50ml sample off.

Stand a further 3 mins. Pour another 50ml sample off.

Taste each sample and record the findings.

Allowing the remaining coffee to cool to 77°F (25°C) and test pH values.

Findings should include the following points:

1. What difference does the type of bean make to the coffee made from
    it?
2. What difference does the amount of roasting make to the finished
    coffee?
3. What characteristics have you found in blended coffees?
4. What blend and roast provides the coffee you like best?

Tea(*Thé*)

Tea has been used as a beverage for over 4,500 years, firstly in China and
then introduced into other areas. It is recorded to have been drunk in this
country during the early days of the Stuart period and became increasingly popular in the mid-17th century.

Tea is the dried leaves of the shrub *Camellia Thea* and is grown in
many tropical areas including China, India, Japan and Sri Lanka. The
majority of our tea comes from China, India or Sri Lanka with small
quantities coming from other areas.

The method of harvesting is to pluck the leaves at intervals throughout
the growing season. The size of the leaf varies according to its age and the
position on the branch. The finest tea is produced from the small top half
of the twig and the bud.

Tea is graded by name according to the quality of the leaf, typical
gradings are as follows:

Flowery Orange Pekoe

Orange Pekoe

Pekoe

Souchong

Broken Orange Pekoe

Broken Pekoe

Broken Pekoe Souchong
Broken Orange Pekoe Fannings
Dust

The flowery variants are available in most of the grades and indicate that the bud of the plant is included in with the leaves. This makes for a more expensive tea than where the bud is left to develop for a longer period.

Orange Pekoe are long, thin, wiry leaves which give the tea made from them a pale colour and a fine taste.

Pekoe — the leaves are shorter and less wiry but the tea has more colour and the taste is rather stronger.

Souchong — made from a bold, round leaf — the tea colour still being pale.

Broken Orange Pekoe — a very popular grade for making a high quality tea. The leaves are small and give a tea of medium strength with good colour.

Broken Pekoe — a rather larger leaf than the above which gives less colour in the cup. Often used in blending.

Broken Pekoe Souchong — larger leaf section but still giving a pale coloured tea. Again often used as a filler.

Broken Orange Pekoe Fannings — a very small leaf which has quick brewing ability with a good colour and a fine flavour.

Dust — as the name implies this is the dust after processing. It is not used in any of the premier tea blends but may be found in the cheaper blendings.

These teas may be blended into any of proprietary blends seen in boxes and packets on the grocer's shelves or may be made into special blends which have a traditional history behind them.

Typical examples of blends and their history are the following:

Earl Grey's Tea An original blend of China teas brought back to Great Britain by the second Earl Grey in 1830.

Darjeeling Tea Claimed to be the best of all Indian teas. It makes a dark coloured tea of distinctive flavour.

Russian Tea A blend of the teas grown in the foothills of the Caucasian Mountains. Usually served with a slice of lemon and without milk.

Jasmine Blossom Tea Japanese tea blended with jasmine flowers. Again usually taken without milk and with a slice of lemon.

English Breakfast Tea A blend of the small leaf teas of India and Sri Lanka. Probably originally developed by the English planters who developed these countries' tea trade.

In addition to the blends of tea named above teas are also purchased by the name of their country or area of origin. Many of these will either use the type names given or use their own markings to denote particular types of the leaf. These are far too complex to list here and any reader particularly interested should consult a good library and obtain a specialist book on tea blending.

The flavour of each individual tea, or blend of teas will vary according to many factors. These include such items as the plantation or the area of ground the plant is grown in, the part of the leaf used to make the tea, the amount of time spent in drying, and the amount of heat used in that process and the period since the tea passed through this process. It is the task of the tea taster employed by the tea companies to select teas which will provide the exact flavour and aroma the firm requires in its tea. A tea taster will have to taste several hundred samples in a day in his selection of teas to be used in the blends required.

The water used to make the tea has an effect upon the results obtained. Hard water will produce a different tea from the same blend than that produced by soft water.

It is usual for the commercial producers to change their blends according to the water of the area they are to sell it in. Messrs XY Tea may be quite different in the hard water areas of London from the blend on sale under the same name in the softer water areas of Leeds, Liverpool or Manchester.

Tea Experiments

Take a weighed quantity of each tea under test. Brew with a set amount of boiling water and allow to stand tasting immediately after brewing and then every two minutes.

Note the tastes of the various blends and compare. Teas used should include commercial blends — China, India, Russian etc. as well as some of the named special blends.

If a stereo-microscope is available it is interesting to examine each tea, before and after brewing under the microscope. Note that in some of the cheaper tea more dust or twigs will be present. In some types the leaf sections are quite large, in others quite small. Compare the results obtained with the above test.

Cocoa, Drinking Chocolate, Chocolate

Cocoa, drinking chocolate and the chocolate we use both as a sweetmeat and as a decorative item are all produced from the same plant, a tree known as *Theobroma Cacao*. There are a number of species of the tree and each produces a bean with different characteristics. The major points will be mentioned in the appropriate places in the next.

The cacao bean was first found in the Amazon basin and is now produced in Mexico, Tropical, Central and South America, the West Indies, Africa, Sri Lanka, Asia and in tropical islands in the South Pacific. Africa is probably the world's largest producer.

The main varieties of the bean used in Cocoa manufacturer are:

Oriollo This has a red or yellow pod with thin walls and large plump seeds which give a bland flavour and good aroma. These beans are used in almost all cocoa and cocoa products.

Forastero This is the commonest of the commercial cocoa types and has a thick walled pod which is melon-shaped and rather flat and purple-coloured beans which have a rather bitter flavour.

Triniario Another common type used in blendings.

The beans are allowed to ferment and partially dry out in the country of origin. They are blended together as required for flavour etc. in our production factories and then after cleaning are roasted. The roasting process changes the flavour of the bean, removes certain acids present, removes more of the moisture present and changes the colour. Finally each bean has its shell removed. (The shells are used in animal feeding stuffs.)

The next process varies according to the product to be made so we deal briefly with each product in turn.

Naval Cocoa
An item not often used in civilian catering but a very traditional drink in the Royal Navy. The cacao beans are reduced to nibs which are then ground and pressed into a block. The portion of slab cocoa is made up with water in the normal way and served with sugar. The drink is very thick and contains a high proportion of fat thus making a very warming drink which helps to keep out the ravages of the night at sea.

Cocoa
The normal cocoa is treated to remove some of the fat by an expression process. The removed fat is called cocoa butter and will be referred to later under the making of chocolate. The amount of fat left in the cocoa will vary from 15 per cent to 25 per cent with the cocoas with the larger amounts of fat being considered to be the better quality. After grinding the cocoa is packed ready for use.

Drinking Chocolate
This is the name given to a type of cocoa which has had other ingredients added to it, usually sugar. It has less fat extracted from it than cocoa so is a more nourishing food beverage.

Both cocoa and drinking chocolate may be made up with water, milk or a mixture of both. They are a traditional evening drink quite often taken at bedtime and from them such specialised drinks as Ovaltine and Bournvita have developed.

The important factor is that cocoa and drinking chocolate are the only two out of the popular beverages we are dealing with which have a food value. Unlike tea and coffee they can provide an important source of nutrients to the body and are thus often offered in hospital meals etc.

Food Values of Cocoa per 100g

Protein	20.4g	Calcium	51.2mg
Fat	25.6g	Magnesium	192mg
Carbohydrate	35.0g	Iron	14.3mg
Calories	452	Copper	3.4mg
Sodium	650mg	Phosphorus	685mg
Potassium	534mg	Sulphur	160mg
		Chlorine	199mg

Chocolate

There are various types of chocolate available for kitchen use. The selection of the correct type for the work on hand is of great importance and will help to provide finished work of the desired quality.

Unsweetened Chocolate

The cacao nibs are ground at a suitable temperature and provide a thick molten mass which sets when cool into a block of unsweetened chocolate. This is principally used as a flavouring medium when added to other items such as white fondant to produce chocolate fondant for decoration of gateaux and similar items.

Plain Chocolate

The unsweetened chocolate is then treated further. Sugar and some of the cocoa butter produced in the manufacture of Cocoa is added and the whole ground together and blended thoroughly to produce the normal domestic plain chocolate and the commercial variety, chocolate couverture.

Milk Chocolate

This is produced in a similar manner to the plain chocolate but has milk added. As water in any form will cause the chocolate mixture to take on special characteristics, the milk has to be specially treated in an evaporation plant under vacuum before it can be added to the chocolate mass. All is then mixed together in the same manner.

Bakers Chocolate or Chocolate Cake Coating

In the manufacture of this product no cocoa butter is added to the block chocolate. Instead other fats are added to make the resultant chocolate easier to use. This type of chocolate can be melted in a pan over a water bath at about 110°F (37°C) and used immediately. It gives a good decorative result but can only be used for moulding work when handled by a specialist.

Chocolate Couverture

As mentioned above this is a chocolate which requires special treatment. Both plain and milk varieties of the chocolate are melted over a water bath to a temperature of 115° to 120°F (50° to 52°C) for plain chocolate and 110°F (45°C) for milk chocolate, stirring occasionally during the melting process. Now place the chocolate container in a cooler area and allow the chocolate to cool to 82°F (27.5°C) for the plain and milk couvertures. At this stage the chocolate should be starting to set around the container. Now reheat and stir gently until the temperature rises to 86° to 90°F (30°C to 32°C). This process is known as tempering the chocolate.

The chocolate is now ready for use and should be maintained at this temperature during use.

Chocolate used for ice-cream coating requires somewhat different qualities from normal chocolate couverture and if this is the purpose a special blend should be purchased.

Storage and Buying

Cocoa is often supplied in sealed tins and where this is the case can be kept in a cool dry store for 6 to 12 months without any difficulty. If the pack is opened or if in a paper package, storage is reduced unless the whole can be tightly sealed. Chocolate, if kept under the same conditions, can easily be kept for a year or more and can be broken into as required provided the package is sealed again after taking out what is needed. Both are, however, expensive items and the purchase of twelve months' supply is not an economical method of purchasing unless the amounts used are very small or the price saved by bulk buying is high. Normally purchases should be made at no less than three monthly intervals and stocks based accordingly.

Proprietary Beverages

A number of proprietary beverages are available on the market, both in domestic and catering packs. They vary considerably in both their make-up and in their intended uses and each should be considered individually. All have their place in one catering situation or another. The malted milks and cocoa-based products such as Ovaltine and Bournvita are used in institutional and hospital catering and in child care work. Some, e.g. Complan, are intended as food supplements for the patient who cannot take full meals in the normal manner. These include various high protein beverages and others which contain vitamin and mineral supplements. A development of the space research programme has been the production of complete foods in powder form which can be quickly made into beverages. These are now being used in hospital treatment for conditions in which the digestive organs cannot deal with food in the normal manner. They are intended as a complete meal and contain all the required vitamins, minerals, fats, protein and carbohydrate required to keep the body healthy. They are often available in various flavours to help promote the appetite.

Fruit Drinks

We have mentioned under 'Fruits' that various fruits are used in the make-up of fruit drinks so do not propose to list these fruits in detail here but possibly some mention of the range and types of fruit drinks will be useful.

Fruit Juices

These are available in concentrated and pure form both with and without sweetening. Some are produced specially for slimming or low-carbo-hydrate diets and so the sweetening agent is of no food value. Others include both an artificial sweetener and sugars, whilst still others contain only sugar as their sweetener. Obviously the choice of which type to use must be made after full consideration of the needs of the consumer. The packs in which these drinks can be obtained also vary considerably in both size and type. Sizes vary from domestic packs containing only single or double portions (which may also, of course, have their uses in certain establishments) to containers holding one gallon, 5 litres or upwards.

Care must be taken to check the storage requirements for each type of drink. Some may be kept in a normal, cool store for many months before use, others must be used within a very limited period and yet others will require storage in a refrigerator. Most must be used within a short period of opening, but the bottled varieties will usually last longest after opening and those with sugar added will also have a longer life.

Frozen, concentrated fruit juices have been available for many years now. These can be very useful in catering where a specific quantity is required each day. If the frozen concentrate is removed from the storage cabinet the night before and then made up with the required amount of water the next day, a ready supply of fresh fruit juice can be available for breakfast or any other meal in a very short time.

A more recent development has been powdered fruit juices. These can, of course, be stored with greater ease than any of the other types. As with most types of powdered convenience foods, exact quantities can be made up with very little skill. Whether or not these newer products taste just the same as the fresh fruit juices is for the user to decide, but this development is likely to be of some considerable use in future years.

CHAPTER 16

Convenience Foods

Convenience foods are largely, but not wholly, a recent development in catering. Before we discuss them in detail we could say that it is often very difficult to know how to classify convenience foods.

A dictionary definition of 'Convenience' is 'Fit for use, handy, suitable, not troublesome, what suits one'.

Under this definition there are a great many foods used in both the home and industry. The unqualified person may think of convenience foods as 'those in a packet' whilst others may include tinned foods or foods which do not require cooking.

We would leave the final definition to the individual but suggest that we would prefer to list convenience foods as those wich save the caterer work.

In this respect we could start with prepared fresh foods such as peeled potatoes which can be purchased ready for cooking as chips, slices etc. The use of these items supplied daily under contract is a practice carried out in a number of establishments in the more heavily populated areas. By using them the caterer can dispense with the storage room and preparation area required for potatoes, he need not buy the the potato peelers which would otherwise be required and he needs less staff for vegetable preparation to supply a required amount of food. Some of these firms will also supply various other raw fruit and vegetables in a prepared form so that the use of the whole facilities of such a firm would mean that space, now used for this work, could be devoted to other needs, an invaluable asset in a crowded kitchen area.

The additional cost of such prepared foods and the possibility of breakdown in supply must, of course, be considered as a disadvantage of the idea but that is up to the individual caterer to determine for himself.

The first form of convenience food was probably meat. When man hunted animals for his food and found that he could not eat all of the animal, he preserved it by drying and/or salting. He could then cut a joint off as required without having to hunt for it, surely a convenience.

If we accept this, then all preserved foods are convenience foods and this will include dried, canned, bottled and frozen foods in addition to the newer types of dehydrated foods. We propose to deal with each, briefly. As mention has been made of the various preservation processes in each appropriate chapter we do not propose to go into manufacturing details but to suggest the reader refers to the appropriate section on each food.

Canned and Bottled Foods

Most canned and bottled foods have been subjected to a heating process in which sterilisation has taken place. They are therefore partly cooked and require less or no cooking before serving. They are usually ready for service and so no preparation work is required. They can be stored in a normal, cool, dry store and have the advantage of always being available for use in an emergency. Cans can often be kept in a good store for many months without any danger of deterioration.

Dried Foods

We would suggest that dried foods can fall under three categories.

1.   Those which are dried to produce a special item of food. In this we would list currants and other dried fruits. They are never reconstituted to form the original fruit but are used in their dried form. It could be argued that these are not properly classified under convenience foods.

2.   Those which, in the drying process, produce a food which is rather different from the original. These would include such items as marrowfat peas, butter and lima beans, prunes etc. They are ready prepared for use and, after the appropriate soaking, can often be used in the same way as they could when fresh but the resultant product is not the same as the original, indeed in some cases such as 'mushy' peas it is more suitable in its new form than in its original one.

3.   Dehydrated and accelerated freeze dried foods

These are processed in such a manner that all of the original flavour, texture and eating quality are retained. They usually require a shorter cooking period than the fresh item and require no preparation before cooking other than to add the water in which they are to be cooked. In the case of many brands of dried potato the only work required is to add boiling water and whisk a short time to produce mashed potatoes. Many of the accelerated freeze dried vegetables are of high quality and are capable of being used in a great many catering situations. As a large variety of vegetables can be stored for a lengthy period and only the required amount made up at the time of preparation then they are of great convenience to the chef.

Another type of food which is dehydrated or subjected to AFD processing are the soups and beverages.

Various methods of dehydration are used in these items. The soup or beverage is made up from the original ingredients and then the water content is evaporated off in various ways, often using a vacuum pan so as to avoid damage to the dish by boiling. The dish or beverage may be rehydrated by adding either cold or boiling water. In some cases a short cooking period is required, in others none at all.

All of these are comparatively recent developments in food production and new foods which may be classified under this general heading are being introduced.

Packet Foods and Dry Mixes

These may appear to be ones which ought to have appeared under the above heading, but as they are made up in an entirely different manner, we would prefer to deal with them separately.

The main foods under this heading are various soup powders and sauce, cake, pudding, scone and pastry mixes. Their use is divided into two different categories.

Soup Powders and Sauce Mixes

Powders from which soups and sauces can be made by the addition of liquids have been in use for many years. The powders are made up and the required flavourings added. Sometimes the recipe will include a proportion of the named commodity in its dried form. In others the flavour only will be added. The cooking period varies with these dishes. A modern development is the use of processed starches which require less cooking and thus enable the powder to be made into soup or sauce within a few minutes. At other times a longer period of cooking, up to 20 or 30 minutes is required. The advantage of these items, in addition to the obvious saving in labour and time over the preparation from a traditional recipe is that the flavour is always constant even with different members of staff undertaking the task on different days. When produced carefully and with full attention paid to detail a very good dish can be produced.

Cake, Pudding and Pastry Mixes

These are made up from the ingredients which would normally be used in the original recipe. Eggs and milk are often added in dried form or the instructions printed on the package may say that these should be added as the mixing is made up. The price should reflect this point. They are designed for use in general kitchen work where no pastry chef or baker is employed for this specialist work. They enable a cook who has not the high skill of the patissier to undertake this work and obtain good results. They are rather different from most of the other convenience foods as we have mentioned because they require exactly the same cooking period as would the same dish made up from basic ingredients.

They have an advantage in that small quantities even down to single cover portions can be made up easily and without any error in minute measurements of ingredients. They have a disadvantage in that there is often a tendency to purchase a large number of different mixes in powder form with the resultant large storage area requirement.

In addition there is a danger that many of the mixes which include eggs, milk, fat etc. have only a short storage life before they commence to loose quality. A final point is that the experienced pastry cook or baker can vary the pastry, cake or pudding mixes at will to produce an item more suitable for use with any situation. If prepared mixes are used then this facility is not available.

Prepared Custard Powders

A development over the past two decades has been prepared custard powders. In these the cornflour is mixed with colour, flavour, sugar and milk powder. When required all that needs to be added is boiling water to produce a custard ready for service.

Frozen Foods

These are used in many establishments and provide a very good supply of easily prepared commodities. The food is prepared ready for cooking and is often blanched in the preparation process and so a shorter cooking period is required. Some are able to be used straight from the storage unit — others require a period of thawing before use. In the vast majority of frozen foods a very high quality is maintained and as with the packet foods single portions may be easily used without the need to prepare a larger quantity of the dish.

Great use is being made of this type of food in those establishments with a large menu choice and they are possibly the most common convenience food used in the catering industry today. Full prepared meals or dishes are also available under this heading.

Advantages and Disadvantages

We have mentioned advantages and disadvantages as we have gone through the various types, but would summarise them as follows:

Advantages
1. Reduced or no preparation time required.
2. Consistent repetition of type and quality
3. Ready availability of most types.
4. Reduced cooking time in many types.
5. Single portion availability.
6. Larger variety of stocks available.

Disadvantages
1. In some cases quality is not always as good as the original dish.
2. In the case of frozen foods, expensive equipment required for storage.

3.   Because they are prepared in a central point the individuality of the establishment or chef cannot be used to advantage.

4.   In a few cases there is a loss of essential nutrients in the processing of these foods.

The question as to whether or not to use convenience foods is one that must be determined by each establishment. Factors which could influence the choice include the type of establishment, labour and space availability and price obtainable for the dishes supplied. Some of these points may be more easily determined after the following experiment has been carried out.

Convenience Foods Experiment

Most types of convenience foods can be tested by using the same basic procedures. The convenience food is made up and compared with a similar dish made up to the traditional methods.

Information Required

In considering the use of such foods the following points should be among those to be considered:-

(a) Ease of use — is there any variation in the time and/or skill required between the convenience food and the traditional method of production?

(b) Time required between starting production and presenting the dish to be eaten.

(c) Storage and purchasing requirements — many convenience foods can be stored more easily and for a longer period than can the ingredients traditionally used in the make-up of the dish — does this apply in this case?

(d) Is there any variation in the kitchen equipment required for the production of the convenience food as against the traditional method?

(e) Finished dish — compare the finished dishes from both the convenience food under test and a similar dish made up by a traditional method. Flavour, colour, aroma, general appearance and the possibility of continuous production of the same dish are amongst the points which should be considered.

(f) Any other points which may apply particularly to the dish under test should also be considered.

At the close of the tests a final assessment of the marks and observations made should be given together with comments upon the use of the product under various catering situations. It must be remembered that a product which would be excellent for one situation may well not be suitable for use in a different situation because of the requirements of the clientele, the cost of the product in labour or in raw materials, equipment required in production, skill of staff required and various other points. All of these must be considered before a final decision is made.

Glossary of French names

We list below the French names for the majority of the commodities dealt with in this book. There are some gaps in our list because there is no French name usually used for such items or because the item itself is only rarely used in French cookery. In a few cases where the commodity has been developed in Britain, the British name is used in the French kitchen.

In some cases it will be noted that there is a great similarity between French names quoted or that the same name is used for two commodities. This is often because the items are both used in the same way or in the same type of dishes.

English — French Names of Commodities

English	French
A	
Almond	Amande
Allspice	Piment, Épice
Angelica	Angélique
Anise (Aniseed)	Anis
Apple	Pomme
Apricot	Abricot
Arrowroot	Fécule de Marante
Artichoke,	
Globe	Artichaut
Jerusalem	Topinambour
Aubergine	Aubergine
B	
Bacon	Lard
Baking Powder	Poudre de Levure
Banana	Banane
Barbel	Barbeau
Barley	Orge
Barley Flour	Crème d'Orge
Barley (Pearl)	Orge Mondé
Barm or Balm (Yeast)	Levure
Basil	Basilic
Bass	Bar
Bayleaf	Laurier
Beans — French	Haricot Vert
Broad	Fève

English	French
Kidney	Flageolet
Beef	Boeuf
Beefsteak	Bifteck
Beetroot	Betterave
Bilberry or Blackberry	Airelle Myrtille
Blackberry	Mûre de ronce
	Baie de ronce
Black currant	Groseille Noire
Borage	Bourrache
Bouquet garni	Bouquet garni
Brains	Cervelles
Bread	Pain
Bream	Brème
Breast	Poitrine
Brisket	Poitrine
Broccoli	Brocoli
Brussels Sprouts	Choux de Bruxelles
Butter	Beurre
Buttermilk	Babeurre
C	
Cabbage,	Chou
Savoy	Chou frisé
Calf	Veau
Calf's brains	Cervelles de veau
Calf's feet	Pieds de veau

English	French	English	French
Calf's head	Tête de veau	**E**	
Calf's liver	Foie de veau	Eel	Anguille
Calf's sweetbreads	Ris de Veau	Egg	Oeuf
Calf's tongue	Langue de veau	Egg Plant	Aubergine
Capon	Chapon	Endive	Chicorée
Caraway	Carvi		
Caraway seed	Carvi	**F**	
Cardamom	Cardamome	Fat	Graisse
Carrot	Carotte	Fennel	Fenouil
Carp	Carpe	Fenugreek	Fenugrec
Catfish	Loup de mer	Fig	Figue
Cauliflower	Chou-fleur	Filbert	Aveline
Celeriac	Céleri rave	Fillet	Filet
Celery	Céleri	Fine herbs	Fines-herbes
Cereal	Céréale	Fish	Poisson
Char	Ombre Chevalier	Flank	Flanchet
Cheese	Fromage	Flounder	Flet
Cherry	Cerise	Flour	Farine
Chervil	Cerfeuil	Fondant	Fondant
Chestnut	Marron	Fowl	Volaille
Chicken	Poulet or Volaille		
Chicory	Chicorée	**G**	
Chives	Ciboulette	Game	Gibier
Chocolate	Chocolat	Garlic	Ail
Cinnamon	Cannelle	Gherkin	Cornichon
Clam	Lucène	Giblets	Abatis
Clove	Girofle	Ginger	Gingembre
Coconut	Noix de coco	Globe artichoke	Artichaut
Cocoa	Cacao	Goose	Oie
Cod	Morue	Gooseberry	Groseille à
Coffee	Café		Maquereau
Coley	Lieu Noir	Gosling	Oison
Coriander	Coriandre	Grape	Raisin
Cornflour	Farine de maïs	Grapefruit	Pamplemousse
Cranberry	Canneberge	Grape sugar	Sucre de raisin
Crawfish	Langouste	Grayling	Ombre
Crayfish	Écrevisse	Grouse	Tétras
Cream	Crème	Gudgeon	Goujon
Cress	Cresson	Gurnet	Grondin
Cucumber	Concombre		
Curry	Kari	**H**	
		Haddock	Aiglefin
D		Hake	Merluche
Dab	Limande	Halibut	Flétan
Dace	Vandoise	Ham	Jambon
Dates	Dattes	Hare	Lièvre
Deer	Cerf	Herring	Hareng
Double cream	Crème double	Honey	Miel
Duck	Canard	Horseradish	Raifort
		Huckleberry	Airelle Myrtille

English	French	English	French
I		Mutton	Mouton
Ice	Glace		
		N	
J		Nectarine	Brugnon
Jam	Confiture	Noodles	Nouilles
Jelly	Gelée	Nutmeg	Noix de Muscade
Jerusalem			
artichoke	Topinambour	**O**	
John Dory	St Pierre/Dorée	Oatmeal	Farine d'avoine
Joint	Relevé	Oats	Avoine
		Olive	Olive
K		Onion	Oignon
Kale	Chou Frisé	Ox Cheek	Palais de Boeuf
Kidney	Rognons	Ox Tail	Queue de boeuf
Kohlrabi	Chou-rave	Oyster	Huitre
L		**P**	
Lamb	Agneau	Parsley	Persil
Lard	Sindoux	Parsnip	Panais
Leek	Poireau	Partridge	Perdreau
Leg	Gigot	Pea	Pois
Lemon	Citron	Peach	Pêche
Lemon Sole	Limande	Peanut	Cacahuète, arachide
Lentil	Lentille	Pear	Poire
Lettuce	Laitue	Pepper	Poivre
Lime	Limon	Perch	Perche
Liver	Foie	Pheasant	Faisan
Loach	Loche	Pie	Pâté
Lobster	Homard	Pike	Brochet
Loin	Longe	Pilchard	Sardine
		Pineapple	Ananas
M		Pistachio	Pistache
Mace	Macis	Plaice	Carrelet
Mackerel	Maquereau	Plover	Pluvier
Maize	Maïs	Plum	Prune
Mallard	Malard	Pollack	Merlan Jaune
Mandarin	Mandarine	Pomegranate	Grenade
Mango	Mangue	Poppy Seed	Pavot
Marjoram	Marjolaine	Pork	Porc
Meat	Viande	Potato	Pomme de Terre
Melon	Melon	Poultry	Volaille
Milk	Lait	Prawn	Crevette rose
Mint	Menthe	Pumpkin	Potiron
Millet	Millet		
Morel	Morille	**Q**	
Mulberry	Mûre	Quail	Caille
Mushroom	Champignon	Quince	Coing
Mussel	Moule		
Mustard	Moutarde		

English	French	English	French
R		Tongue	Langue
Rabbit	Lapin	Tripe	Tripe
Radish	Radis	Trout	Truite
Raspberry	Framboise	Truffle	Truffe
Red Cabbage	Chou rouge	Tunny	Thon
Red Mullet	Rouget	Turbot	Turbot
Rhubarb	Rhubarbe	Turkey	Dinde
Rice	Riz	Turmeric	Curcuma
Rye	Seigle	Turnip	Navet
		Turtle	Tortue
S			
Saffron	Safran	**V**	
Sage	Sauge	Vanilla	Vanille
Sago	Sagou	Veal	Veau
Salmon	Saumon	Venison	Venaison
Salmon Trout	Truite Saumonée	Vinegar	Vinaigre
Salsify	Salsifis		
Salt	Sel	**W**	
Sardine	Sardine	Walnut	Noix
Scallop	Coquille St-Jacques	Water	**Eau**
Semolina	Semoule	Watercress	Cresson de
Shallot	Échalote		Fontaine
Shin of Beef	Jarret de Boeuf	Whitebait	Blanchaille
Shrimp	Crevette grise	Whiting	Merlan
Sirloin	Aloyau	Whortleberry	Airelle Myrtille
Skate	Raie	Wild Duck	Canard Sauvage
Sloe	Prunelle	Woodcock	Bécasse
Smelt	Éperlan		
Sorrel	Oseille	**Y**	
Soya	Soja	Yeast	Levure
Spice	Épice		
Spinach	Épinards	**Z**	
Sprat	Harenguet	Zest	Zeste
Squid	Calamar		
Strawberry	Fraise		
Sturgeon	Esturgeon		
Sucking Pig	Cochon de Lait		
Sugar	Sucre		
Sultana	Sultane		
Swede	Rutabaga		
Sweetbread	Ris (de veau)		
Syrup	Sirop		
T			
Tarragon	Estragon		
Tea	Thé		
Teal	Sarcelle		
Tench	Tanche		
Tomato	Tomate		

Index

Game   92-7
Garlic   149
Gels   163-4
Gherkin   15
Glacé cherries   48
Glucose   144
Gluten   116
Ginger   154
Goose   90-1,97
Gooseberry   33
Grape   44
Grapefruit   43
Ground nut   53
Grouse   95
Guinea fowl   92
Gums   164-6
    Marine   165-6
    Synthetic   166
    Vegetable   164-5

Ham   86
Hare   93
Hazel nut   52
Herbs   147-151
Horseradish   149

Jams   168-9
Jellies   168

Kohlrabi   14

Lamb   79-82
Leeks   14
Lemon   43
Lentil   7
Lettuce   10
Lime   43
Loganberry   34

Maize   124
Marrow   15
Melons   45
Milk   54-8
Mint   149
Mushroom   30
Mustard   11

Nectarine   37
Nutmeg   154

Nuts   50-3

Oatmeal   123-4
Oats   123
Oca   20
Oils
    Marine   132
    Vegetable   130-1
Onion   12,20
Orange   42-3
Oregano   150

Parsley   17,150
Parsnip   16
Partridge   94-5
Pea   6
Peach   37
Pear   41-2
Pepper   155
    Sweet   15
Pheasant   94
Pineapple   44
Pistachio nut   53
Plum   38
Pork   83-7
Potato   17-20
Potato flour   126
Poultry   87-92
Preservatives   170-2
Preserves   166-9
Pumpkin   15

Quail   96

Rabbit   94
Radish   11-12
Raspberry   34
Rhubarb   45-6
Rice   121-2
Rye   126

Sago   125
Salt   156
Semolina   117-8
Shellfish   107-12
Soya bean   7
Spinach   9
Spices   151
Strawberry   34

Sugar   139-46
    Beet   141
    Boiling of   144-5
    Cane   139
    Glucose   144
    Honey   144
    Maple   139
    Refining of   141
    Types of   141-3
    Uses of   145-6
Swede   16
Sweet potato   20

Tangerine   43
Tapioca   125
Tea   184-6
Tomato   13
Truffle   30
Turkey   91
Turnip   16
TVP   24-8

Ulluco   20

Veal   78-9
Venison   93
Vinegar   156

Walnut   53
Water   178-80
Wheat   114-8

Yam   20
Ysano   20